C0-AZU-259

Writing
Useful
Reports

ROBERT E. TUTTLE & C. A. BROWN

Writing
Useful
Reports

PRINCIPLES AND APPLICATIONS

New York
APPLETON-CENTURY-CROFTS, INC.

Copyright, © 1956 by

APPLETON-CENTURY-CROFTS, Inc.

All rights reserved. This book, or parts thereof, must not be reproduced in any form without permission of the publishers.

677-5

Library of Congress Card Number: 55-9483

PRINTED IN THE UNITED STATES OF AMERICA
E 88887

Foreword

THIS BOOK is a detailed formulation of principles and techniques that have been successful in report writing courses. We believe it will prove useful to those who must write reports in business, industry, and professional life, and to college students.

The approach to report writing that is presented has evolved directly from learning to help people to write better reports.

Current books use one of three approaches, or a combination of them. One group teaches how to write a variety of "types" of reports. The implication is that all reports may be classified, and that the task of the writer is to determine the class into which a report will fall and to write accordingly. In actual practice, the report writer finds that reports are not named according to these types, or that he cannot find a type to fit his situation. Hence he either resorts to standardizing on one type which does not fit many situations, or simply imitates both good and bad features of the reports he finds in use in his own organization.

A second approach results in what is actually a style book. The chief emphasis is on format and mechanics. These books often include what is basically a handbook of English. But style varies widely from organization to organization; and after all, correct style should be an aid to content, not an end in itself.

A third and very useful approach is aimed at an elementary college level. These books concern themselves primarily with fundamental composition—process exposition, definition, classification, and so on. Enough is said of "long" and "short" reports to give an idea of a few satisfactory patterns. For simple report situations, these books are enough to go on, and they provide a fine basis for more advanced instruction.

All of these approaches we have tried at various times. Fortunately, we were working in a situation where we could see the actual result of our teaching as it was applied in business and industry.

These things became increasingly clear:

1. Almost anyone could write routine reports where standard form and content had been established. These gave no trouble. However, it was found that format and style vary widely from one organization to another and even within departments of the same organization. It follows that if any organization wishes a particular style or format, it is its responsibility to instruct its own personnel.

2. The more important a report situation, the less often any ready-made formula would fit it. And with only types or formulas as guides, the report writer had no basis for decision. Hence his decisions were often wrong.

3. Conferences to decide on a report presentation invariably moved eventually to a discussion of how the reader would use the report and what he needed to make a decision.

The implications were clear. In report writing, as in other fields, the technician might be able to get along with formulas. But the man working above that level needed a solid grounding in basic principles which would serve as a guide to enable him to master nonroutine situations.

This book is a formulation of the method we have found most effective in developing such professional competence. Its thesis is simple. The report writer analyzes the report situation, with emphasis on the probable use of the report. He then examines the means at his disposal—the potential functional elements of reports—and selects or modifies to fit the situation. The first part of this text helps him to do so by describing a technique for analyzing the report situation and by making explicit the means at his command. The second part contains sample reports, fully analyzed, to enable him to develop flexibility in applying the principles and means. Practice suggestions and other study aids relate the sample reports to the individual chapters.

At first glance, such an approach appears to proceed from the complex to the simple. In fact it does not. Anything can be better understood if it is first looked at whole and its over-all function recognized. In practice, the approach helps make sure that the writer at least considers whether a particular device or element will help the reader. If instead the writer starts with a simple routine report pattern, and then adds to it, he tends to modify it only when absolutely forced to do so. Hence he makes the least change, not the best one.

The approach was proved effective with quite different groups. The principle of use was first emphasized by Brown in connection with report writing courses for supervisors and engineers. About 1946 the approach was developed and formalized by Tuttle, and used in a college course for second-semester Junior engineering and business administration students. A sequence course was also developed for Senior business-administration students.

Simultaneously, much was being learned of the great variation in report situations through experience with our Institute Fifth-Year Program. Graduates from our four-year resident curriculum may apply for an additional one-year nonresident program and thus become candidates for degrees. Each candidate conducts a research project at the plant where he is employed and reports on his results. The projects range from the theoretical to the very practical, and hence the reports of them must often be specifically designed to fit the particular situation. Our work as advisers to over 1,500 of these students demonstrated further the need for the report writer to have such an understanding of report principles as would permit intelligent flexibility in reporting.

By 1948 both authors were teaching the Junior course, and their increased understanding from plant contacts was jointly used to modify and refine the approach. A formal presentation of the principles involved was then given by Brown at the 1949 meeting of the American Society for Engineering Education at Rensselaer Polytechnic Institute, and copies of the talk received wide distribution. Since then many other presentations have been given before professional organizations and at various special institutes.

The text itself has been written by Tuttle, and he is hence solely responsible for its effectiveness or lack of it. However, the authorship is truly joint. Much of the first four chapters is from the Rensselaer presentation of Brown. And we have worked so closely together on the project over the past fourteen years that it is utterly impossible to say whose ideas are whose. Also incorporated are countless valuable suggestions from instructors who have used the material, from the many who have seen the first portion of the manuscript over the past four years, and from men in many plants.

To them go our sincere thanks. Our colleagues Grady G. Stubbs, William B. Thomas, and Marvin H. Swift have reviewed the language and content of the text critically and in detail. Their comments have been invaluable. Much also owes to our former students—Juniors, Seniors, and Fifth-Year. It was a student, for example, that pointed out to us that even simple form reports have prefatory material—in the directive that goes out when the form is first created. It has been a pleasure to work with our students and to learn from them.

Finally, our thanks go to those who have helped by

providing the reports which illustrate this text. They include the writers of the reports, those that helped us in obtaining clearances or who gave those clearances, and the companies who owned the reports. Individual acknowledgments to them follow.

The following authored the reports which have been used as samples: D. C. Apps, E. Borker, N. L. Haight, A. A. Havlena, E. L. Handley, V. E. Hense, George Kingsbury, H. H. Miller, D. G. Morse, E. E. Nelson, R. B. Schenck, J. A. Simons, R. W. Stanley, K. A. Stonex, J. W. Vogel, R. F. W., and B. E. Wright.

The following either gave final clearances and permissions or aided in obtaining them: A. A. Alderman, C. R. Anderson, H. H. Barnes, Margaret D. Blickle, Charles Bruce, C. A. Chayne, George Coburn, P. A. Carlstone, G. R. Cowing, C. A. Dilley, L. W. Elder, H. F. Hatfield, V. E. Hense, C. E. Hilton, B. L. Lowe, D. G. Morse, E. E. Nelson, D. M. Shackelford, K. A. Stonex, D. R. Tuttle, and J. W. Vogel.

The following companies, corporations or divisions allowed their material to be reproduced: American Business Writing Association, American Society of Mechanical Engineers, Buick Motor Division, Clevite Corporation, Delco-Remy Division, Fisher Body Division, General Foods Corporation, General Motors Corporation, General Motors Institute, General Motors Proving Ground, International Harvester Company, Pennsylvania Power and Light Company.

GENERAL MOTORS INSTITUTE
Flint, Michigan

R. E. T.
C. A. B.

Contents

Part II: APPLICATIONS

PART I

Writing Useful Reports

1

Why Write Reports?

A WHILE BACK some of us had been planning to go over to Central Office in Detroit. The meeting was on Thursday, and on Monday my boss asked me just who was to go. I told him I didn't know, and he said I ought to.

. . . So I found out.

But then I couldn't find my boss. So I left a note on his desk that said: "Going to Detroit Thursday—You, me, Stubbs, and Davis."

The rest of the afternoon I spent digging through a 420-page affair called *A Proposed Quality Control Program.*

Now if I'd ask you what that 420-page affair was, you'd probably say, "Sounds like a report to me."

It was.

But what about my note to the boss?

It was a report too.

In fact, a good share of the information we pass back and forth every day can be called "reports."

Because the word has so broad a meaning, it is hard to define. About the best that can be done is to say that a report is any communication aimed primarily at conveying facts, or generalizations purportedly based on facts.

Granted, this definition isn't too helpful. That is probably why, when we are asked to write a report, most of us want further specifications. If they exist, or if our boss knows exactly what he wants and patiently explains, then we are lucky. But the more important a report is, the less likely

3

we are to find ready-made specifications for writing it.

This and the following chapters are intended to help you design your reports to fit any situation.

Being able to do so is essential in almost any organization today.

Even in a small organization, reports are important. One friend about twenty-five used to keep telling me that they weren't. He didn't mind filling out a few forms, but he couldn't see sitting down and actually writing something. He worked as assistant to his dad, who owned an automobile dealership in Canada. Naturally, he felt he could always talk to his dad, and if he filled out a few forms and had a good bookkeeper, why more reports?

Then one winter his dad got sick, went to Florida, and left Jim in charge. Pretty soon Jim found he was keeping a record of the major decisions and changes he was making. When he needed help, he wrote to his father, reported the facts, made his recommendations, and asked for an O.K. And when his dad came back, Jim gave him a written summary of what had happened. He wrote more "reports" in those three months than he thought he would write in a lifetime.

Of course the situation was unexpected, but it resembles pretty closely what happens all the time in larger firms. The larger the firm, the more important it is to write things down. We can't see people when we want to. When we do get to see them, they don't have much time to spend with us. Someone interrupts, or the telephone rings, and we don't get the whole story told.

So we write it down.

We gain several advantages. Our facts are there in our boss's office—on his desk. He can look at them when he finds time. He can read the whole story. The issues and facts are in proper relation—we don't get tangled up in sidelines the way we may when we're talking. The boss can make his decision after thinking it over instead of right away. He has something to refer to if he happens to forget.

To gain some idea of how many reports are required for the everyday operation of a big organization, look at any organization chart. Take one like that on the following page, which shows only a small part of one organization—just enough to demonstrate the general idea. There is a steady flow of information up, down, and across, and even within some of the blocks shown.

For instance, *Up.* A labor-costs man reports a difficulty to the superintendent of standards. If it is something the latter can't decide, he reports to the manufacturing superintendent. From him it may go to the plant manager, and even on up to the president. Finally, on some matters the president reports to the directors or to the stockholders. At all levels, this steady upward flow takes place every day, week, month, and year. Most items go up only one level, of course. Any particular thing tends to stop (a) where a competent decision can be made, or (b) where it becomes consolidated with other information to give a bigger picture.

The flow *Down* is just as steady, though usually the volume is less. The president may tell the plant manager of a new policy of the board. He passes it on to the manufacturing superintendent and tells him to implement it in his area. The latter in turn tells his superintendents, who tell their foremen. The directive generates other directives that cover smaller areas in greater detail. Each man tells those just under him the part that applies to them and what they are supposed to do about it. By the time the order gets to the lower echelons, incidentally, the report tends to become oral. Also by this time, the original statement of the policy has probably disappeared. The policy is being expressed in changes in many minor procedures all over the plant.

Meanwhile, across the organization, other information is

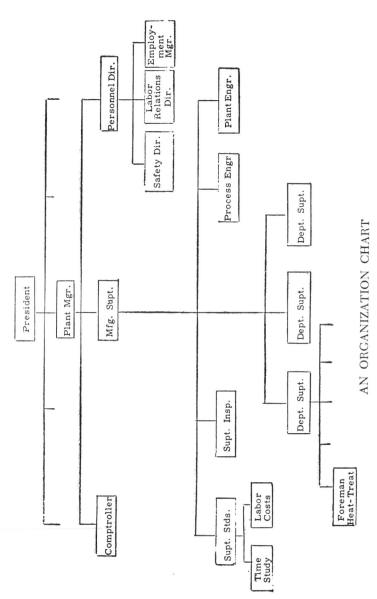

AN ORGANIZATION CHART

moving in all directions. The foreman of heat-treat is reporting any accident both to his direct superior and to the safety department. In turn, the safety department representative may be pointing out new hazards. Simultaneously, inspection is reporting defects to a department superintendent, and another superintendent is reporting a grievance to labor relations—and so on.

All the while, many reports have stayed within the department in which they originated. They may later become parts of a larger report, or they may just be put away for future reference.

In general, only routine, noncontroversial matters are reported *Across*. Those that go *Up* are ones containing information that the immediate superior needs to see the picture of the area he commands, or ones requiring decisions outside the jurisdiction of his subordinate. Those going *Down* report the success of the department in meeting goals, or give new directions or objectives that affect its operation. Those that remain at home concern matters the department head is competent to decide, or that he wants for his records or for the operation of his department.

Obviously no one can keep all these things in his head. That is why, the bigger the organization, the more likely we are to put things down in writing.

2

What to Use in Building
the Report

HARDLY ANYONE ever puts information on paper simply for
the sake of doing so. It requires effort.

We decide to report something because we have been
told to, or because it is part of our job—about the same
thing—or because we know something that someone else
needs to know for our good or the good of the organization.
The one who gets the report is the final judge of its success. There is no use telling him something unless he takes
some action about it, now or in the future. A report is
written to be used.

The reader is most likely to use it if it is clearly related
to his needs and if it answers questions he wants answered.

What kinds of questions are these? Because they are
"natural" ones, writers have been answering them for centuries.

Hand anyone something he doesn't expect, and what is he
likely to say?

"What are you giving me *this* for?"

You answer him that it is going to be a big help to him,
and that you know it is because you've had experience with
it. If you do the same sort of thing in a *report,* you have
written a *preface.*

If not the first, his next question will be, "What is it anyway?" Or if by now he knows it is something written, "What's it all about?"

The answer to this question is an *introduction*.

Next comes, "What about it?" The answer roughly constitutes the *body*. Often, because it is the longest part, it is broken into paragraphs, sections, or chapters. (In this discussion all these will be called "developing sections.")

Certainly he is going to ask one more question—"So What?"

Your answer to that is the *ending* or *conclusion*.

These are the functional or structural parts that we can use in writing reports. Various things we can do with them (including leaving them out) will be discussed later:

Functional part	*Chapter*
Prefatory material	5
Introductions	6
Endings and conclusions	7
Developing sections	8

Developing sections are the meat of the report. They may contain facts, data, evidence, or simply a chain of reasoning. How this content can be handled is discussed in Chapter 9.

Good illustrations and clear writing help the reader understand the facts. Proper acknowledgments help him judge their worth. And to help him find his way around in a report, we can use a table of contents, a list of illustrations, an index, and headings. All these we will look at in Chapters 10 through 13. Two additional chapters discuss the related problems of locating certain facts and making them permanently accessible through good records.

In order to make all these principles more clear, this book has a second part. It consists of sample reports, each of which is individually analyzed. At the end of each chapter are specific suggestions as to how to use these samples.

The general idea is this. After you have read the chapter on introductions, say, turn to the reports in Part II. (Their arrangement is explained on page 277.) The analysis of each report has material under the first heading called "Report Situation." Read this first. Then skip to the heading of "Introduction," where the report is analyzed in terms of the principles of Chapter 6 of Part I. Check the analysis against the actual wording of the report introduction to see how the principle is worked out.

Don't use any of the reports for an exact model and slavishly follow it. If you learn the principles at all well, you can write a better report than any of these—you can write a report specifically designed for your particular report situation.

The sample reports have variety. Their authors range from a corporation president to college students, their length from part of a page to over one hundred, their subjects from steel to potatoes.

Whatever the subject area—business, industry, agriculture, engineering, government, or education—report principles are the same. So are the techniques that make reports easy to use. But you will get most out of your study if you see the techniques applied to reports in your own professional field. Assemble some by following the practice suggestions at the end of this chapter.

Now back to our illustration. After you have studied the sample introductions, analyze the other reports you will collect when you follow the practice suggestions at the end of this chapter. Decide if each has the best introduction possible in view of the situation for which it was written.

Talk over your analyses with other people. You'll get more out of your study, and you'll have a check on your own judgment.

Before we can make any analysis, however, we need a

base to work from. And we need some rules of operation, or guides. These are taken up in the next two chapters.

PRACTICE SUGGESTIONS

Gather a collection of reports that are directly related to your field of specialization. The best sources will be business, industrial, or other organizations in your own field. Do not plan to use these reports as models, but as examples to analyze. For that use, it doesn't matter whether they demonstrate good or bad reporting techniques.

You will find reports easiest to gather if you explain the following:

1. Why you wish the reports—for study and analysis to improve your own ability to write good reports.
2. That you want various sorts of reports—long or short—from different levels of the organization. Showing the samples in Part II of this book will help.
3. That you don't need *recent* reports on current operations. Old reports will do perfectly well.

    The reason for this step is that many reports concern problem situations or costs. On both of these any organization has a right to be sensitive. However, none of us mind very much if people know of our past shortcomings after everything is under control.
4. That you will keep confidential the names of people, suppliers, or other organizations mentioned or evaluated in the reports. You can do the same with figures designated as confidential.

    If you make this stipulation, of course you are ethically bound to carry it out. The best way to eliminate names or figures is to cut them out of the report with a razor blade.

The best source of reports depends on what your job is right now.

1. If you are a full-time student, you are using this book as part of a course. Your instructor will have some sample

reports. In addition, you or your friends in the class will have connections with organizations that are concerned with your area of specialization. The connection may be through past employment, through a parent, or through someone you know in your professional field. Ask them for assistance, using the guide lines suggested above.

In addition, libraries contain some longer and more formal reports.

2. If you are a student in a cooperative program, enlist the help of your past supervisors. Also helpful will be the man who is the contact between your school and the company with whom you cooperate.

3. If you are working full time, tell your immediate superior what you are doing and ask him to help.

3

A Base Pattern and Some Guides

As a base of operations, we can take the most traditional arrangement of the elements which were talked about in the last chapter. We will ignore for a time the things scattered throughout the report—facts, illustrations, and headings.

The pattern then is:

> Title page
> Prefatory material
> Table of Contents
> List of Illustrations

  I. Introduction
  II. Developing sections
  III. (These will vary—
  IV. We will assume three of them)
  V. Conclusion
    Appendix

How do we change this pattern to get a report that is easy and satisfying to read?

To find this out we need the best answers we can get to four questions. Answering them also tells about the general content of our report. They are:

> 1. What kind of material is it?
> 2. Who is going to use this report?
> 3. How is he going to use it?
> 4. Where do I stand in the picture?

13

1. *What kind of material is it?* The amount of the material or subject matter affects both the basic pattern and what we put in each functional part.

   You'll remember that, at the first of Chapter 1, I had been asked by my boss to tell him who was going to Detroit for a meeting. My report contained a three-word introduction—"going to Detroit" and a five-word body—"you, me, Stubbs, and Davis."

   If I had used all of the functional parts—preface, introduction, and the works—and you were my boss—what would you have thought?

2. *Who is going to use this report?* The reader's position, personality, and location are some of the things about him that may affect the report. Most top executives want things down to a page or two. Winston Churchill and Dwight Eisenhower are examples. Such executives are too busy to read much more than that about any except the most important problems. And so things which go to them are checked and rechecked, sifted and boiled down. In effect they get reports which are simply "introduction—conclusion."

   Personality? Once I worked for a man whom I didn't dare hand a report containing just "introduction—conclusion." The minute I did he was in his boss's office trying to get action, and when a conclusion was questioned he had no facts to support it. I took to giving him reports that had all the data, with the conclusion well in the back.

   Location? The farther the reader is from the writer, the more data he is likely to need. He can't call the writer in to question him, or send for the pertinent file.

3. *How is he going to use it?* A simple illustration is this—If the report is likely to be read once, acted

upon, and filed as completed, it needs no index. If it will be used for constant reference (and is long), an index is essential.

4. *Where do I stand in the picture?* This usually can be translated to mean, "How much confidence does the reader have in me?" If he has a great deal of confidence, giving him my conclusion may be enough. But if I am a young, new employe, chances are he'll want to check the data very carefully before he commits himself.

The more in detail we can answer the four questions, the better report we can build. Here, for example, are some of the things that could help us:

About the material

a. How much is there?
b. On what basis does it rest? (Is it something I, as writer, can be assumed to know about, or is it something essentially new? Did it come from accumulated learning and experience, or does it result from a project, investigation, or experiment just completed?)
c. To whom does it "belong"? (Have I read it, or heard it, or is it my own?)
d. Is it routine, drastically important, or somewhere in between?

About the reader

a. What are his knowledge, experience, and education? (What can I assume he knows without being told? How much mathematics does he know? Is he familiar with my technical and "shop" terms?)

b. What is his temperament? (Is he a believer or a doubter? Does he like things in a hurry or does he prefer to browse, absorb, and even quibble? Is he sensitive to criticism?)

c. What is his responsibility in the matter? (Is he going to have to take the blame if I am wrong?)

d. What does he think of me?

About the use of the report

a. Is it to be filed away for uncertain future use? (This happens. A project is done, action taken. But someone might want to refer to it later. We don't know if they will, but we summarize the project in a report and put it away.)

b. Will it become part of another report? (Use a format to make consolidation easy.)

c. Will it be the basis of a decision? (Better give enough data for the reader to decide.)

d. Will it be read once, or frequently referred to? If the latter, as a whole or in parts? (Heads, kind of table of contents, and index depend on the answers.)

About how I stand in the picture (the writer)

a. What is my intention? (Do I want a decision, or simply to pass on information?)

b. How much do I know? (Can I use my own material or must I use that of others?)

c. How much time do I have? (If I was given half a day, my report can't be as complete or elaborate as if I had a month.)

d. What does the reader think about my ability, my competence in the field, my dependability, my experience and my judgment? (What these *really are* is, of course, important. But what the reader *thinks* really counts, especially if he is my boss. If he has full confidence in me, I may just give him my conclusion. If not, it's best to give the full facts.)

e. What help or equipment can I get to reproduce the report or prepare the illustrations? (Typed or printed? Photographs or drawings? These and other physical factors are affected here.)

Three things are true about the lists above.

First, the four factors, or *variables,* are all complex, not simple.

Second, the factors are interrelated. Each bears on and affects the others to make the total report situation. In other words, the relation is organic—the factors cannot be completely separated out.

Third, *because* the situation is complex and organic, no list can ever be complete.

The list is nevertheless useful. If we answer the questions before we even start to write any report, and if we learn how to use the answers, we can't go far wrong.

PRACTICE SUGGESTIONS

1. In Part II, the first section of the analysis of each report deals with the report situation. To get an idea of how situations vary, compare those on pages 279, 354, 418 and 428.

2. Think back over the last three or four reports you wrote. These may have been for your boss, for some organization to which you belonged, or for an instructor. In terms of the four questions or guides, rebuild each report situation just as completely as you can.

Using the Guides

Now TO APPLY the guides to the base pattern:

> Title page
> Prefatory material
> Table of Contents
> List of Illustrations
>
> I. Introduction
> II-IV. Developing sections
> V. Conclusion
> Appendix

TWO DERIVED PATTERNS

There are two extreme relationships in which we, our reader, and the report material may stand. The first is the problem-solving or experimental situation. We are dealing with a situation where no one knows the answer until something new is tried. After we claim to have discovered the answer, we must report to a reader who will raise all sorts of questions. The second is the information-giving situation. We are considered by our reader an authority on the subject, and he is anxious to know what we have to say.

Each situation completely infects the contents of the resulting report. Each functional part takes on special characteristics. This is true even though the reports both take the general pattern shown above.

There are many possible variations in each part, as we shall see in later chapters. But for the moment let us fill out somewhat the patterns of the two extremes.

One warning—AS STRONG AS I CAN MAKE IT. These are simply two full patterns at opposite poles. They are NOT "types" of reports. *About the best way in the world to get confused about reports is to try to make your material fit some prearranged type.* Reports have been classed into any number of such types: experience, observation, research, progress, completion, descriptive, analytic, investigation, test, conclusional, recommendation, informational, routine, periodic, special, evaluative, examination, appraisal, and many, many more. Unless some of these terms happen to be used in your organization, the best thing to do is to forget them.

In business and industry, reports are mostly named by what they report. They are called trip reports, dynamometer reports, service reports, policy-holder complaint reports, competitive-parts reports, test reports, inventory reports, and sales reports. The same is true in any other professional activity.

It would hardly be worth the effort to learn a pattern for every possible type of report. This is especially true because we can also find so many different patterns for each "type."

What these are, then, is simply two possible patterns.

THE FIRST PATTERN

Here is sketched in the first pattern—that *reporting results of an investigation:*

> Title page
> Prefatory material
> Table of Contents
> List of Illustrations

 I. Introduction
   Background
   Statement of problem
   General procedure or method
   Divisions of report (if different from steps in procedure)

 II. ⎤
 III. ⎬ Developing sections (These are in the order suggested at the end of the introduction)
 IV. ⎦

 V. Conclusions (These answer the problem)
   Appendix

In a report that takes this arrangement, interest is in a problem and its solution. Laboratory experiments, tests—any report trying to find an answer—could in theory take this pattern.

To get to the conclusions your reader would have to go all the way through the report. He would be willing to do so if the report were short. If it were, it would not need many of the parts given. If he were a teacher checking a student's technique, he might even read a long report. He might also do so if he were very interested in all the facts and had plenty of time.

But if the report ran to more than a few pages, no executive or manager would have time to read it.

Thus we get back to the fact that a report is written *to be used,* not necessarily to be read. With a mystery novel or a short story the reader starts on the first page. He enjoys himself following the plot and trying to guess how it will come out. The author tries, within certain ground rules, to hold him in suspense. The reader has fun in a mental game of hide-and-seek. But he enjoys it as a recreation. *It doesn't make any vital difference how the story comes out.* If the reader feels like it, he can put the story aside.

A report is not like that. *How it comes out is the most*

important thing about it. And the reader is a busy man. He should have to read only as much as he needs to read. For him, the pattern has to be rearranged.

THE SECOND PATTERN

Here is the *pattern giving information:*

Title page
Prefatory material
Table of Contents
List of Illustrations

I. Introduction
    Background
    Purpose of report
    Divisions of report, in order

II. ⎱ Developing sections. (These exactly correspond to
III. ⎰ the divisions of the report named at the end of the
IV. ⎰ introduction)

V. Conclusion. (This is either a short concluding paragraph or a summary)

In a report that takes this arrangement, the interest of the reader is centered in the facts. There is no problem. Nothing is being tested. No procedure is in question. Someone who knows something is simply telling it to someone who doesn't.

To get anything out of such a report, again the reader would have to read it all the way through. This limits it to about four situations:

First, when the story to be told is short. Let's say it can go on a single page—in practice, usually much less. Then, of course, many functional parts given here would be superfluous. Second, when we are teaching someone something. Textbooks, manuals, and booklets of directions or information to employes fall in this group. Third, when we are telling something to someone who already knows it—but we have to prove that we know it too. Most student "papers" and reports come here. Fourth, papers read to tell professional colleagues something we think they ought to know, or sent to a professional magazine for the same purpose.

Note that, except for manuals and instruction booklets, about the only time this pattern is used in actual practice is when the report is very short. We'll see why later.

As an aside here, notice the handicap a young man is under when he has to write his first report. For years, as a student, he has written a kind of paper or report that is exactly what isn't wanted. And he has been trained from textbooks which—quite logically for them—use exactly the same pattern. Even his answers to examinations followed the pattern. Small wonder if he has trouble!

THE REARRANGED PATTERNS

When these two patterns are rearranged for the busy man, we put first those things he will need most and hence be most likely to use. The introduction is immediately followed by the concluding section. When the reader has finished these, he has the most important ideas of the report. If he believes us, and this is all he needs to know, then he will not read the rest of the report. On the other hand, there may be points on which he wants to check more carefully. In that case, he turns to the particular place in the report where the detailed facts or reasoning may be found. Here he expects to find everything that is significant in reaching the generalization on which he wanted further information. Yet he does not usually want to go through our "arithmetic" or to see the raw data or facts before they have been sorted out and arranged. Hence we put material of this type in the appendix. The material is there if anyone wants to see it, but it does not get in anyone's way.

The arrangement and the general content of the functional parts become:

For the report of an investigation:

> Title page
> Prefatory material
> Table of Contents
> List of Illustrations
>
> I. Introduction (background, statement of problem, general procedure or method, divisions of report)
> II. Conclusions (the outcome—usually the things needed to make a decision. Often *recommendations* also result; they are placed here too)
> III-V. Developing sections (These contain all the data, facts, findings, and reasoning needed to support the conclusions)
> Appendix (supplementary matter, detailed calculations, arrays of raw data, and similar material most people won't need)

For the report centered on giving information:

> Title page
> Prefatory material
> Table of Contents
> List of Illustrations
>
> I. Introduction (background, purpose, divisions of report)
> II. Summary (the main facts and interpretations)
> III-V. Developing sections (full explanation of all the significant facts and interpretations that the reader would want to know about)
> Appendix (primarily reference material, sometimes minor details, glossaries, additional background material)

The summary can be placed in an earlier position, such
as right after the title page or just after the list of illustrations. Then it is often called an "abstract." These variations
will be discussed in Chapter 7.

THE "THREE-LEVEL" REPORT

A report such as the two we have just looked at is sometimes called the "three-level" report.[1] The idea is that a report this elaborate is rarely read by only one person. Almost
certainly it concerns important matters that must be passed
upon by several people. Each of these is on a higher level
of responsibility, and each is more remote from the report
situation. The report can start at any level of any organization. It will keep going till it gets to the hands of whoever
has the authority to make a decision on the matters it concerns. For the sake of explanation, and quite arbitrarily,
suppose we say it will have three readers at levels of increasing responsibility. Again arbitrarily, we'll call these levels
the *supervisory, executive,* and *administrative.*

Not only the order of the report but many of its other
characteristics will be affected. Take for example a problem-
centered one that will reach these three levels. Here is
how some of the parts will be influenced.

INTRODUCTION

Our immediate supervisor unquestionably knows the
background of the problem and its general nature. Probably
a very brief statement would be enough for him. On the
other hand, the executive (*his* boss) is a step removed, and
needs in addition an idea of the significance of the problem.
This means some background. Certainly it means a very
exact statement of the problem. For the administrator, even

---

[1] Richards, Thomas O. and Ralph A. Richardson, *Technical Writing,*
Research Laboratories Division, G.M.C., Detroit, Michigan: 1941.

more "fill-in" may be necessary, since he is even further away and may be hearing of the problem for the first time.

Our superior is quite likely a technical man in the same area as we. For him, we could have stated the problem in technical terms without hesitation. But the man on the executive level quite possibly is not from our specialization or has not worked at it for a long time. And it is almost certain that the administrator came up the ladder a different way. Yet the executive must pass on our report, and the administrator must make the final decision. It follows that the language cannot be technical. It must be such that any reasonably intelligent man can understand.

The fact was emphasized to me just the day before I wrote this. I had finished speaking to a group which included a number of men on high levels in their organization. After the talk one man came up to comment, and we began to speak of a mutual friend who worked directly for him. The executive expressed considerable concern for my friend's immediate future. The executive was moving up, and Frank would normally be expected to take the job. But, said the executive, he was afraid he would have to recommend someone else. The reason was that Frank had never been able to write reports that could go to the general manager. They were always too technical. Frank's superior had to rewrite every one in terms intelligible at that level. Frank would be held back because, "There had to be someone who could tell the general manager what was going on in that department."

The introduction would also have to be short. Neither the executive nor the administrator would wish to spend more time than absolutely necessary to grasp the problem.

CONCLUSIONS

All that has been said about the introduction applies equally well to the conclusions. All three readers would be interested in them, for they would be the basis for final decision. They should contain everything needed to make the final decision, but they should not be wordy. And neither the executive nor the administrator could be expected to make a decision upon them unless he knew what they meant, so their language must be nontechnical and clear. Finally, they would have to be "keyed" to the text, so that if a conclusion were questioned, any of the readers could turn immediately to the pertinent supporting data.

DEVELOPING SECTIONS

The developing sections would contain all the data necessary to support the conclusions. It is unlikely that even the supervisor could carry all the facts in his head. Probably too, he would want to review them carefully to see that they were accurate, and to brief himself in case his superior raised questions. He must be able to use the report to defend the position it takes.

The executive likewise will want to review the facts. Probably he won't look at all of them, but he will wish to consult those sections where he doubts the conclusions or recommendations.

The administrator is much less likely to turn to the body of the report. On the other hand, he may. Or he may hand the report to someone on his staff and ask that the data be checked. Or he may pass it on to someone in another department who is also concerned.

Several things follow about the developing sections of the report. First, the opening paragraphs must be clear. The problem or purpose of each section must be stated so that it can be understood by nonspecialists in the field. Second, all important interpretations must be in equally clear language. Third, at any point the reader must be able to understand what is being done and why—though it need not be expected that he know exactly *how* or that he follow the detailed calculations. Fourth, the outcome should be stated so that he can understand it.

APPENDIX

Probably none of the three readers will check the appendix. It is likely, however, that the supervisor may ask someone else in the department to review the calculations. And the appendix does complete the story of the report, so that everything is gathered in one place. Later, the appendix may become extremely valuable to another man who is assigned the same sort of project.

Better than any other, the three-level report demonstrates the importance of considering who is going to use the report, and how.

SIMPLER REPORT SITUATIONS

Fortunately, so far as time we must spend organizing and writing is concerned, most report situations are much simpler than the "three-level" situation. Possible situations are literally infinite. But a few examples will show typical effects of applying our guides to the appropriate variation of the basic pattern.

FIRST SAMPLE SITUATION

Here the *material* with which we are dealing is complicated—the report will be long. The outstanding feature is that our report is dealing with an abnormal matter. Something has broken or should break normal routine. An operation is out of control. A change in procedure is needed. There has been a sharp rise in scrap or customer complaints. We have failed to meet schedules or norms. Something we are doing can be improved. The report will therefore concern "what is wrong" and "what we should do about it."

The *reader* of our report is our immediate superior—our

boss. He will *use* the report to make a decision which will affect the operation of his department. Here he has full responsibility and control. He is just as well acquainted with the technical aspects as we are.

As *writer* we have had to develop the procedure we used and the data which resulted. Our boss has full confidence in our ability and judgment, but the decision is very important.

How will the pattern be affected by this situation?

Actually, this report will resemble very closely a three-level one. Because it will be long, it will require full apparatus of title page, table of contents, and list of illustrations. Prefatory matter, however, will reduce to simply reminding our superior of the assignment of the project. The introduction will state the problem, general procedure, and order of discussion. But since the reader knows the situation and is a technical man, we reduce background to little or none, and we use technical terminology quite freely.

The same holds true of the conclusions, which may now be stated in technical terms.

The developing sections will need to state detailed procedures and the data, so that the accuracy of the conclusions can be checked carefully. But since we are writing to a technical man, we can safely use technical terms, curves, charts, and so on, without explaining elaborately what we are doing or what they mean. These make convenient short-cuts.

The appendix will still be the place for detailed calculations and other supplementary material.

One warning—some bosses *always* want the explanations and nontechnical language of the three-level report. If it turns out that they must pass the information upward after all, they don't want to have to do anything to the original report.

SECOND SAMPLE SITUATION

Now suppose the *material* was not so extensive. Then the handling of title page, table of contents, list of illustrations, and prefatory material would become very simple. In fact, the report would probably take some variation of memorandum form. Except for length, the introduction, conclusions, developing sections, and appendix would remain the same.

THIRD SAMPLE SITUATION

Here the *material* we are dealing with is relatively routine. It is in an area in which our superior has complete trust and confidence in us. The entire problem is therefore within our area of responsibility and skill. Hence our word will be accepted. If we are wrong (as everyone is sometimes) we will hear about it later.

The resulting report is almost certain to be short. Again elements preceding the introduction will nearly disappear. The introduction itself will reduce to a brief statement, possibly to just a subject line, and it will be immediately followed by the concluding section. That will be all. We will do little or no explaining of how we arrived at the results. Certainly our superior will not expect to go carefully over the calculations and detailed procedure.

FOURTH SAMPLE SITUATION

Now let's take a situation that occurs in any department or office. We have some routine figures or facts that need to be reported every day. Examples are records of material on hand, of amount and type of scrap, of absentees, of manhours lost, of how routine schedules are being met, and so on. The material of the report is routine.

These reports often stay within the department. Sometimes, in routine fashion, they are sent to other departments.

An example would be a simple "Notice of Rejection" made out by an inspector. A copy of the original might go to the production department concerned, or it might be used to make up a summary of figures for the day. In either case, any reader is very familiar with the situation and with the report itself. As writer, we are merely performing one of our routine and expected jobs.

Here a standard blank or form would obviously be the most efficient way to make our report. Title page, preface, table of contents, list of illustrations, and introduction would reduce to a heading for the form, perhaps a routing, and a place for signature or initials. Conclusions would be one word—"rejected"—probably printed on the form and simply checked. Data would be name and number of the part and reason for rejection. That would be the entire "developing sections" plus appendix. In short, we have a simple form for filling in minimum data.

Reports such as these make up the vast majority of all reports. They provide information necessary to show how things are going. Later they may be used for summary reports which show figures for particular periods. These summaries can then be checked against norms or projections. But such simple reports call for little or no special action.

The samples we have just gone over show how the basic patterns and guides can be used. To use them in writing any report, the general procedure should be this:

First, get all the data that you can on the *material, reader, use,* and *writer* of the report. Then look at each of the functional parts of the report. Ask if in this particular report situation this part is needed. If the decision is "yes," determine how much is needed, and where it should go. Then you are ready to consider final form.

The chapters that follow are to help you make the decision in respect to each functional part.

PRACTICE SUGGESTIONS

1. In Chapter 16, page 277, each group of reports is arranged so that the report situations are progressively simpler. Skim rapidly through each group. For each report, first note the report situation.

2. In the reports mentioned in Suggestion 2 of the last chapter, what was the order of the functional parts? Would you make any changes now?

3. Sort the sample reports you have collected according to which pattern they most closely resemble—information or investigation.

4. Record the order of parts in the sample reports you have collected. In view of what you know of the report situation, should the order be changed?

5

Using Prefatory Material

ONE OF THE four questions which we found people asked when we handed them something was "Why are *you* giving *me this?*"

The answer to the question constituted prefatory material. Examining the question shows that we are simply being asked to make clear the variable factors in the situation. *"This"* is the *material, "me"* is the *reader,* and the *"you"* in our question is the *writer.* The *"why"* implies use, and indeed the idea of use is implicit in the whole question. It might even be asked, "What do you expect me to do with this?"

In other words, the reader needs information which will help him feel at home with the situation and help him evaluate the report.

When a toastmaster or chairman of a meeting "introduces" a speaker, he is really giving, not an introduction, but prefatory material. Usually the chairman tells us who the speaker is and why he is qualified to talk on the subject. (In a speech I listened to recently he was a former member of the State Department who had just returned after fourteen years in the Near East.) Then the chairman explains why this subject should be of especial interest to this audience at this time. (The Near East is in a critical geographic position, and our government has commitments there.) The chairman may even say that the speaker has only twenty minutes in which to talk! When the chairman finally pronounces the speaker's name we feel fairly confident that he knows what he is talking about, and we understand why he should be talking to us in particular.

Such material may be a long formal preface like that found in a printed report to the general public, or there may be none at all. The general principle is that the farther the reader is from the writer, the more prefatory material he needs.

In practice, it is best to do the actual *writing* of the prefatory material last. As we shall see in the next chapter, doing so helps us avoid putting in it material which ought to go into the introduction. But if the report situation is anything except the most routine, we should *plan* the preface *first*. We cannot really judge how to handle the rest of the report without making a complete analysis of the variables in the report situation. Planning the prefatory material forces us to make this analysis.

This chapter therefore discusses:

1. What are some of the things that I may need to cover?
2. Which of these should I tell about this time?
3. Where in the report should I do it?

POSSIBLE CONTENT

Prefatory material may need to cover any of the points in the following list:

THE REPORT SITUATION

1. The occasion for writing, such as
     an assignment
     need of a reader or user
     a situation that needs correction
2. How this occasion led to this particular project or report.

3. Why the material was selected, treated, or organized as it is—in terms of the use the reader will make of it. (Notice that just a statement of how the material is organized is not prefatory. The criterion is whether the organization is explained in terms of why it is good for the reader.)

THE READER AND USE

1. Who the reader is to be.
2. What he is expected to know.
3. What he is expected to do about it.
4. How he can use the report.
5. Why the material is good for him.
6. Why the arrangement of material is good for him. (Compare "3" above.)

THE WRITER

1. His authority.
   degrees and titles
   present job
   past experience
   time he devoted to project
2. His personal feelings or reactions.
3. The people who supported him. (Acknowledgments of a broad or personal nature. Usually these give person, title, and nature of aid. Acknowledgments not only do the gracious thing of giving credit where it is due. They also clearly imply that the experience and ability of these others have been added to those of the author.)

As you examine prefaces, you may want to expand and modify this list. If so, go right ahead—it is merely a working tool. But beware of one thing. Many prefaces contain material that is not prefatory. Sometimes strictly introductory material is combined with them. At other times they contain a summary of results or recommendations. The latter practice can serve to give special emphasis to some phase of the project. But if no such emphasis is needed and the report itself is well arranged, such overlapping is not desirable.

PRINCIPLES FOR SELECTING CONTENT

To tell which of the points listed above need to be covered in a particular report, go back to your analysis of the report situation in terms of the variables. Then apply the guides to the above list.

It is possible that your final decision will be that most of the points will be omitted. It is also possible that you will decide to cover them all. Most of the time, however, you will decide to omit some and include others.

In the rest of this subsection, the points listed above are restated as questions. Following each question are concrete suggestions to use in making your decision.

THE REPORT SITUATION

1. *Does the reader need to know the occasion of the report?*

   "Occasion of the report" refers to the particular motivating factor that caused it to be written at all. The question could be rephrased as two. Need the reader know whether the report was assigned by him, assigned by someone else, or initiated by you? Does he need to know why you thought it was important to undertake the project or make the report? Here are specific guides for making the decision:

   a. The more unusual the report occasion—the less routine—the more elaborate explanation the reader will need.

  b. Conversely, a routine situation will need no statement of occasion beyond the title of the report. People are used to getting the report all the time and expect to get it.

  c. The wider the audience—the greater the number of potential readers—and the less definite it is who the readers will be, the more necessary is a detailed explanation of the occasion.

  d. Conversely, if the report is to your superior, and was assigned, the statement will be brief. You may not even indicate the fact that the report was assigned, especially if submitting it is part of your regular duties.

  e. The length at which you state the occasion will bear a direct relation to the total length of the report.

Except for very routine reports, it is a safe and desirable practice to state the occasion. Many superiors require it on the grounds that a report should be complete in itself. The boss should not have to look up a record to get the facts of the assignment. This information is easy to provide, either in a special line devoted to it or in a phrase in the opening sentence of the report.

One more thing—if you initiate a report yourself, the project becomes "unusual," and you will need to give space to explaining why. This is a corollary of item "a" above.

2. *Does the reader need to know how the original occasion developed into this particular project or report?*

  a. If you were assigned one task, but could perform only part of it, the answer would surely be, "yes."

  b. If the project that led to the report started with a relatively minor matter that led to a much larger one, the answer is again, "yes."

    c. If the reader is likely to ask, "Why this study and not some other in the same area,"—again, "yes."

    d. Otherwise, "no."

3. *Should the reader know why the material is selected, treated, or organized as it is?*

    a. Usually, "no." The effectiveness of the organization or treatment should be expected to stand on its own.

    b. "Yes," if you need to give the reader a sales talk to show why any of these features will be especially useful to him.

    c. "Yes," if in your organization reports of this sort are usually handled in one way, and you are using another. Even here, however, it is preferable if your way is so *obviously* better that it speaks for itself.

THE READER AND USE

1. *Need you tell who the reader is to be?*

    a. Except for the most routine, "blank-filling" kinds of reports, "yes."

    b. The more indefinite and general the readers, the more space you devote to telling to what reader the report will be useful. The fewer the readers, and the more surely you and they know who they are, the less space.

    c. In most instances, simply use some method to address the report to the reader—the salutation of a letter, or the name after a reference line "submitted to."

2. *Should you say what the reader is expected to know?* Outside of manuals, it is rarely desirable to tell what the reader must know to understand the report. In some reports the point is covered by referring to related studies, the implication being (though it is not

expressed) that the reader needs to know about them too. It should never be done in a manner that might insult the reader.

3. *Should you tell the reader what to do about your conclusions?*

   a. If action is necessary, it is occasionally proper to point out this fact in the prefatory material and even repeat some of the main conclusions or recommendations of the report itself. Remember that this is done only when special emphasis is necessary.

   b. You may wish to tell to whom the information is to be transmitted or who is to take action. This is a characteristic of reports giving information, which are traveling *down*. ("Please call the attention of your people to these new procedures.")

4. *Should you tell the reader how to use the report?*

   a. Generally the subject of the report will indicate in what area it is useful. Obviously, a report which produced the answer to a problem should be used in taking action on that problem.

   b. If the report structure is complicated or unusual, the reader ought to be told how to find items in it most efficiently. In manuals this often becomes a section called "How to Use Your Manual."

5. and

6. *Should you explain why the material is good for him or why the arrangement is good for him?*

   This is tricky, because doing so may result in "talking down," which will get the wrong result. Usually, you can safely explain how the information will help him in his job, or why the material or arrangement is good in a general way. Again this happens primarily in reports going *down*.

THE WRITER

1. *Should you give your degrees, titles, present job, past experience, or the time devoted?*
   a. Generally, give all of these only in reports to the public or in others similarly going outside your own organization.
   b. You should almost always give your name and department. Use your job title if the reader may not know who you are.
   c. The closer you are to the reader, the less you need to tell of your experience.
   d. Usually skip the time factor. The amount of time spent rarely excuses a bad job or increases respect for a good one. One exception—if a time limit were set in the assignment, it can be casually mentioned while reviewing the facts of the assignment (occasion).

2. *Should you mention your personal feelings and reactions?*
   a. This depends pretty much on who your reader is. Will he care about them? Sometimes it is effective: "I feel it very important that we take action as soon as possible, because . . ."
   b. Sometimes this can be a gracious way of thanking someone for a productive assignment—you can mention how much you got out of it or how you appreciated the chance to do it. But watch this one carefully. It may sound naïve, or as if you are apple-polishing.

3. *Should you acknowledge people who helped you?*
   a. If the help contributed to the technical substance of the report, you are obligated to do so. Besides, then they are likely to help you again. Give name, job title, and type of assistance.

   b. For other types of assistance, use your judgment.
      Sometimes flowers or candy to your secretary are
      more appropriate than a mention in the report.

Two final cautions on the use of prefatory material:

1. It should be kept in proportion to the rest of the report.
   The shorter the report, the less prefatory material.
2. Before you decide to include any item of content,
   scrutinize it carefully. Then express it as simply, clearly,
   and directly as possible.

We are now ready to answer the last of the three questions
we asked at the beginning of this chapter.

PLACEMENT

Prefatory material is found in a wide number of places,
and it is not always found in any one place even in the same
report. Here are some of the possibilities, with an idea of
when each can be suitable. Notice that the *reader* and the
material are the dominant factors in any decision.

IN A PREFACE

Prefaces are regularly used in technical books such as textbooks. They are also suitable for certain types of report.
Guides are:

   a. The report is more than a few pages long.
   b. The readers are general. There is no particular person
      or group to whom the report is addressed, and while
      we can guess the type of people who will read it, we
      have no certain idea who they will be. The more
      readers, and the less they are specified, the more likely
      we are to call this type of material a *preface*.

The preface is almost always placed immediately after the
title page. In form it is headed with the word "Preface,"

sometimes has the author's name at the end, sometimes is given a place or date line, and sometimes has title or position after the printed or typed name.

IN AN ACKNOWLEDGMENTS SECTION

When the necessary acknowledgments are very detailed and lengthy—say nearly a page or more—they should be separated from the rest of the prefatory material. They appear in a separate section which either follows the preface or is placed in the appendix.

IN A FOREWORD

Guides for deciding to use a foreword are the same as for prefaces, with these differences:

a. If your readers have less technical knowledge than you, or the report is more informal. "Foreword" sounds easier than the Latinate "Preface," so you use the other name.

b. When the preface is written by someone other than you. The reader expects a preface to be by the author, unless it is clumsily named "Publisher's Preface," or something of the sort. "Foreword" is more loosely used, so the reader has no particular mind-set in respect to it. For example, "Foreword" is used when it is thought desirable to say things about the author that he could not gracefully say for himself. Another instance is where some higher executive may want to introduce the report to the general audience. This happens a great deal with manuals and other reports giving directions. Then "Foreword" may even be replaced by a descriptive line such as "A Word From the President" or "To Our Employes."

Not all forewords are prefatory. The term is also used as an informal substitute for introduction.

The foreword is usually placed in the same position as a preface, and it follows the same general form. Occasionally some author goes "hogwild," and you see a report that has a preface, a foreword, and an acknowledgments section, one right after the other. Generally this is unnecessary.

IN A LETTER

In reports a letter is more commonly used than is a preface. It is called a covering letter or a letter of transmittal. Guides for use of a letter are these:

a. The report is more than a few pages long.
b. The reader or readers are known. The letter may be addressed to a professional society or some other group. Usually, however, it is addressed to the first official reader.

There are a number of variations in the use of these letters. Where reports continue *upwards,* some readers add a letter of their own and transmit the report to the next level. They place theirs ahead of the original letter. Others remove the transmitting letter and substitute one of their own. And some writers use more than one to start with. They may, for example, reproduce the authorizing letter verbatim, and then add their own. Unless there is some overriding reason, however, it is best for the writer to try to do the job in one letter. Too much preliminary material can kill even the best report.

The letter may be placed in any of several positions. Right after the title page is most common. Other times it comes before the title page, and sometimes it is not bound with the report at all, but simply clipped to the outside of it. In the latter case, the letter is not expected to stay with the report after its first reading.

The form of the letter also varies. Normally it takes standard business-letter form, with or without a letterhead. In other companies, the interorganization letterhead or memorandum form is used. All are equally good, and which to use is simply a matter of preference or custom. Whatever the form, the actual signature of the writer should appear at the end—unless the report is reproduced in many copies. The position or title of the writer usually follows his signature.

The fact that prefatory material is put in a letter is a matter of form, not of content. The content of a letter of transmittal includes whatever prefatory material is needed. The letter is not something peculiar or different, in spite of its formidable sounding name. It may consist of no more than a sentence or two. Here is the entire body of one I wrote yesterday:

> As you requested, the Special Activities Advisory Committee met yesterday to consider space requirements for these activities. A preliminary report of our findings is attached.

On the other hand, the content of the letter may be very elaborate, as in the example on page 576. The thing to remember is that a letter of transmittal is merely a form for presenting prefatory material. Just like other prefatory material, its content is determined in terms of the guides on pages 35 to 40.

ON THE TITLE PAGE

In reports long enough to require a title page, the name of the recipient and author, together with their titles, may appear there. If so, they follow lines which say, in effect, "submitted to" and "by."

IN OTHER TITLE POSITIONS

In shorter reports where there is no separate title page, the information about the author or reader which usually goes there may appear under the title on the first page of

the text. Other prefatory material gets one of the positions
discussed below.

IN REFERENCE LINES

Where the report is short, the whole thing may take letter,
or more likely, memorandum form. Then various reference
lines may be used to give either merely names, or names
plus titles. These include possibilities such as "To," "From,"
"Authorized by," "Suggested by," "Test performed by," "Reported by," etc. Placement depends on local custom.

IN THE INTRODUCTION

In short reports, both where reference lines are used and
where they are not, other prefatory material appears with
the introduction. This material then must be very brief. It
usually concerns the occasion of the report: *"Here is the report you requested . . ."* or *"As vacation time draws near
again . . ."*

NOWHERE AT ALL

Short routine reports have no prefatory material other
than initials or signature. Everyone knows everyone else
concerned, the occasion occurs often and regularly, and it
would be foolish to waste time giving any unnecessary
information. In a sense, however, even these routine reports
once had prefatory material—in the original directive on the
use of the form.

OTHER POSITIONS

Occasionally reports are printed in magazines or other
serial publications of technical societies. Generally the
writer is then simply asked to furnish prefatory material on
a separate sheet. He has no hand in it from then on, but
he may find it in print later in several places. It may appear

as headnotes under the title, footnotes on the first page of the article, boxed or otherwise separate from the text in its early pages, or even in a special department of the magazine which is devoted to telling about contributors. And if he ever has a long report printed for public distribution, he may find such material on the book jacket.

About the latter we need not worry. For everyday reports we simply need to use the guides of this chapter and, by means of them

1. Decide what content is needed.
2. Visualize the length of the report.
3. Check local custom.
4. Determine the best placement and form.

PRACTICE SUGGESTIONS

1. The first group of reports in Part II begins with one that uses a letter, in memorandum form; the rest in that group have very little prefatory material. Study the reports and their accompanying analyses to help establish the general principles involved. For each report, read the analysis of the report situation and prefatory material. Then look at that material itself. Begin on pages 279 and 284.

2. Prefatory material is also shown in other reports in Part II. With these, read and analyze the prefatory material *first.* Jot down your analysis of where the material is located and what it contains. Also write down what you think the report situation must have been. Then compare your results with the analysis given with the reports.

   Begin on pages 366 and 370.

3. An illustration of a letter which contains summary material that overlaps the report is shown on page 576. One showing overlapping with the introduction is on page 434. Only in instances such as these is overlapping either desirable or necessary in a well-planned report.

4. Now examine your own collection of reports. Use the material in this chapter as a checklist on *content* and *position.*

It is best if you can also check your findings with those of other people.

Ask yourself whether the writer of each of your reports selected the best placement and content for prefatory material, in view of what you know of the report situation. Try some other schemes to see if they seem better when actually written down.

5. An acceptable form for a letter without a letterhead is shown on page 371. One with a letterhead is on page 425. Memorandums adopt forms such as are shown on pages 348, 354 and 414.

6. By the way, where is the prefatory material in this book? I played around quite a while with it. First I thought I'd just use the material at the end of Chapter 2 right where it is now, and hide the rest in back. Then I decided acknowledgments *had* to go up front in this instance. Why? For what readers is the present preface intended? For whom the end of Chapter 2? Why is some material repeated?

6

Using Introductions

ANY READER wants to know what the report is all about. To tell him is the function of the introduction. At one extreme are the complicated and long introductions which may precede a three-level report. At the other extreme, there may be no introduction, its function being accomplished by the title of a form.

In this chapter the plan is to start with the two variations of the three-level report described in Chapter 4. Then, as the writer, reader, use, and material change, we will see introductions reduced to the very minimum elements. First this will be done for a report that results from an investigation, project, survey, or test. Then will come the one reporting information.

IN REPORTING INVESTIGATIONS

THE THREE-LEVEL INTRODUCTION

The pattern of the introduction of the three-level report resulting from an investigation can be expanded from that outlined in Chapter 4. The result would be:

Background [1]

    History and development of problem
    Theory or principles on which problem rests

---

[1] Only *some* of the items listed under background appear in any one three-level report. Occasionally other items also appear.

General need which produced this problem
Importance of the area or problem
Definitions

Statement of problem or objective of the project or study
General procedure or method of solution
Purpose of report—very brief
Divisions of report

When and *how* should each of these be used?

Background

GENERAL. Any question about the use of background returns us to the reader, the use, and the material. It must be as much as the reader needs, but it must not wear him out. It also must not be out of proportion to the rest of the material in the introduction. Many long reports give too much background. To avoid doing so, try these steps.

1. State the problem *first*.
2. Get a clear idea of your reader or readers. (If you don't know him, you will know what his job is. Picture him in your mind, or even use the trick device of finding somewhere a picture that corresponds to your idea of him, and put it in front of you.)
3. Now ask—what is the *very least* he needs to know *before* he can understand my statement of the problem? How much to understand its essential importance and significance?

What you put down is the background material. Place it just ahead of the statement of problem.

Often what you have *not* put down will seem very important to you, even if you know it is not essential to the statement of the problem. You feel that at least one reader will understand better if you tell him more, or you feel that the material is too valuable to lose. If so, perhaps it can be used—but keep it out of the introduction! Remember that your readers are busy men. They must be able to stop, if they want to, whenever they clearly have the answer they need. But you don't want them to stop because they give up.

Some possible positions for extra background material are these:

1. Sometimes it can go to Section III—right after the conclusions. Place it here *only* if you think all or almost all of your readers will need it. If there is any doubt, use another choice. Put it this way: If your most important reader decided he would like to see the detailed steps of your solution and began to read the body of the report, *do you want his attention on this background or on what you did?* Don't smother your project!

2. Sometimes background can be split into smaller bits and put with related sections. To test if this is good, suppose your reader doubted one conclusion and turned to the appropriate section. Would the background dominate the section? If it was at all long, it would again get in the way of what the reader was trying to find out.

3. In most instances background can go in the appendix. Then you refer to it in the introduction and at any other place your reader might need it. In a way, it puts the decision on his shoulders. Probably if any one reader is likely to need it, but not others, the appendix is the best position.

4. Much of the time it can be completely omitted. This is the solution if the material is readily available in some other place. Then your text can simply refer to it.

So much for background in general. Now for some of

the specific kinds of background and what to do and what to avoid with each. Remember that the general remarks apply to all.

HISTORY. Occasionally the reader needs to know about earlier attempts at solution of the same general problem. The typical flow of thought might go something like this (though the wording would differ and the concrete facts be supplied):

> During World War II there was a shortage of trained supervisors. This plant felt the effects. They showed in high labor turnover, in sharply increased grievances, in absenteeism, etc. To supply the shortage, supervisors were recruited from other plants. This did for a while. Then with the Korean situation the same problem came up. A college graduate program was tried, with these results . . . Today the situation is more acute, and these programs have broken down. To see how they could be modified and supplemented, the study reported here was undertaken.

Note that the history led up to the present problem, which now will be stated more exactly. Note also that it did not attempt to show the entire history of the development of problems of supervisory competence since Adam began to be supervised by Eve!

The last remark is not facetious. Too many people who write reports (and textbooks) think they should start with the dawn of history. One report which came across my desk began with a discussion of how the caveman moved rocks. It even showed a drawing of him doing it. A few pages took me through centuries of unhistorical history to the present day and to the fact that "material handling" problems still exist. In another couple of pages I found that the project dealt with *one* problem in *one* part of *one* department of *one* plant—should or should not a certain item be palletized!

The best rule is to leave out any history which does not

bear *directly* on the problem. If this hurts your historical sense too much, or if it is desirable to give a lengthy discussion of really pertinent history, try some of the solutions under "General" above. If it just hurts, try the appendix. If it really counts, try Section III or breaking it up.

THEORY OR GENERAL PRINCIPLES ON WHICH PROBLEM RESTS. What is meant by "theory or general principles" can be illustrated by an actual report on statistical quality control. After a perfectly legitimate statement that statistical methods had been successfully applied in certain areas, the report then went into an elaborate discussion of basic theory. Then it got around to saying that the project was an attempt to apply this theory to certain parts produced in a particular production area. This theory went handily in the appendix of the revised report, replaced in the text by a single paragraph stating the principles involved.

In such instances involving basic theory, a good textbook is usually available. You already know that at least the original reader will understand your report without explanation. The others do not want to become experts in that area, and wouldn't have the time if they did. Give them just enough to know what the report is about.

GENERAL NEED. By "general need" is meant a general problem or situation which led to the specific problem of the project. An example might be saturation of a particular market with your product. The result would be falling off of sales. This would lead to your particular problem—a market research to see if a demand existed or could be created in a certain new area.

Like other background the statement of general need leads directly to the statement of problem. It is there so that the reader can get an accurate idea of where your project fits in the general picture. It keeps things in proportion.

The more this need can be expressed in concrete facts and figures, the more significance it will carry. Indeed, it is better to leave "need" out than to be so general no one will believe you. In any event keep it short. If you spend much time on it, people will expect your report to deal with the *whole* problem.

Importance of Problem. Stating the importance of the problem is giving "need" from another angle. Your project deals with an area that is perennially important (say, cost of production), though no acute larger problem exists. Don't blow this up unduly. The mountain may seem to bring forth a mouse.

Definitions. Often definitions appear in the background when they should not. The only definitions that should go in an introduction are those involved in the statement of the problem. Definitions needed in *developing the solution* belong either at the point of use or in a glossary. And in a three-level report, specialized terms would not appear in the conclusions. There is, then, no reason for defining them in the introduction.

Choice and Position of Background Parts. Hardly ever are *all* these kinds of background needed. Since the purpose of background is to emphasize or clarify the problem, simply choose whichever of these you think will be most effective.

Any kind of background can come either before or after the statement of the problem. I strongly recommend the earlier position. If background comes after the statement of problem, the reader has to go from a smaller concept to a larger one and then back. Giving him background first keeps his thoughts moving in one direction.

Statement of Problem

The specific problem or main objective is the kernel of any introduction to a report that concerns a project, test, investigation, survey, or similar study. It is the only reason the study was made. It follows that if it is not clearly stated, no reader can be expected to understand the rest of the report. In fact, if the statement of problem is not clearly formulated early in the project being reported, the chances are that it was a sloppy project. You can't solve a problem unless you know clearly what the problem is. You can't reach an indefinite objective.

Neither can the reader judge conclusions unless he knows precisely what they are conclusions about.

It follows that the problem should be formulated in a single clear statement. A connection is first made with the background, because it was used to lead up to this sentence in such a way that the problem *would* be clear. One of the means of making the connection is a phrase or sentence. For example, after the background you might write, "The project reported here was therefore undertaken. The specific problem was . . ." (Or, "Its specific objective was . . .").

This statement serves as a lead or topic sentence for further clarification. Sometimes simply restating the problem in other terms clarifies it.

Other devices are:

1. To give a breakdown into subproblems or subobjectives.
2. To limit the problem; that is, carefully tell what it will *not* cover.

Sometimes you need to do both.

The entire discussion should be brief. Details are not given here. The purpose is to state the general problem as concretely as you can. If necessary, you can give elaborate details of the main problem later in the report (Section III, if you haven't assigned it to something else). Details about subproblems or subobjectives should go to the part of the report that gives details of their solution.

The "statement of problem" with which the report of an investigation deals will not always be called "Problem."

Sometimes the terms "Object" or "Purpose" are used instead. If so, "object" means "object of the project," not "object of the report." Likewise "purpose" means "purpose of the project," or "purpose of the test."

Both terms are good in practice, but in studying reports they tend to get the statement of problem confused with the statement of the "purpose of this report." Since investigations, tests, or projects always seek an *answer* or *solution,* "problem" is the least confusing term.

The term "Scope" is also sometimes applied to that part of the statement of problem which gives subobjectives or limitations of the problem. The term will not be used here in talking of reports of investigations, in order to avoid confusion with its use to mean "extent of coverage in this report."

General Procedure

An account of the general procedure or method of solution comes next. For, once the reader knows the problem, he wants to know if it was solved in a sensible way.

The same things hold true for it as for the earlier parts. Be brief, but concrete.

Give something about the major techniques or steps used. If the steps are described in detail in later sections, simply name them in the introduction. However, they must be named in a way that means something. To say you "analyzed" something, or "made a survey," means nothing unless you tell the technique used in the analysis or survey. (For instance: They were analyzed by this method, or in these respects; or a survey was made of 10,000 customers, selected at random from the owner list, by means of a questionnaire aimed at determining so and so.)

Sometimes the complete details of the procedure can be given in half a page to a page. If so, it might as well be done in the introduction. Usually, however, the details of the method must go to the body of the report.

Here are some of the ways to determine where.

If just one procedure was used throughout the report, put it in an early section. Again Section III will do if not used for detailed background or detailed statement of problem. If it has been assigned, Section IV is logical.

If several different procedures were used in different parts of the investigation, put the account of them as close as possible to the data or facts they evolved. For example, early in a section. Or, if a section is made up of subproblems, put them with the problem they concern. Or if, say, the data of three sections resulted from one method, and those of another three from another method, put each method in a separate section just ahead of those sections containing the data it evolved.

If the procedure is detailed and long, the reader will not remember it from an account given in the introduction. He needs the account at the point of use. And putting it there helps keep the introduction short.

Purpose of Report

The purpose of a report of an investigation is to report the results of the investigation. That is all you say and all you need to say.

Divisions of Report

The last part of the introduction gives the reader a very brief sketch of how the rest of the report is organized. If the report follows the steps of the procedure as just outlined, say so. If it deals in order with each of the subproblems or subobjectives previously given, say that. If the arrangement is more complicated, review it by naming the topics discussed in the order in which they occur.

Always give the location of the conclusions.

Though often omitted in otherwise good reports, this assistance to the reader is very important. As you can see from the preceding paragraph, a number of arrangements are possible, and some may even be suggested by prior parts of the introduction. The reader will therefore feel more at home with the report if he knows what to expect. The report will seem to unfold naturally.

SIMPLER INTRODUCTIONS

To get the right introduction for situations that are simpler than one which requires a three-level introduction, use the following steps:

1. Establish the "content" of the four guides: What is the material? Who is the reader? What is his use of the material? Where do you stand in the picture?
2. Review in succession the things which go into the introduction of a three-level report, and ask if they fit the new report situation.

Here are some examples of what will happen in varying situations. Each situation has no particular title, so they are merely numbered progressively.

1

GIVEN:	*Material*	Not routine. Some unusual situation has come up.
	Reader	Immediate superior.
	Use	To help him make a decision in a matter which concerns his own department. He can make the correction or do whatever needs to be done without further approval.
	Writer	Anyone in the department who saw the problem and *initiated* the study. He is reporting on his own, not because the problem was assigned.

SOLUTION: *Background*   Use less than in a three-level report because the reader knows the department. But since he didn't see the problem himself, so far as is known, give enough background so he realizes that it is a significant one.

Other elements   Same as three-level.

2

GIVEN: *Same as 1, except*

Writer   Now he was assigned the report.

SOLUTION: *Background*   Omit most or all of it. (Some prefatory material may be used to remind the reader of the assignment.)

Problem   Make it brief, usually just as assigned.

Other elements   Same as three-level report.

3

GIVEN: *Same as 1, except*

Use   To file as a permanent record for an indefinite but much later use.

Writer   Anyone in the department, but the report could be either assigned or initiated. It would make no difference.

SOLUTION: *Background*   Between that of the three-level report and that for your immediate superior in 1. The later reader will be a man of the same technical or professional specialty, but he won't know what situation existed in the department when you wrote the report (perhaps five years before he looked at it).

Other elements   Same as three-level report.

4

GIVEN: *Material*   The thing being reported is routine. An example would be a report of a customer follow-up interview. A standard laboratory test is another.

Reader   Immediate superior or a co-worker whether in the same department as the writer or in another. He regularly receives such reports as part of his job.

Use   To help the reader do something that is part of his regular job assignment.

Writer   Reporting such matters is part of his regular job.

SOLUTION: *Background*   None needed.

Problem   Very brief. (To give a customer follow-up interview or to test the tensile strength of a particular sample sent in by another department. This would be stated in the title or in a subject line, as in a memorandum.)

Procedure   If standard, name it. If any variations, explain them.

| | *Purpose* | Omitted. The reader knows it from the title or head of the report. |
| | *Order* | Omitted. The reader knows the standard order for all routine reports of this sort. It may even be preprinted as standard heads on a memorandum form. |

5

GIVEN:	*Material*	Routine as can be.
	Reader	Anyone in the organization who gets this routine information.
	Use	Immediate action, record keeping, or filing for part of a later summary report.
	Writer	Getting and reporting this material is part of his routine job assignment.
SOLUTION:	*Problem*	Identify what was checked, if it is not identified in the title of the report. (This means to fill in the blanks asking for identifying data.)
	Procedure	Name the standard test, if not already printed on the blank.
	Other elements	Not used. Notice such a situation calls for a form that has already been developed. If none exists, develop one.

IN REPORTING INFORMATION

THE THREE-LEVEL INTRODUCTION

The expanded pattern for the introduction of the three-level report giving information looks like this:

Background

> History of the subject matter
> Preliminary theory or principles
> Importance of the subject
> Preliminary definitions
> Identifying facts

Statement of purpose
Scope and limitations of report
Divisions of report

Our discussion of when and how these are used in the introduction can be much briefer than it was for the report of an investigation. Because the two patterns come from the same basic pattern, what applies to one applies in most respects to the other.

Background

GENERAL. In the introduction to the report centered on giving information, selecting background is the biggest problem. Almost any kind of material may be right for certain occasions and certain readers. In selecting background, then, it is necessary to form a very clear idea about the reader and his probable use of the information.

Fortunately, three-level reports in this pattern are frequently assigned rather than initiated. We wouldn't, for example, send such a report to our superior unless he asked for it or unless it was a regularly expected thing. Hence the nature of the assignment will give a clue as to what background is needed. Suppose, for example, you were asked to assemble all possible information on the probable future supply of critical materials. You would have been given the assignment because you were thought to know most about it, because it was in the area of your specialization, or because you had best access to the information. The assignment would also probably give you some idea of how the information was to be used. Knowing that, you would concentrate on the background needed to show the real significance of the material you decided to present.

Other three-level information reports will travel *downwards* rather than up. This is true even if the person who reads them is not below you on the organization chart. For your report may have been given to him by his superior, to whom you originally reported, after he had reviewed and approved it. The annual report a president sometimes makes to his employes is an example. He may not write it, but he signs it. Here the background again is determined by the reader—what will be likely to make him want to read the report?

In an introduction of this sort, the statement of purpose is the dominant part. It should be used as the starting point. In actual writing, then:

1. Formulate the statement of purpose in a clear sentence.
2. Get a clear idea of the reader, especially of his interests and knowledge.
3. Then ask—what is the *least* he needs to know to understand the purpose *and* to think it matters?

Any other material you think he might possibly need or want can be put in an early developing section or in the appendix, or be split among various sections dealing with particular phases of the subject as the need for it arises. It should not be allowed to overpower what you want to contribute to the subject. Thus if your subject is *Future Sources of Critical Materials,* don't spend so much time on the history of the development of existing sources that your reader forgets that he is supposed to learn about future sources.

HISTORY. In the introduction, limit history to that which shows the importance of the subject.

PRELIMINARY THEORY OR PRINCIPLES. The introduction should contain only the preliminary theory needed to understand the purpose of the report or the significance of the following summary.

IMPORTANCE OF THE SUBJECT. Background showing the importance of the subject is the most frequently justified. It answers the natural question, "Is this worth reading about?" The more concrete it can be, the better. Tell, for example, a few of the most important uses of critical materials and the effects of the shortage. But don't try to be exhaustive.

PRELIMINARY DEFINITIONS. Terms used in the title, in the statement of purpose, or in the statement of scope must be defined if the reader does not know them. For example, what is a *critical* material? Other definitions belong in a glossary or at the point of first use of the term defined.

IDENTIFYING FACTS. Some subjects require identifying facts to give the reader a concrete idea of what is being discussed. Thus a report written to retail men to describe the outstanding features of a new retail outlet would need to tell such things as its location and its volume of business.

Statement of Purpose

The statement of purpose tells what the report is going to do about the subject. It expands or specifies the idea of the title. For example, in the report on critical materials, the purpose might be to tell what the existing sources of the materials are, to evaluate their present yield, and to estimate the possibilities of their development. In the report on the new retail outlet, it might be to describe how it was planned, its outstanding features, its success in operation, and the possibilities of duplicating it. Or it might be any one of these.

Note that the purpose is expressed without reference to the reader, even though he is clearly in the writer's mind. Except in prefatory material, it isn't a good idea to say that you are writing for the layman, or the young man, or those who don't know anything about the subject. If you drag the reader in at this point, you almost always insult him. It is all right to assume you are an authority by taking an authoritative tone, but it is bad to imply to the reader that he doesn't know anything.

Likewise, any personal reasons you have for writing the report should not appear here. They belong in the preface too. In the introduction the reader wants to know as exactly as possible what the report is about.

Scope and Limitations

If the exact limits of the discussion to follow are not clear from the statement of purpose or from the "divisions of report" to follow, the next step is to describe those limits. These are not the limits of time or your ability or available material—those are prefatory. They are the explanation of what is or is not considered in the report that follows.

Divisions of Report

Sometimes the statement of purpose or scope tells the reader just how the rest of the report is organized. Often, however, it does not. Then the remaining step is to give him this information. For example, in the report on critical materials, the sections of the report might have dealt, in order, with the three phases that were given in stating the purpose. On the other hand, you might have decided to devote a section to each material, in which case you would name them in the order in which they were to be discussed.

If the summary follows the introduction, tell the reader here.

SIMPLER INTRODUCTIONS

Simpler information reports make up the majority of all reports. To get an appropriate introduction to such a report, reduce the pattern just as for a report of an investigation:

1. Determine the reader, his expected use of the report, the material, and where you stand in the picture.
2. Review the things which can go in the introduction to such a report, and ask how they fit the report situation.

Specific applications will parallel those for the report of an investigation. The more familiar the reader is with the subject, the less background he needs. Indeed, he may need none. The more routine the use, the less necessary a statement of purpose, scope, or arrangement of the report. At the simplest extreme is the short, routine report regularly sent by the writer to the same reader, in a standard order of arrangement. Here all that will be left of the introduction may be the title of the form which contains the report.

IN OTHER APPLICATIONS

The same principles can be applied to other types of writing on technical subjects. Manuals, directions, and similar pieces of writing use introductions that follow the information report pattern. Articles in professional magazines may take either pattern, but may place more stress on the background elements, especially importance. The reason is that the reader's need of the information is not so urgent because it does not so directly concern his job. And when no immediate need appears, and the reader is in no hurry, as when he reads an article in a general magazine, more stress must be placed by the writer on devices for gaining interest, and even the purpose may appear only by implication.

PRACTICE SUGGESTIONS

1. First study introductions of the reports of investigations. Begin on pages 279 and 294. The introductions and analyses are on the following pages:

   As you do so, tabulate the number of times each item, on pages 47-48 appears—kind of background, statement of problem, and so on. Notice that the statement of the problem investigated is the keystone of these introductions.

2. Do the same with the reports giving information. Begin on pages 366 and 374.

   Again tabulate how many times each item appears, but use the list on page 60. Notice that the statement of the purpose of the report is the keystone of these introductions.

3. Look especially at the handling of these items of background:

   History—pages 532, 546
   Theory or principles—pages 390, 398
   General need—pages 279, 294
   Importance—pages 322, 326
   Definitions—pages 279, 294

4. Analyze for yourself introductions of the reports in Chapter 17. Begin on page 447. Then compare your analyses with those given with the individual report. You may not always agree. If so, discuss the disagreement with others and then make your own decision. Watch the ones on pages 473 and 491-495—they are tricky.

5. Now you are ready to examine the introductions of your own collection of reports. Should missing parts be supplied? Is the order in a logical progression? Is prefatory material unnecessarily mixed and confused with introductory material?

   Rewrite any that you find unsatisfactory.

6. An unusual way of handling "order of discussion" is shown in the report on pages 470 to 487. What do you think of the device?

7

Concluding

ONCE THE reader knows what a report is about, he is anxious to know how it came out. His reaction is a practical instance of the same sort of urge that makes you want to turn to the last pages of a mystery novel just after the murder has been described. The developing parts of a report are useful only to explain the outcome. Hence if the reader is willing to accept your statement of the outcome at once, he has no use for the developing sections.

Put in another way, the concluding section of a report is the answer to the problem that gave rise to any investigation. Or it summarizes the significant factors that justify the purpose of a report giving information.

That is why the concluding section regularly is placed just after the introduction, even though it must actually be *written* after the developing sections.

Since the concluding section is what a report exists for, planning it requires real thought. Again our guides must be used. Let's see what happens when we apply them to the customary concluding sections for the two patterns of a three-level report.

CONCLUDING THE INVESTIGATION PATTERN

The final outcome of any project or investigation will be facts, inferences from those facts, or recommendations as to how to solve the problem. All are in a real sense *conclusions,* for they are the outcome of applying a certain procedure. But there is a difference in their degree of remoteness from the raw data. Hence it is useful to distinguish them with the terms *findings* (or *results*), *conclusions,* and *recommendations.*

For, example, if you don't feel very well and go to a doctor, he performs certain tests. He takes your temperature and finds it to be, say, 101. This and what he learns from other tests and procedures are raw data, which, summarized, are *findings.* On the basis of these he makes the inference that you have malaria. This is a *conclusion.* Finally, he tells you what to do. This is a *recommendation.*

IN THREE-LEVEL REPORTS

Placement

THE RELATION OF CONCLUDING ELEMENTS

Not all three-level reports have all of these elements in their second section. When all do appear, they are not necessarily in the order named above. That is, they may not appear in the order in which they were reached. Here is how to tell what to do:

1. If all findings are in one group, all conclusions in another, and all recommendations in a third, try them in *reverse order.* The principle is the same principle of *use* which led to the placement of conclusions right after the introduction. The recommendations are the biggest outcome. If the reader accepts them, he need not read further. If instead he asks "Why?", he finds his answer in the conclusions. If of any conclusion he then says, "I'm not sure it's true," he can immediately go to the findings on which they were based.
2. Sometimes the reader cannot understand the recom-

mendations or appreciate their significance without seeing how they grow out of the conclusions. Likewise, sometimes he cannot understand the conclusions without a summary of findings. If so, the order is findings, conclusions, recommendations. But notice I said *understand*, not *believe*.

There is one other time this order is used—when the reader is known to reach snap judgments. Then to protect both him and yourself you have to start with the findings. But whenever that occurs, you have such an unusual situation that you may have to place the entire concluding section at the end of the report, abandoning all the advantages of inverted order.

3. Sometimes the concluding elements break into triplets. That is, one finding leads to one conclusion, which leads to one recommendation. If so, group them in those triplets. Which element is put first depends on the same considerations discussed in 1 and 2.

4. Sometimes the data cannot be summarized in findings, for the summary would be too long. At other times, the conclusions grow from a chain of reasoning rather than directly from findings. If so, no summary of findings is used. Otherwise, the treatment of the concluding section is the same as when all three elements are present.

5. Sometimes there are *only* findings, sometimes *only* conclusions, and sometimes both these but no recommendations. Under such circumstances, disregard any missing elements and proceed to arrange the section on the same principles as before.

USING SEPARATE SECTIONS

In very long three-level reports, the concluding section may seem too long. Then it is a good idea to use three short sections instead. Their order will follow the same principles as if they were in one section. If you adopt this plan you must tell the reader so at the end of the introduction.

ORDER WITHIN GROUPS

Whatever groupings you use, you may find that some conclusions are specific ones, and others general. For example, some conclusions may grow out of each specific section of the report. When you compare these conclusions, you draw further ones which apply to the whole problem. In accordance with the principle of use, place these general conclusions first—they are the most important ones.

Opening

With so many different possible arrangements of the elements, it is obvious that no reader will know what to expect unless he is told. Hence in a three-level report you cannot rely on the section head alone. You must have an opening sentence or two to tell the reader which elements to expect and how they will be arranged.

Content

How much of the outcome of the report should go in the concluding section? Here is a real problem. You cannot go into too much detail or you will lose the objective of saving the reader time. On the other hand, chances are that he will not read most of the developing sections. Anything it is really significant for him to know must go up front.

Part of the answer here depends on how the particular reader has reacted in the past. Part will depend on his known interest in the problem. Generally, keep the concluding section as short as you can while still including everything he *has* to know about the outcome of the report in order to make a sound judgment.

The difficulty of drawing the line between too much and too little shows the importance of placing general conclusions and recommendations first. It gets your main story to the reader, it permits him to stop when he feels like it, but your secondary matter is right at hand in case he feels like using it.

To keep down the length, argument hardly ever should appear in the concluding section. The conclusions serve as the argument for the recommendations, and the summary of findings is the argument for the conclusions. Where the study does not really have findings, however, it is sometimes necessary to tell one or two of the most important reasons for each conclusion.

Form

In any concluding section, the objective is to get the vital outcome told in the easiest way for the reader. Tables, graphs, and charts that summarize often help. The text is then used to point out the highlights in the accompanying illustrations.

Lists also help. If each conclusion and recommendation is set apart and properly numbered, the reader sees it quickly. And he sees it as a single, simple item, so that it is easier to grasp and evaluate. (The value of such devices is discussed further in Chapter 10, "Using Illustrations.")

If the reader accepts the conclusions, he stops reading the report. But if he doubts one of them, he wants to find the supporting evidence as quickly as possible. Any long report should therefore have its conclusions *keyed* to the related spots in the report. The reader can then turn immediately to what he wants to know.

Two methods are used.

First, where the specific conclusions correspond to the sections, they can be grouped in Section II under heads

that match the section heads. The reader can then turn
to the pertinent section.

Second, where another type of grouping is used, each
outcome can be keyed by page number. If this is done, the
opening of the concluding section should contain a statement to the effect that numbers in parentheses after each
item show the page of the report on which substantiating
evidence may be found. (The page given is the *beginning*
page of the pertinent discussion.)

Duplication of Outcomes

One result of giving specific findings, conclusions, and
recommendations in Section II sometimes worries writers
of reports. That is the fact that specific outcomes may duplicate word for word those which appear within or at the
end of developing sections of the report. You will not
worry if you remember that a report is written to be used.
When the reader uses the concluding section, he wants
to get the important outcome. He will not use the body
of the report unless he doubts an answer or wants to trace
in detail how it was reached. When he turns back to trace
the evidence he is led step-by-step to each answer. Seeing
that same answer at the end of the proof serves to complete
the thought pattern. It is like a mathematical demonstration that ends Q.E.D. And if he reads the entire section,
the conclusions gathered at the end are a logical summary
of what has gone before. Hence repetition of this kind is
not a fault.

Special Problems

Some types of report materials create special problems
in stating conclusions because they have a whole structure
or system as the final result. If the problem is a new layout
for a manufacturing area, for example, the real outcome is
the new layout. If the problem is to create a satisfactory

design, the outcome is the new design. If to improve a procedure, a new procedure. Yet any of these will usually be too long or too clumsy to appear right after the introduction.

The solution depends on the nature of the materials. Suppose the solution is verbal. You might, for example, have set up a new system or procedure. The reader will want to know two things. First, is it any good? Second, exactly what is it? So you do two things:

FIRST, set up your conclusions. How you arrive at them we will see later in discussing organization of data. But certain things will surely be true. First, there will be certain objectives or end results which any satisfactory system must achieve. Second, there will be certain functions that must be performed by any system. And third, there must be standards of judgment—measuring sticks which are called criteria. They might include such things as cost, flexibility, speed, freedom from error, and so on. Moreover, any proposed system must be judged in terms of whether it is better than some other possibility—the old system or other alternatives. The concluding section therefore must summarize the findings in respect to the alternatives, draw comparative conclusions, and recommend the procedure decided to be best. These findings, conclusions, and recommendations are treated just like any others.

SECOND, write up the complete procedure or system in exactly the way you would do it if you planned to hand it to someone and say, "Put this into effect at once." (That is just what you hope your reader will do.) The most convenient place for the reader to find the account is right after the conclusions section. So the system is outlined in Section III.

The reader asks the same questions about any layout or design. The difference is that the final outcome is graphic instead of verbal. The solution is substantially the same:

FIRST, set up conclusions as before. The design must accomplish something (objective), there will be certain critical points (like functions), and you will have certain criteria to judge how well these are taken care of. So far, then, your method of handling the concluding section can be the same as for a new procedure.

SECOND, you must place the completed drawing or drawings somewhere. If it is one drawing, it is too big for Section III. If you break it down, it may take several pages, and it is clumsy to have several pages of illustration breaking up the basic text. The solution therefore is to place the graphic material somewhere else in the report—usually the appendix—and refer the reader to it in the concluding section.

Another special problem is the use of abstracts in investigation reports. It will be discussed at the end of this chapter, along with the abstract for the report giving information.

SIMPLER CONCLUSIONS

Treatment of conclusions changes very little when a report is simpler than a three-level report. Provided, that is, any conclusions at all are given (some reports consist of title plus data). The reason is obvious. If there is anything almost any reader is sure to want to know about any problem, it is the answer.

One difference will be in content. If your reader has great confidence in you, he may be willing to accept the recommendations without conclusions or findings. Or perhaps only the findings will be omitted.

A second difference may result in dovetailing elements of the concluding material with the parts that remain after the introduction has been reduced.

Typical arrangements are:

Problem
Conclusions and recommendations (These may reverse)

Procedure
Results (or Findings)
(Possibly followed by detailed data)

Problem
Procedure
Conclusions, etc.
Results (or Findings)
(Detailed data)

Problem
Procedure
Results
Conclusions
Recommendations
(Detailed data)

In practice, almost any mutation of these may occur. Occasionally, indeed, conclusions precede the statement of problem. The order in which results, conclusions, and recommendations appear is determined in exactly the same way as for a three-level report. Where the procedure goes is determined partly by its length and partly by whether it is needed to understand the conclusions and recommendations.

A third difference from the three-level report will be the frequent omission of a topic sentence that introduces the conclusions and tells their order. This happens when the conclusions are too brief to make such a guide necessary. Likewise, as the report gets shorter, keying the conclusions is less important.

A final difference—though we haven't considered this aspect here—comes when the reader is a specialist in the subject. Then technical terms and short cuts may be used in all three types of concluding material.

CONCLUDING THE INFORMATION PATTERN
IN THREE-LEVEL REPORTS

In the pattern for a three-level report of an investigation, the reason for putting the outcome right after the introduction was to give the busy reader a quick view of the whole. The information pattern has the same objective. One technique is to place a summary right after the introduction. Another is to place a summary somewhere *ahead* of the introduction. In the latter position the treatment may be slightly modified, and the result called an "abstract." Abstract is also used for a quite different type of summarizing element.

Let's look at each of these in the order named.

The Summary

CONTENT

The content of any summary hinges directly upon the purpose stated in the introduction. If your purpose had been to describe a new process, the summary would give the novel features and main steps of the new process. If your purpose was to describe the progress made by your department in the last year, the summary would list the main accomplishments.

Length is determined by how much you think the reader will be willing to read and how much you want to leave with him. Errors in judgment result in too general a summary or too long a summary.

Too *general* a summary can be avoided by asking yourself, "If the reader stops here, what important thing will he miss because I left it out?" Or ask, "If this is all he reads, will he have any concrete idea about my subject?"

If the summary seems too long, try working in reverse.

(This is the best procedure to use anyway.) First, put down all the things you think are essential for the reader to remember after he has finished the report. Be as concrete and factual as possible. ("The department saved $38,000 by nine types of savings in three areas." Not "The department made a considerable amount of savings in widely divergent areas.")

Your summary will now be too long. Taking a dim view of your reader's interest, set an arbitrary length you think he will surely read. Now try rewording to gain space without losing any fact or idea. (Your whole summary concerned a department, so your sentence can become, "$38,000 was saved in nine ways in three areas.") When you have condensed as much as you can, match the relative importance of each fact or generalization. Reluctant though you may be, cross out the less important ones. ("$38,000 was saved in three areas." Or, if necessary, "$38,000 was saved.") Note that, for brevity, a figure was used even though it comes at the beginning of a sentence.

As you weigh each idea against the other, the summary will finally come to the prescribed length. And holding yourself to a set length is good practice, as sometimes you will be *told* how far you must digest your facts. But the job will not have been easy, and will have taken a long time. A really good, compact, informative half-page summary of a twenty-page report may well take longer to write than the twenty original pages.

If you have enough space, sometimes you can use the same device used in the investigation pattern—place a general summary first, followed by a more detailed summary of each of the phases mentioned in it. You then assure yourself that the reader will get the general idea, and you make more detailed information very accessible to him.

FORM

Simple, easily read tables are just as helpful in a summary as in the concluding section of the investigation pattern. So are lists. They should be used to condense information or to make particular items stand out individually.

Keying parts of the summary by page number to the body of the report is not so easy nor so necessary as keying conclusions. Items in a summary may grow out of progressive section-to-section development, hence summarize primarily the last section or two. This makes keying difficult. It is less necessary because the reader is accepting you as an authority. He does not turn to the developing section in a spirit of doubt, but to get the whole story. If he is curious enough to go beyond the summary, he is more likely to read the whole report, or to read selected sections which he can easily pick out from the table of contents.

Nevertheless, if the result is not clumsy, it is a good idea to key the summary to the parts of the body.

ENDING THE REPORT

Because a report of this nature may be read all the way through, it may seem awkward to stop at the end of the last section without any device that gives finality to the report. To repeat the summary as a last section also seems awkward. One solution is to use a brief ending. It merely recalls to the reader the dominant idea of the introduction. That is, it uses the same type of closing device which we used back in the days when we had to write themes in school.

The Abstract (Summary Type)

The summary abstract, sometimes called the "informative" abstract, is primarily a summary separated from the rest of the report and placed before the introduction. Sometimes it is still called a summary, and it has a wide variety of other names. Two features mark it—position and content.

It is placed just before the introduction, just before the table of contents, or just before the prefatory material. If it were taken out, the report would still look like a complete report.

It is informative in content. It tells, not just what topics the report covers, but what the report *says* about the topics —it is a very short report on the same topic.

Use

In this position, the abstract or summary accomplishes the purpose of giving a quick picture of the main facts of the report. In two circumstances it is more desirable than a summary following the introduction:

1. When it will be separated from the report or reproduced for separate distribution. The abstract will be sent to people who need to know the main facts, but have no reason to know the details. Or if they do get interested, they can send for the whole report.
2. When it is the customary form used in the organization for which the writer works.

Content

Because the abstract must stand by itself, it varies in one way from the summary following the introduction: its opening sentence must give some idea of the purpose of the report. This is done by using a topic sentence or two to introduce the primary idea of the report.

When the term "abstract" is used, some people add another proviso—that it maintain the same proportions as the original report. The abstract then is like a pocketbook-size photographic reproduction of a large oil painting. All the parts, outlines, and main features are there, but the details are dropped out. In practice there is no need to follow this rule rigidly.

FORM

Summarizing tables and lists are used with the abstract also, though in practice less often. Probably this is because of the attempt to maintain proportion or to get greater compactness. If you think they will be helpful to the reader, use them.

ENDING THE REPORT

Using a summary before the introduction *and* another just after it is superfluous and confusing. Hence if you use the one way to get the quick picture, do not use the other.

To get completeness to the whole report, again use a simple ending. Or, if you call the out-of-position summary an abstract, you may decide to use a more detailed or list summary at the end of the report. If you do the latter—which I myself don't recommend—remember that most of your readers will never get to it. It follows that anything really important must go in the abstract.

The Abstract (*Review Type*)

The "indicative," "review," or "descriptive" type of abstract does not really perform the same function as a summary or an informative abstract. It "indicates" the *topics* covered in the report, but says little or nothing of what the report says *about* those topics. Sometimes it gives a judgment as to the value or completeness of the report. It is not a picture at all, but an outline sketch. It is intended to be used separate from the report (or as a "teaser" for a report printed in a magazine). It is very short, ranging from a sentence to perhaps a hundred words. All the reader knows when he has read it is whether the report covers the type of topic in which he might be interested.

Obviously, it does not give the same *kind* of quick view that we have been talking about earlier in this chapter. Hence it is not an integral part of the pattern of any report, though it may be used with either of the base patterns or their variations. When such an abstract is bound with a report, just after or just before the title page is the best position.

In reporting an *investigation,* the indicative abstract is simply added to the basic pattern in one of the same positions already given for the informative abstract. If in reporting information the introduction-summary arrangement is used, the review abstract is again simply added. If an informative abstract is used, the indicative type is called the abstract, and the informative abstract renamed a summary. The review abstract comes first.

Some writers mix the two types in a single abstract, trying to accomplish both functions. This practice improves the usefulness of the indicative variety—provided it doesn't add too many words. But it weakens a good informative abstract and prevents it from performing its real function in a report.

SIMPLER SUMMARIES

In reports that are less complex and complicated than the three-level, the one thing which happens to summary elements is that they get shorter and shorter. The same relative position to other parts of the report is maintained. When a report is but a single page, however, the summary sometimes appears in its natural position only—at the end. And when the report is intended for more technical readers, more technical terms may be used in the summary.

As with the investigation pattern, the reason for the relatively little variation from the three-level prototype is simple —the *outcome* or the *main facts* are what any reader, at any level, is most certain to want.

Which leads us to the other thing that may happen—a report may be nothing but a summary. All the other parts are in the files (or head) of the writer.

PRACTICE SUGGESTIONS

1. The first four reports of investigations in Group One of Chapter 16 have the introduction-conclusions arrangement. So also do those on pages 434, 470, and 564. Notice particularly

    a. The difference between the "summary of findings or results," "conclusions," and "recommendations."
    b. The relative position of these elements, when more than one are used.
    c. The relative position of general and specific conclusions.
    d. How the conclusions are introduced.
    e. Whether the conclusions are keyed to the body.
    f. The relation between the order of conclusions, the order of sections, and the order predicted in the introduction.

    Set your findings up in a table.

2. An introduction-summary arrangement is on page 375. An indicative abstract is on page 437. The "digest" on page 395 is a mixed abstract. Note the comments on each.

3. Note that the summary reports on pages 418 and 424 do not themselves have summaries.

4. The reports on pages 470, 489, and 532 all use different devices to give the "quick picture." Look at their introductions along with their conclusions. Which seem most effective?

5. Analyze the concluding elements in the reports in your collection. Are there possibilities of improvement?

6. To study the technique of the simple "ending," examine the first and last of magazine articles in general magazines.

8

Organizing the Developing Sections

As WE SAW in the last chapter, although the concluding section of a report appears right after the introduction, it must actually be written last. Conclusions are based upon data, evidence, and reasoning. Summaries are based upon detailed facts or information which they summarize.

Such material is developed in the main part or body of a report. In a long report the body is broken into "chapters." In shorter reports we may feel that "chapter" is too dignified a title, and hence we may use the term "main division." Here "section" will continue to be used for both. On the sections rests the validity of the conclusions or the significance of the summary.

Developing sections in a report of an investigation are not necessarily themselves reports of smaller investigations. Some may simply give information. The information may consist of a detailed account of a process, of the background, of the existing situation, or of a number of other things. Similarly—though not as often—a report which has the basic pattern of an information report may have a section that tells of an investigation. (An example is described on page 404).

This chapter deals with the possible orders in which the main sections can be arranged and then discusses the patterns these sections take in reporting an investigation or giving information.

DETERMINING ORDER OF SECTIONS

Regardless of the kind of report, the sections have to be put in a sensible order. What that will be depends on what will be easiest for the reader. The principles are the same in both the investigation and information-giving situations. Here are some possibilities.

SOME USEFUL ORDERS

Chronological

One of the simplest orders is chronological. In reporting information, simply follow a time sequence. Describing any process takes this order. Or on reporting progress of an international conference, you might report by successive weeks. Another simple example is minutes of a meeting. Similarly, in telling how you carried out a project, you could put first the step you actually first took, and so on.

This order is so easy to write that it gets overused. For example, if you were asked to lay out and equip a modern kitchen for $10,000 and then wrote a report on it, you might use a chronological order. Suppose, though, you interviewed four hundred people on their ideas of a model kitchen. Would it be best for the reader for you to report interview by interview or to group information about the answers under "opinions about stoves," "opinions about refrigerators," and so on? (This would be a functional order.)

Spatial

The spatial order is simply according to position. To report on how a building is arranged, describe it room by room, or in a project to test efficiencies, report plant by plant.

Functional

Another order is by function or functional part. It can look just like a spatial order. Thus if you dealt with departments according to where in a plant they were housed, you'd have a spatial arrangement. If you arranged things according to what they did (accounting, purchasing, and so on) you'd have a functional arrangement. But if all functions were housed separately, you might end with the same sections as if you had used the spatial order. The functional order is often combined with the order of importance—the most important function is reported first.

Order of Importance

Here the arrangement is according to relative significance. You might put first the plan you thought best, then the next best plan, and so on. Or you might report first the phases of the project on which you were most successful.

Other Orders

Many other orders and principles of arrangement are possible. The "general to particular" starts with a discussion of general principles, then shows progressively detailed applications. It is the "deductive" method.

The reverse, or "inductive," starts with applications and "induces" principles from them.

Starting with a simple case and moving to more and more complex is another order. And we even have psychological orders—we put first what we think will most satisfy the reader, in view of his known likes and dislikes.

In general, we select the order most suitable to the material.

SUPPLEMENTARY ELEMENTS

After the order of main sections has been decided upon,

some supplementary sections may need to be added. These may come *before* the others, or in an appendix, depending on how necessary they are to the other sections. They include extensive discussions of such things as history, definitions, basic principles, and so on, which we talked about on pages 46 to 52. If in a report of an investigation a section must be given to the over-all procedure because it is too long for the introduction, it comes here too. Occasionally a whole chapter must be given to telling how a problem was "pinned down" in a preliminary investigation. Perhaps criteria need to be set up and justified, and so on.

All such preliminary material is placed just ahead of the other sections *if most readers will need it.* Otherwise it goes to the appendix.

BASIC PATTERNS FOR SECTIONS

Because the sections of a three-level report are generally long, they need strong organizational elements to help the reader get through them. The objective is to help him know where he is going, and to get him there as easily as possible. As in the whole report, the difference between a section reporting an investigation and one giving information is in the point of view. The former centers on a problem and its solution; the latter just gives the facts as the writer sees them. The major patterns are:

INVESTIGATION	INFORMATION
Opening (problem centered)	*Opening (purpose centered)*
Developing subsections	*Developing subsections*
Results, conclusions or recommendations.	*Summary or "ending."*

Notice that neither of these is in the inverted order of the whole report. The inverted order is used to give a quick picture. If the reader turns to any section, he wants the whole story. He has questioned a conclusion and wonders how we managed to reach it. Or he wants to know more about one of the subjects already summarized. Your job, then, is to lead him to the proper outcome step by step. Putting the outcome at the last gives him the satisfying sense of having reached the goal the opening pointed out to him.

Now to expand the patterns and see some of their variations.

FOR AN INVESTIGATION

The Three-Level Section—Full Development

OPENING. The first part of the section reporting an investigation is problem-centered. The statement of the problem may be all that is needed, for the main introduction or preceding sections may have given the reader enough background. At other times, more special background is needed. And if the section is long, the reader must be told how it is organized. The full pattern for the opening is:

> *Background*
> *Statement of general problem of section or phase of investigation covered.*
> *Breakdown into subproblems or into phases discussed, in order of their discussion.*

Into this pattern is sometimes placed an account of the general procedure of the section.

The *background* will consist of the same kind of material used in the main introduction. That is, it may be history of the development of the problem, basic theory or principles, explanation of a general need, a statement of the importance of this phase, or definitions needed to understand the section but not needed before. The main point is to remember to put in only what is necessary for the reader to understand the problem of this section. Anything else goes later in the section—or to the appendix.

Next state the particular *problem* considered, or the phase of the study with which this section will deal. Do so briefly if possible, but above all, clearly.

The next step varies. Suppose, for example, the chapter is made up of a series of tests, each with its own special procedure. Then simply list the tests. (If their nature is clear, just say eight such tests were made.) This both breaks down the main problem and gives an idea of the order of reporting. (If you want, you can add "Results are reported here" or something of the sort.)

Suppose instead the section consists of a series of tests or phases each of which was run or examined by the same method. Then there are two choices. If the procedure can be described in a brief paragraph, put it right after the statement of problem. If it takes longer, put it right *after* the rest of the opening.

Finally, suppose the whole project employed one basic procedure, which was described in the main introduction or in an earlier section of the report. Then procedure is simply left out, or the reader merely reminded that the same one is still being used.

DEVELOPING SUBSECTIONS. The next step is to present the data, evidence, and reasoning in an organized manner. This is done in the subsections. These must be divided by using some single principle and must be arranged in a sensible order. Use the same principles used to set the order of the main sections—spatial, chronological, or whatever is best. If necessary, add to the resulting subsections auxiliary ones such as background, just as for the main sections (page 85).

There is no need to maintain the same principle of order *within* different sections. (Section III may be in chronological order, Section IV in functional.)

The subsections which result are organized in one of two ways. If they are long enough, they are organized exactly like main sections. If not, they take one of the patterns discussed below under "The Simpler Section."

CONCLUDING. Each section ends with an over-all conclusion. It may simply gather in one place the concluding elements from the subsections. It may be a comparison of the results of the subproblems, leading to a new and larger conclusion. Or possibly, the answer to each subproblem has produced the next subproblem, so that the conclusion of the last subproblem also serves as the section conclusion.

Just as the conclusion of the report as a whole, the section conclusion may be made up of a summary of findings, of conclusions proper, of recommendations, or of a combination of them. Unlike the whole report, however, if more than one of the three is used, they either take the order named, or each individual conclusion is followed by its own recommendation. Logical order is never reversed. The reader goes to the body of the report when he wants the whole story, not the quick view.

The Simpler Section

Even in three-level reports, not all sections are long enough to need the full pattern. In any report, the amount of material is one factor governing how much of the pattern is needed. The other is what the reader knows, either from what he learned earlier in the report or from what he already knew. If he needs no background, the pattern becomes:

Opening

Statement of problem
Phases of problem (order of discussion)

Procedure (if needed)

Other developing subsections
Conclusion (Findings, Conclusions, Recommendations)

If there isn't much material, and the section is short, chances are that the reader can see all the subsection heads at a glance. Then the breakdown into phases isn't needed. Probably the problem can be stated in just a sentence or two. The pattern now becomes:

Problem
Procedure (if needed)
Subsection A
Subsection B
Subsection C
Subsection D
Conclusion

If all the subsections were short—or the whole problem didn't need to be divided—but the actual data needed interpreting, the pattern would be:

Problem
Procedure (if needed)
Data (called possibly "Findings" or "Results")
Interpretation (called possibly "Discussion")
Conclusion

Many short reports take exactly this form.

The final step comes when the problem can be stated in a brief phrase. Suppose also this section used no special procedure and the data needed no interpretation. Then all that is left is:

Problem (a phrase)
Data
Conclusion

All these (and even some interpretation) might be combined in a single paragraph.

FOR GIVING INFORMATION

The Three-Level Section—Full Development

What was said of the section reporting an investigation applies to that giving information, except for the different orientation of the material. The principles involved are the same as for the whole report, except that the functional parts are in the order named, the concluding part being last.

OPENING. The opening appears right after the chapter or section head, generally with no subhead of its own, occasionally with the subhead "purpose." Whatever heading device is used, the elements are the same as in a main introduction.

First supply any special *background* or other orienting material that may be needed. Perhaps it will be necessary to call attention to how this section relates to the main topic. (Sometimes this can be accomplished simply by showing the connection with the preceding section.) Perhaps special definitions are needed. Exactly what to put in can be tested by using the same questions used for the main introduction. (Pages 50-52.)

The main part of the opening will be a sentence or two devoted to making clear the specific *purpose* of the section. This is again done in the same way as for the major introduction. The statement may be short, but it is the absolutely essential part of any section opening.

A section opening may carefully define the *scope* of the following discussion, but it does so much less frequently than does a major introduction. The reason is that when the limits of the entire discussion are set, the parts automatically take on similar limitations. It is usually enough simply to name the topics of the section in the same *order* in which they will be discussed.

DEVELOPING SUBSECTIONS. The sequence of the subsections

of the section depends upon the reader and material, just as did the sequence of the main sections.

If a subsection is long, it will need a formal introduction similar to that for the section. It will likewise need its own ending. Otherwise, a topic sentence will be quite enough.

CONCLUDING. The section is concluded with a summary or ending, exactly as an entire report would be. The difference is one of length, not of general principle.

The Simpler Section

As developing sections become shorter, the functional parts receive less elaboration and emphasis. The entire body may be a single paragraph. Here are some skeleton outlines showing the direction the reduction takes:

EXAMPLE 1. This outline is for a long section in a three-level report, and consequently uses a full pattern. The assumption is that the section will take several pages, and that each subsection will in turn consist of a number of paragraphs.

> SECTION (CHAPTER) HEAD
> *Background*
> *Purpose*
> *Scope and order of discussion*
> A. *First developing subsection*
>
>> Opening—purpose and order of discussion
>> Developing sub-subsections. (Each will be a paragraph or so in length, taking the order of
>>> Topic idea
>>> Facts and information
>>> Ending or summary)
>
> B. C. D. *Other developing subsections,* in same arrangement as A

　　E. *Ending or summary.* If the latter, it will gather
　　　 together the summaries of the subsections, or
　　　 will condense them in an over-all summary.

EXAMPLE 2. Here the material is not so long or complex.
That is, each developing subsection will be but a paragraph
or two in length.

　　　　　　SECTION (CHAPTER) HEAD
　　　　Background (less or none)
　　　　Purpose
　　　　Order of discussion
　　A. *First developing subsection*—a paragraph or
　　　 two
　　　　　Topic idea
　　　　　Facts and information
B. C. D. *Same as* A.
　　E. *Ending or summary.*

EXAMPLE 3. Here the material is even less extensive. Any
needed background will have been handled entirely in the
main introduction or in a special section devoted to it.

　　　　　　　SECTION HEAD
　　　　Purpose
　　　　Order of discussion (Unless all subheads can be
　　　　seen by the reader at a glance, as subheads of
　　　　the section.)
　　A. *First developing subsection*—a single paragraph
　　　 consisting of topic idea plus facts.
B. C. D. *Same as* A.
　　E. *Ending or summary.*

EXAMPLE 4. If the entire section will consist of only one
or two paragraphs, the organization becomes:

SECTION HEAD

Topic Idea
Developing facts

Note that the summary or ending has disappeared. The next thing to go is the topic idea, which is expressed only in the section head:

SECTION HEAD

Developing facts

To sum up, the longer the developing section, the more nearly it will approach the organization of an independent report, except that the concluding section appears at the end. The shorter the section, the fewer organizational elements are needed.

PRACTICE SUGGESTIONS

1. First look at the tables of contents on page 287, 325, 372, and 443. According to what principles are the major divisions arranged? (You will find the division made according to alternatives with the best one first; the same division, but in the order of increasing complexity; general to specific; and functional order.)
2. The tables of contents on pages 287 and 372 show the subsections. What is the principle of order in each?
3. What method is used to open and close each of the sections reproduced from these reports?
4. Outline the sections beginning on pages 405 and 554. What principles of order are used (a) in the section, and (b) in each subsection? What does the opening of each one cover? The close?
5. Trace the gradual simplification of the organization of the reports in Group One. Jot down in a table what you find. Begin with pages 279 and 306. Do the same with Group

Two. Begin with pages 366 and 382. In both groups, which reports really have no sections?

6. Outline completely each of your own group of sample reports. For both sections and subsections check the method of opening and closing, the method of order used to arrange the parts, and the extent to which they follow the appropriate pattern.

9

Presenting the Facts

WHEN YOU tell someone that something that you say is true, you soon find that you stand in one of two relations to him. He either believes you at once, or he wants you to explain why what you said is true. This difference is the reason for the basic division given in Chapter 4 between reports which pass on information and those which tell the results of an investigation.

In the information-giving situation you are regarded as an authority. You expect your reader to accept your facts without serious question. Of course, when you write, you may want to encourage your reader to accept your word. Then, as we saw, you may tell him in the prefatory material about the experience you had in the field. If you also used other authorities, you may tell him so there or in the text by means of footnotes and similar devices. But it remains true that the attitude of the reader is not going to be one of questioning your facts. You are in approximately the position of someone writing a textbook to students.

Where you are reporting the solution to a problem, the situation is reversed. Your answer will be accepted only if you arrived at it in a sensible way. Your procedure and your interpretation of the evidence will be areas of challenge.

This chapter deals with how to meet this challenge by effective reporting. First is considered how to report procedure; and second, some principles and pitfalls in reporting and interpreting evidence.

Notice that the chapter will be concerned with problems of reporting. It will not discuss methods of determining facts by various scientific techniques. It is up to you—and to any other professional man—to be able to set up valid methods of investigation and reasoning in your own field.

But this much is equally sure. If you cannot follow these principles in reporting your procedure and evidence, you must have used a bad procedure and have bad evidence.

REPORTING PROCEDURE USED TO OBTAIN DATA

In an investigation, three sorts of procedures may be used. First, a procedure is used to obtain data. Second, a procedure is used to process the data into a convenient arrangement or into a summary of findings. Third, a procedure is used in interpreting the data and drawing conclusions. Not all investigations use all three sorts, but all use at least one of them. The first portion of this chapter will concern mostly the procedure used to obtain data. What is said of it applies to the other two kinds of procedure also. Special pitfalls in reporting them will be discussed in connection with the stage of the investigation with which they deal.

IMPORTANCE

The less routine the report situation, the more important it is to report the procedure carefully. If you are writing a routine report resulting from some routine tests, if you have performed these tests successfully in the past, if your reader knows the tests, and if he has confidence in you, then there is no need to do more than name your procedure. The less routine the procedure, the less experience you have had with it, the less the reader knows about it, and the less confidence he has in you, the more important it is to trace the procedure in detail.

How important it is to report a good procedure well has

been driven home to me many times. Last week was an instance. I was sitting in on a conference where some high-level executives were reviewing a progress report on a project in which they had a keen and vital interest. If results could be obtained, there were tremendous implications in improved operations and eventual savings. Though tentative results were given early in the oral report, and were in front of us in the written one, not a single question was directed to them for over three hours. Every question was directed to some phase of the procedure. Only when it was thoroughly understood—in both its strong and its weak points—did the discussion move to the results and their interpretation.

An aside is worth making here. The report was a brilliant and impressive one. But what was most impressive was the careful command the man making the report had of the procedure he had used. He knew where it was weak, where strong, and why. He never pretended to have more than he had. He carefully pointed out where inevitable weak points in the procedure would affect results, and to what degree. As he answered questions it was possible to see the group's confidence in him grow. *They knew,* by the time he had finished, that his conclusions were exactly what he said they were.

No piece of data—no conclusion—is any better than the procedure used to arrive at it. A wrongly calibrated instrument will give wrong results. An inadequate sampling procedure gets inadequate or contaminated data. If your work is to be properly judged, then, your procedure must be a good one accurately reported.

THE EXPERIMENTAL IDEAL

In a laboratory, tests can be made under controlled conditions. Historically, one of the criteria of a good experiment therefore became that a good experiment should be repeatable. That is, given the same conditions, the same equipment, the same procedure, and so on, the test should give the same results regardless of who performed it. This criterion resulted in a corollary criterion for good *reporting* of a test. Procedure should be reported so that it could be exactly duplicated with no further information or instructions. This remains the scientific ideal. If you hold it in front of you, you cannot go far wrong.

PRACTICAL VARIATIONS

In actual practice in business and industry, especially outside of the research laboratory, this ideal often cannot be attained. It is hardly likely, for example, that any two offices will have practices so identical that what is done in one can be exactly repeated in another. It is more likely that instead both will have the same *type* of problem to be solved in the same way, but with variations. So in a plant— we will not have the same layout problem this year that we had last. Details of our procedure will have to vary.

Another factor also comes into the picture. In actual operation it is frequently not possible to hold constants so constant as in the laboratory. Moreover, we cannot stop operations while we carefully vary one element at a time.

But the fluidity of the operating situation makes it even more important that we carefully account for all unusual features in telling of the procedure. If someone wants to use our procedure elsewhere, he must be able to see which features do and do not apply. And if we cannot eliminate fluctuation in certain variables, our reader needs to be able to take this into account in evaluating our results.

The practical question to ask then, is, "If another person were faced with this situation in another place, have I described what I did and why I did it so clearly that he could go ahead on his problem in the same way?" If the answer is "yes," then the procedure is adequately reported. If it is "no," we need to fill in the gaps.

BLIND ALLEYS AND FALSE LEADS

The final procedure evolved should certainly be reported completely and all in one piece without confusing side issues. However, many times we try things which don't work out. Yet they may have seemed a logical approach before we tried them. On other occasions we consider certain techniques that have been used in similar situations and discard them on logical grounds.

Generally it is a good idea to preserve a record of such false steps. If they were simply silly or stupid (all of us make mistakes), we can bury the account in our own files. But if the procedure is one which looks logical for our problem, then somewhere in the report (the appendix will do) it is a good idea to tell what happened. To find out that something doesn't work is often just as valuable as to know what does. Moreover, if the reader happens to think of this procedure, and you have not mentioned it, he will not know you discarded it for good reasons. Telling him about it strengthens his confidence in what you finally evolved.

If the procedure is the best that can be used under the circumstances, but has limits or weaknesses, be sure to point them out. Be sure also to keep these in mind when interpreting the results, and to remind your reader of them. Otherwise he may misinterpret your conclusions. Also explain, of course, why this is the best procedure practically possible.

PLACEMENT OF ACCOUNT OF PROCEDURE

The positioning of the account of procedure has been discussed in connection with the introduction of three-level and other reports and in the last chapter. These and some other special positions can be summarized thus:

In three-level and long reports

1. Always briefly in the introduction.
2. Completely in the introduction if the account is short and the same procedure was used throughout the project.
3. In Section III (or another early section if III is devoted to further background or to detailing of the problem).
4. At the appropriate place in individual sections where it concerns only one part of the total problem. That is, where varying procedures are used with different aspects of the project, tell about them at the point of use.
5. Unless very important to the significance of the final procedure, tell about false leads in the appendix.

In other reports

1. After the statement of problem if the account is short or necessary to interpret the conclusions.
2. Otherwise just before the detailed data.

REPORTING AND INTERPRETING EVIDENCE

WHAT IS MEANT BY DATA OR EVIDENCE

In any investigation, a procedure is used for gathering the facts. These facts result from the procedure, and if a different procedure was used, different facts might result. For example, if you look at a drop of blood with no instrumentation besides your hands and eyes, the data are that it is a red liquid. If instead you use a microscope, you find it to be filled with objects of certain structure, which you can then describe or draw. The data have changed because the procedure has changed.

At one extreme, the data that result from a controlled laboratory procedure are measurable in quantitative terms. We have milligrams, degrees of hardness, and so on. At the other extreme is a survey of the opinions of a limited number of people. There a questioning procedure simply results in recording a few people's opinions. There may be no way of measuring the relation of those opinions to fact. But what resulted from each procedure were *data.*

Evaluating and interpreting data or evidence leads to *conclusions.* If a reader is to be able to judge the validity of the conclusions, he must see the data on which they are based and be able to follow the reasoning process which led from the data to the conclusions.

How to report data and how to report the evaluation and interpretation of it therefore involves five questions:

1. Should the "raw" or "primary" data be reported?
2. How much of the data should be reported?
3. How detailed should be the account of the processing of the data?
4. How much should be told of the process of evaluation?
5. Where in the report should these things be accomplished?

These questions have no set answers. Yet before any report can be completed, they must be answered. And they must be well answered. Personally, I have seen more reports rejected, sent back for correction, or placed aside without action because these questions were wrongly answered *than for any other reason.*

To get the best answers for any report situation, *apply our guides to that particular situation.* Analyze the material, the reader, the probable use of the report, and where you (the writer) stand in the picture. The following paragraphs will give some answers to the first four questions in the order listed above. The fifth question will be answered in connection with the others.

1. *Should Raw or Primary Data Be Reported?*

Raw or primary data consist of the actual things observed. Perhaps the clearest example I can give comes from a very painful personal experience. (Names, I might add, are definitely fictitious.)

Back in World War II, I had been working in the Air Corps as inspector for a squadron commander. He had come to place a good deal of confidence in my judgment and rarely questioned my reports. At length I was commissioned and then became group technical inspector. Proud of my new job and of the people working for me, I undertook my new duties with great enthusiasm. This was somewhat cooled when the group colonel, Colonel Johnson, got my first reports. You see, he gave them back.

As a matter of fact, after he read three items aloud, he threw them at me.

The squadron colonel had objected to them. As Colonel Johnson put it,

"You say the hardstand's dirty. Colonel Leeds says it's clean and always was.

"You say there's an engine in bad condition by the hardstand, not pickled. Leeds says they just took it off the plane.

"You say some damned Technical Order hasn't been complied with on the carburetor air scoop. He says it has.

"One of you's a liar. Get out!"

I took a quick trip down to the hardstand with my crew. The revised report contained items like

Hardstand condition—oil drum tipped over in northeast corner. Oil spilled. Thirty square feet of hardstand deteriorated— gives when walked upon. Machine gun clips lying about. Fifty-seven found under right nacelle. Right tire of plane contains three cuts. Ten clips showed no spot without rust, suggesting they have been there some time.

The other items were similarly revised.

What was the difference? Actually, the first report contained judgments or generalizations. It contained nothing which showed what I had *seen* to form the judgment. When Colonel Leeds disagreed, his different standard of judgment could not be questioned—there were no *facts* that Colonel Johnson could consider.

The story not only illustrates the difference between primary data and an inference from them. It also shows two types of situation which affect how much primary data we put in. Before my promotion, I had worked for the same man for some time. He had grown to respect my judgment because when he questioned it I had been able to support it with facts. But Colonel Johnson was a different reader. He had no real reason to accept even a minor inference without supporting data.

Generally, at least *some* supporting raw data should be given (a) whenever any reader of the report may not have full confidence in the writer's judgment, (b) where there may be differences about either the processing or the evaluation of the raw data, or (c) where the outcome of the report is of importance. It follows that a three-level report will always contain raw data.

At the other extreme, the more confidence the reader has in you, the less controversial the report problem, and the more routine the report, the more likely it is that the raw data need not be reported. Excepted here, of course, are the very simple, very common, very routine reports which do nothing *but* record raw data in suitable blanks already provided.

Where should the raw data go in the report? The answer depends upon two things: the extent, and whether they were substantially changed in processing

If the raw data can be reported in a short space, in relation to the rest of the report, there is no reason why they should not appear in the body of the report where they are used or their processing is shown. When put there, they need not be in the original form in which they were taken. For example, they may be arranged in a list, table, or graph. If they are simply re-recorded, not processed, they are still raw data.

If the raw data have been processed in an elementary way only, it is not necessary to show how they were processed. They may, for example, simply have been added. Then, provided the reader trusts the writer's ability to add, they need not appear in the report at all.

Often only enough of the raw data need appear in the body of the report to show how they were processed to get the summary data. The rest are then placed in the appendix. This position is also used when there is a reason for preserving the data, even though their processing is routine. It might be thought, for example, that the individually recorded items might be used later in further research, even though all that was needed here was a total or group of totals.

Unless the raw data are extremely bulky, or unless it is absolutely certain that they will never be used again, it is a good idea to preserve them somewhere. Except where noted above, the usual position is in the appendix of a long report or at the last of a short report. The truth is, that unless they are gathered with the report, they are likely to be lost. Even important file drawers get cleaned out—often a little bit at a time. No one has to read such appendix material, but it may become a useful mine of information in some further research.

Of course company files or some other repository must be used if the data are very unwieldy. Consider, for example, what the length (and expense of printing) of the famous Kinsey reports would have been if all the thousands of original interviews were recorded in an appendix!

The first reader of a report often helps in the decision here—ask him where he wants the raw data preserved.

2. How Much of the Data Should Be Reported?

This question has been partially answered in dealing with the first question. However, in addition to raw data, we usually have processed data. Processed data result from operating on raw data. We may add the raw data, average them, put them through formulas, arrange them in statistical arrays, classify them, put them on curves, and so on. The objective is to get them in more convenient form for interpretation and evaluation.

All such processed data belong in the developing sections of any three-level report. Indeed, the purpose of most developing sections of such reports is to display the processed data, explain how they were reached, and interpret them. No reader who wants to check the validity of the conclusions can do so without them. Hence they should not go to the appendix.

One exception is sometimes made. When there are many pages of such processed data, and all are the same in nature, samples may be placed in the body and carefully interpreted. The rest are then put in the appendix. A curious or interested reader then knows how to interpret for himself any concerning which he has questions. Groups of performance curves illustrate a type of processed data often treated in this way.

Even in short reports going to a reader in the writer's own department, the processed data are often preserved. It is not that the reader will doubt the summary of findings or the conclusions reached, but rather that the easiest way to preserve the data is with the final report. If, however, the report will be short-lived—that is, if immediate final action will be taken—there is no reason to give any processed data other than the summary of findings. And even this, as we saw in Chapter 7, can often be omitted.

3. *How Detailed Should Be the Account of Processing the Data?*

Again, how routine or unusual was the processing, and how do we stand in respect to our reader?

If we are dealing with standard data, which we process in a standard way, and our boss knows perfectly well that we know how to process them, there is no need to do more than name the process we used. Now this happens a good deal of the time, but it hardly ever happens in reports important enough to be three-level. If the processing is at all unusual, or if there are any obscure or debatable points about it, we report the details. And even in routine matters, except at the higher levels, an account of how the data were processed is omitted much less often than is commonly supposed. It was once put this way in a letter to me from a man who has a great deal to do with reports:[1]

To a vice-president, things are either black or white. This must be, because many decisions have to be made on the moment, and the vice-president does not have time to sort out the various shades of gray to determine which are blacker than white and which are whiter than black. Consequently, the facts presented to him, and upon which the decision must rest, are of necessity useful only when they have been filtered and condensed to the point where the executive can see immediately that they are relatively black or relatively white.

The vice-president dimly recalls the days when he was one of the people engaged in the filtering process, and he suffers from the misconception that everything would be clearer and simpler if people would only make it so, while as a matter of

[1] Letter dated April 4, 1952, from K. A. Stonex, Head, Technical Data Department, General Motors Corporation Proving Ground, Milford, Michigan. Used by permission.

fact his viewpoint and approach is one of experience and evolution, and the facts of life are just as they always were. Someone still has to weigh and balance and analyze the details, and someone has to institute and maintain procedures to assure that details are evaluated.

. . . countless hours of special help and individual consultation must be sweated out . . .

. . . The 600 or 800 engineering employees in ———— spend most of their time sorting out the different shaded factors in engineering development problems so that they are consistent and well ordered before the chief engineer sees them. If this were not so, he could get along with a staff of six or eight. Because he has more than a few on his staff, we must assume that their functions have been justified economically.

Furthermore, industry requires in practice that the engineering graduate have a few years' experience before it trusts him to make any but the most trivial decisions. Our young engineer is supervised very closely at first, and both the work and the reports on the work are supervised in detail until we are satisfied as to his responsibility and competence. As time goes on and the boy proves himself, the degree of supervision is relaxed continuously over a long period of time until the boy eventually matures into a vice-president or something else, when he in turn requires that people bring to him their facts all neatly sorted out and bundled up into piles of nicely matched shades.

In any report except those which *for us and the reader* are routine reports, then, the sensible thing is to report the processing of the data in full. And if our status is that of a learner in the department, it will not hurt to put even our detailed calculations where they can be found, but where they will not be in the way if they are not wanted.

This does not mean to go overboard. A distinction must be made between significant and insignificant processing of data. Generally, for example, it doesn't matter whether you record your data in pencil or in ink, on blue paper or on white, on cards or on notebook paper. The results will not be affected. But if in reducing raw data you use one class-interval instead of another, you may influence how the classified data may be interpreted.

As a check on whether your reporting is complete enough up to the point of interpretation of data, you might try the following rules of thumb:

a. Are the raw data sufficient to allow the reader to reprocess them by another method, if he does not like mine, without any fear that vital data are missing?

b. Is my description of how I processed the data sufficiently detailed that the reader can interpret them himself, drawing his own conclusions, without fear that anything was dropped out, distorted, or contaminated by the processing I used?

Where should the account of how the data were processed be put in the report? The answer depends on the reader. If you know he wishes to check every detail as he goes along, it belongs in the appropriate developing section. If he is almost certain not to want to check in detail, you may just name the processing method in the body and place the details in the appendix. Generally, you will arrive at some compromise between the two. All unusual or nonroutine processing will be reported in the developing sections. Sample calculations may also be placed there. Standard calculations, or repetitious calculations applied to different data of the same sort, will go to the appendix of a long report or to the last section of a short one.

MISUSING TERMS. In processing raw data, whether mentally or on paper, many writers lose exactness and fall into what are really *fake* quantitative terms. They end up talking of "many," "few," "high rpm," "the average wage" and so on. These terms are dangerous and betray inadequate reporting of the actual processing. They convey nothing exact to the reader. If twenty people were killed by an explosion, and all were your friends, you would think a great many were killed. But if the same number were killed among unknown aborigines on a remote island, you might think they were lucky to escape with so few casualties. In a fractional horsepower motor, twenty rpm is a low figure. If some wrestler were whirling you about his head at the same rate, it would seem high. If you and I and the Aga Khan took our average yearly incomes, the figure might misrepresent the actual income of you and me, and so on. In giving quantitative interpretations of raw data, we should try to use exact quantitative terms. If we use comparative terms, we should give some basis for the comparison. In any case, we must define carefully what we mean. The same goes for averages or any other statistical phenomena—we must give an idea of how they were arrived at and of the ranges involved in the unprocessed data.

Qualitative terms may also be meaningless if not carefully defined and interpreted. What is "dirty," "smooth," "careless,"—or "beautiful"?

4. How Much Should Be Told of the Process of Evaluation and Interpretation?

Some reports give only data—the objective of the project they report is only to determine facts. Others process the facts to make them easier to handle, but may end with no more than a summary of the processed facts. Still others not only process the facts, but evaluate or interpret them. In other words, they report conclusions.

Everyone knows that the same facts do not always lead to the same conclusions, even when there is agreement on the facts. A worker might have a high accident rate. I might conclude to fire him, you to send him to a psychiatrist. Or better, remember the last argument you had in which there was no question about the facts, but a great deal about what they meant.

Facts must often be judged as to their worth or meaning. Such judgments are made in terms of standards established early in any investigation.

One standard is our objective or objectives. We start out to solve a problem, or check a hypothesis. Some things we try, say, do not solve the problem, or do not prove the hypothesis. Even here we set up some measuring stick as to whether the hypothesis is proved or not, the problem solved or not. The reader must be told what these measuring sticks are.

Most problems are not so simple as to have a single solution. Any of several may meet our objectives either completely or in part. Some do it better than others. In many projects, therefore, we set up standards of judgment called "criteria." These are the standards against which we will measure proposed solutions suggested by the facts. Criteria frequently used are those of cost, consistency of result, safety, speed, and so on. Each may in turn be broken down. Thus cost may be broken into machine cost, material cost, labor cost, and so on. Any proposed solution will be measured in terms of some unit or quality which can help us evaluate in terms of these criteria. Thus we use dollars to measure cost, minutes to measure speed, positive clearance of hands to measure safety, and so on.

The criteria are either standard, or given to us in the assignment, or established by ourselves. Before we know what the data show, we must do our best to determine if the criteria apply and are adequate. Hundreds of accounting people have frustrated production people by determining their efficiency in terms of inadequate criteria. (They compare two departments, for example, without taking into account that one has new machinery, the other machinery on its last legs.) We must then determine the relative importance of the criteria. We must also establish the validity and adequacy of our measuring units. The next step is to measure any proposed solution against either an ideal (even absolute) solution, or against other proposed solutions.

It follows that our reader will not be able to understand the value of our proposed solutions unless we have set up clear criteria, told him where we got them or why they were applicable, and shown their relative importance. He then expects to see the measuring units or qualities applied to the data to give conclusions. In terms of the cost data assembled, which method is the cheapest? Which is the safest? Which is the fastest?

This interpretation of the data in terms of the problem must be done systematically and with great care. It must be reported in the same way. The only exceptions are where the criteria and terms of measurement are accepted routine.

Since the interpretation is critical, it always appears in the body of the report.

Good interpretative procedure prevents drawing conclusions which assert more than the data show. A further check is to examine each resulting conclusion and ask, "Have I proved *exactly* that?" Over-extrapolation, as it is called, can also be detected by checking for sweeping adjectives—"all," "most," etc. A final check is to ask, "Do I mean this is true in respect to the data obtained in this project only; or do I mean it is certain to be true in respect to any data that *could* be gathered bearing on this project?"

It all boils down to this. If the reader has gone into the body of the report, he wants to check how you arrived at your conclusions. And there are three critical points. The first is the procedure used to get the raw data, the second is the processing employed to get the raw data into usable form, and the third is the reasoning used to get from the processed data to the conclusions. He will be looking for holes. Your job is to leave him none. And if some must be

left, you must point out where they are and why they are
there.

PRACTICE SUGGESTIONS

1. The reports in Part II show different degrees of reporting procedure used to obtain the data—from very complete
   accounts to none at all. You will find these variations:

   a. Very complete accounts with quantitative data
   b. A complete account, with some of data subjective
   c. A complete account where data are not quantitative
   d. Briefer accounts
   e. Three-level reports with no procedure given and no
   raw data
   f. Reports in which procedure is simply named

   Examine the reports beginning on pages 279 and 308. Read
   the "Report Situation" and the discussion on "data." Then
   turn to the report and record the following:

   a. Does the procedure deal with obtaining, processing, or
   interpreting the data?
   b. Are any raw data presented? Where? (Developing
   sections? Appendix?)
   c. What form do the data take? (Lists, tables, photographs, paragraph form, etc.)

2. Make the same analysis of your own group of sample reports. In view of what you know of the report situation,
   did the writer make the right decision?

10

Using Illustrations

Every technical, business, and professional man has more than one language. Besides his verbal native tongue he uses mathematics and graphic devices. Each language can do some things better than can the others. If used to supplement each other in the right way, they give the maximum in clearness, exactness, and brevity.

Ordinarily the basic structure of the text of reports is verbal. Much of the mathematical and all of the graphic material is used as illustration rather than as part of the text. If such illustrations are to perform their proper function, they must meet certain tests:

1. They must be useful.
2. They must be properly integrated with the text.
3. They must be located at the point of greatest convenience.
4. They must be selective in the information they present.
5. They must not distort the facts.

The rest of this chapter discusses these tests and the principles which lie behind them. Generally, the tests apply equally to all reports. But a few principles for adapting them to the reader will close the chapter.

Appended to this chapter is an example which illustrates the principles.

DETERMINING WHEN ILLUSTRATIONS ARE USEFUL

Illustrations are useful whenever they can give a more clear, exact, compact, or detailed picture than can ordinary language. A photograph is better than text for giving an over-all view, or for showing relations of size, or of parts to a whole. It also can give some kinds of evidence effectively, such as data on microstructure—or on accidents. A table can condense a great many figures in a relatively small space, and it can be arranged for making easy comparisons up and down columns, or across rows. A schematic drawing easily displays basic functional relationships. A line graph allows the plotting of a large number of figures in a small space, or allows for comparison of variables over a period of time. Mechanical drawings give exact relationships in fine detail, and so on. Illustrations ought to be used whenever they perform any such useful function.

On the other hand, they should not be used merely to prettify the report or to give it added bulk. Each should be tested by asking what it contributes to the report. If the only reason for using it is to "add interest" or because it is handy, it should be left out.

Otherwise, it will probably help.

RELATING TEXT AND ILLUSTRATION

Text and illustrations are in one sense independent, in another reciprocal. Thus the text should read so that it makes sense without the illustration, but the illustration should add detail or clearness to what the text says. And when the reader has turned his attention to the illustration, he ought ideally to be able to read it without any text; yet the text should help him interpret and understand the illustration.

An illustration cannot help the reader if he does not know it is there when he needs to use it. Personally, I still regard one book on my shelves with disfavor because its writer failed to perform this very elementary duty—it's a good book too. The book discussed the Civil War and was tracing movements and battles. I found no reference to a map, even in a list of illustrations. So I went to my shelves and took down a number of other books till I found enough maps to get me through the pages of the first book.

I found a beautiful map later—buried right in the very middle of the appendix!

Under certain circumstances—for instance, in reports to a nontechnical reader—the illustration is so simple and is placed so close to the explanatory text that no reference is needed. However, in most reports, the minimum reference possible is the standard "(See Fig. 12)." This is usually not enough. The reader wants to know *why* he is supposed to see "Fig. 12" and what he is supposed to see in it. One report written by a metallurgist showed an extreme example of the misuse of this technique—he was just out of college, by the way. In the report he mentioned "ferrous metals" and then said to "(See Fig. 12)." His boss did so, and there found a list of ferrous metals. The boss wondered a bit why he was supposed to need refreshing on what ferrous metals were. But more important, his time had been wasted in turning to something he didn't need.

A good reference then, even a short one, should at least tell the reader what the illustration is about. The only exception is if the illustration immediately follows the text.

Even with a clear illustration, the point may be missed. Where this seems at all possible, the text should interpret the illustration and call attention to the most significant points in it. A reader will most easily see or find what he is told about.

This is not to say that *everything* in an illustration should be explained in the text. It would be a waste of your time and the reader's time. No one would reproduce in text form all the data in a complicated table. But the text should tell how to read and interpret the table, and point out the most important things that it shows.

Once the reader gets to the illustration, he should be able to read it with a minimum of reference to the text. Certainly it should have an identifying title. He should not have to go back to the text to find out what the illustration is about or what the units of measurement are. If all parts are labeled clearly, if units of measurement are shown, and if the whole is clearly captioned, the illustration will do its job best.

Finally, it can be taken as a general rule that the less the reader knows about the subject matter of the report or of the specialized field in which it is written, the more help the text must give him, and the clearer the illustration itself must be.

PLACING ILLUSTRATIONS

GENERAL PRINCIPLE

The general principle for placing any illustration is "as close as possible to the text with which it belongs." This is where the reader will need it. In practice, this principle must be modified. Sometimes part of our readers will need the illustration, but others will not. Sometimes it is too bulky to go into the body. Sometimes there are typographical disadvantages. So let's take a look at some of the possible positions to see how the general principle is applied.

APPLICATIONS

1. CUT INTO THE TEXT. Here the illustration is placed on the same page with text. Text may be above it, below it, on either side of it, or all around it. Theoretically this is ideal,

for it gets text and illustration just as close together as possible.

The arrangement has the *advantage* that the reader has both illustration and text together and cannot miss the illustration. No awkward reference need be made. Space may be saved.

Disadvantages outweigh the advantages in some instances. In a typed report, a mistake in drawing or mounting the illustration will ruin the page, and it must be retyped as well as redrawn. The same result may occur if the illustration is done first—a mistake in typing necessitates redrawing. And if the typing is done by someone else, or worse, if one person does the typing and another reproduces the illustrations (as for multiple copies), the text and illustrations frequently don't get together anyway. Finally, in printing a report, such an arrangement may add expense.

2. ON A FACING PAGE. An alternative is to place an illustration so that it faces the text which explains it. The reader then looks from one to the other without difficulty. In a report typed on one side, the illustration must necessarily come ahead of the page that discusses it. Since the back of the illustration is a right-hand page, we must place the figure number and title on it. Otherwise the reader sees only a blank page at first and may be momentarily puzzled. We repeat the identification on the illustration itself, so that the reader can see it when he actually turns to the illustration.

The *advantages* of the arrangement are obvious for reports typed on one side. The reader can see the illustration as he reads the explanatory text—he is not required to turn back and forth. The disadvantages of cutting an illustration into the text are eliminated. Reference remains easy.

But new *disadvantages* are created. If the textual explanation takes more than one page, the reader must turn back anyway, and little has been gained. And the arrangement is very awkward when two or more illustrations come together. Unless *all* illustrations can be faced without such awkwardness resulting, it is better to face none.

If the text is on both sides of a sheet, as in ordinary printed books, we add the same disadvantages that the cut-in illustration has.

3. On an Adjacent Page but Not Faced. The arrangement which is most satisfactory most of the time is to place the illustration on a page adjacent to the text but not facing the text. The position should be *just after the last page that contains text describing it*. It should be *after* the text refers to it so that the reader does not see the illustration first and wonder what he is to do with it. If several pages of text discuss it, it should be *after the last page* for convenience in turning from text to illustration and back again. As an experiment, take any typed and bound report. Pretend that the *second* of six pages contains an illustration to which all six pages refer. Try reading, turning the pages and flipping back and forth to the page supposed to contain the illustration. Now pretend that instead the last of the six pages contains the illustration. I think you'll see what I mean.

The *advantages* of this arrangement are relative only. The illustration is not so far from the text as to be hard to find. Using text and illustration together requires some flipping of pages, but not much. Awkward reading positions are minimized. Finally, it allows for uniform placement of illustrations in the body and helps the general appearance of the report.

The *disadvantages* are that some flipping of pages is required, and that care must be used in telling the reader that the illustration is there. Especially if it is just after several pertinent pages, an exact page reference is needed. This makes for some awkwardness in typing—a blank must be left and the page number inserted when the location of the illustration is known.

4. IN THE APPENDIX. Illustrations may also be placed in the last pages of a long report, usually labeled "Appendix," or in the last pages of a short report, usually unlabeled.

With *advantages* must be included those times when the appendix position *must* be used. An illustration *must* go to the appendix when it is unlikely that most readers will use it. Very elaborate tables of raw data are examples. Bulky folded items must go there. When several pages of illustrations would normally come together if they were placed as close to the text as possible, some of them must be moved to the appendix. Also, if an illustration must be referred to throughout the text, the appendix may be the most convenient place for it.

There are sometimes other advantages. If a report is typed one place, and the illustrations are assembled another, the simplest thing to do is to number the illustrations in sequence, and refer to them in a text with those numbers. Then when the text and illustrations come back from the processors, all the writer does is to slap them together. As a matter of fact, whenever I have found this practice in use in any organization and have traced it to its origin, ease of assembly is the primary justification given. In short reports it is not an inconvenient arrangement, as little page flipping is required. In long reports with many illustrations it is inexcusable practice. The reader either wears himself out finding where he was in the appendix, or tires his finger by using it as a bookmark.

The *disadvantage* of the appendix position can be seen from the last remark. It violates the general principle of keeping a necessary illustration as close to the point of use as possible. For any convenience to the reader, it requires textual reference by exact page number.

5. THE ATTACHED ENVELOPE. Sometimes bulky folded

illustrations, and sometimes all illustrations, are attached to the report in an envelope. The reader can take them out and use them whenever he sees fit.

This is most convenient for the first reader. Later readers find an empty envelope or find the illustrations out of order.

6. In the Files. Obviously this position is not in the report at all. It must sometimes be used for bulky and clumsy illustrations, such as a drawing the size of a bedsheet. If the report goes outside the department in which the material is filed, however, this solution is a poor one, even when it is the only one possible.

SPECIAL PROBLEMS

Some situations come up with enough frequency to be worth special discussion. The general principle to use in solving them is still convenience in use. We make things as easy as possible for the reader. Here are some of them.

Folded Illustrations. If an illustration must be folded it should be arranged to unfold toward the right or up; or if both, toward the right *and* up. It unfolds to the right because most readers turn pages with the right hand. It unfolds *up* because if it should fold *down* it would push the reader away from the pertinent text.

If there is more than a single fold, an accordion fold is best. The reader can unfold the illustration in one motion without danger of tearing it.

Sometimes a reader must refer to the same illustration while he reads several pages of text. It is most convenient for him if he does not have to peer under other pages to see the illustration. Arrange it so that when it is unfolded only a blank or nonessential part is covered by intervening pages.

Long important reports are sometimes sewed and bound. They are then trimmed to even the edges. If this is to be done, fold the illustration to give enough margin to prevent the folded edge from being cut.

Likewise, don't fold the edge you intend to be loose so far in that the illustration will be sewed shut, thus forcing the reader to peer into a kind of tube in order to read it.

MARGINS IN GENERAL. If the report is to be placed in a cover or bound, all illustrations should be planned from the first to leave enough margin so they can be conveniently read at the bound or "fastened" edge.

LARGE ILLUSTRATIONS. If an illustration is very large, it is not convenient to place in the report. If the report is to go outside the department of origin, placing the illustration in the files is not, as we saw, a good solution. Even when the report remains in the department, it is often desirable to have it all in one cover. If possible, the large illustration (usually a drawing) should be reduced. Details are often lost, but the reader can see the general outlines. Then the original drawing can be split into parts and included. While this solution is not ideal, it is practical in a surprising number of cases.

PLANNING TO FINAL SIZE. The solution mentioned in the last paragraph is easier if it is planned for from the start. This is true of all illustrations. More margin can be left on the drawing paper than usual. Photographs can be printed on standard 8-½ by 11 size. (A thinner paper which comes in sheets or rolls and can be trimmed to size works well for this.) In printing, margin can be left for titles and figure numbers.

SEQUENCE OF ILLUSTRATED PAGES. Sometimes a number of pages of illustrations—a dozen graphs, for instance— would normally fall together in the body of the report. The reader, stopped midway through a section of the report, must turn twelve pages before he continues reading the text. (Let us hope he was not stopped in mid-sentence.)

Two solutions are possible. One solution warns him that the next twelve pages are graphs of the data. The warning is placed at the last of the page of text just preceding the illustration, or under the caption of the first one. It is an awkward device, but it does enable the reader to get fairly easily to the page where the text continues. The other solution is to place one of the pages in the text where it belongs, put the others in the appendix, and explain to the reader in the text, giving a page number reference. This procedure permits the reader to see the nature of the illustrative material, and if he wants to see the rest, he can find it without trouble. If he does not want to see it, he can continue his reading uninterrupted.

MAKING ILLUSTRATIONS SELECTIVE

No matter what kind of illustration is used, it should be selective in what it presents. Photographs, for example, should be planned so they do not contain extraneous matter which draws attention from what they are intended to illustrate. One case in point is a photograph I saw which was taken during a lunch hour. It was to illustrate the new arrangement and brightness of an area. But it was dominated by some unusually disreputable-looking characters eating lunch. Another was of a female operator's hands, to show an operating position. Instead of straight down, it was taken from the side, slightly to the rear—and the good-looking girl was wearing a sweater. Both photographs were interesting, but not in the way intended.

Likewise, tables should be checked to see that they contain only the pertinent data. There is no sense for line graphs to contain fine grid when it will not be used in reading them. Curves can be smoothed out when no significant data will be lost. The main idea is to plan and execute illustrations so that they contain only what the reader needs—only the things which throw light on the problem under consideration.

AVOIDING DISTORTION

Quite accidentally an illustration may give a false impression. To return to a previous example, if too fine grid is left in a graph, the reader may try to interpolate when the data are not susceptible to doing so. Or take two bar graphs, one showing 90 units and the other 100. If they are started at zero, the difference is one-tenth of that of the longest one. Start them at 50, and the difference *looks* like one-fifth of the longest one. Even though both are accurately labeled, the reader may get an entirely erroneous visual impression. All illustrations are capable of giving such unfair impressions unless carefully planned.

ADAPTING TO THE READER

The reader of technical reports, even on the administrative level, expects to find them full of illustrations giving data. The technical reader may find these the most valuable part of the report. The administrator does not expect to be able to understand them completely. Even though we help him with interpreting text, the most he expects is to get the general idea. But this is not true of summary tables or other illustrations used in the concluding section of the report. Such illustrations are useful, but they lose their value if the reader does not understand them. Hence they should contain only the most significant facts, and the text must interpret them to show that significance.

The same is true with many reports which give information to employes, stockholders, or the general public. The best practice here is to simplify the illustrative material as much as possible. Line graphs should not plot more than two or three variables. Tables should contain few rows and few columns. More photographs can be used, with emphasis on giving a more general picture and even creating interest.

The whole chapter can be summed up thus—select and plan illustrations so that the particular reader you have in mind can understand them, and can use them as easily as possible.

PRACTICE SUGGESTIONS

1. The pages appended to this chapter illustrate each of the five points in the chapter. Point by point, examine the example. Ask

   a. How are the illustrations useful?
   b. Are they integrated with the text
      i. By brief reference?
      ii. By reference which tells what they show?
      iii. By explanations high-lighting and interpreting them?
   c. Where are they located in respect to the text? Is this a convenient location?
   d. Do they contain any unnecessary detail?
   e. Can you detect any distortion?

2. Do the same for the reports whose illustrations are discussed on pages 336, 352, 384, 500 and 550 in the order named.

3. Beginning on pages 279 and 334, check through the treatment of illustrative material in all the reports in Part II. Note lists of illustrations in them also.

4. Finally, examine your own collection. What changes might be made to improve the reports?

EXAMPLE OF USE OF
ILLUSTRATIVE MATERIAL

From a Report on Weight Distribution
1946-1947 Cars

The difference between the 1941-42 group and the 1946-47 group on the basis of the curb weight distribution is shown in Figure II. It is apparent that the curb weight distribution on the front and rear wheels of the 1946-47 cars differs only slightly from the immediate pre-war group. There is an increase in the average of only from 51.6 to 52.0% on the front, and there is some shift within the range of the cars in the 50-51% class interval into the 51-52 and the 52-53% class intervals, but on the whole the distributions are nearly similar.

With the full five passenger load, three rear and two front, there is, however, considerable shift in weight as shown on Figure III. The mean of the 1941-42 cars is 46.95% of the loaded car weight on the front wheels, while on the 1946-47 group the mean has increased to 48.5%. In the 1941-42 group frequencies are greatest in the class intervals of 46-47 and 47-48%, while in the 1946-47 group the number of cars falling in the 48-49% class interval is considerably the greatest.

The differences between the distributions on Figures II and III mean, of course, that the passenger weights are somewhat farther forward on the 1946-47 cars, that is, the passenger load center of gravity is somewhat farther forward.

3

PERCENT OF WEIGHT ON FRONT

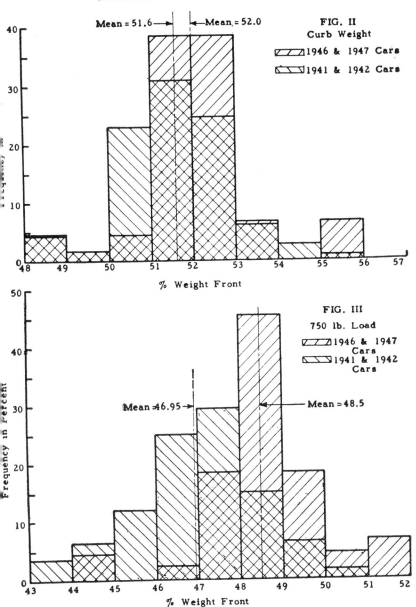

The data of Figures II and III are expressed in percentile form on Figure IV. These curves represent the cumulative heights of the bars for the several distributions shown in Figures II and III. The cumulative percents are plotted on the vertical scale at the left of the chart, at the class intervals indicated on the scale at the bottome of the chart.

The percentile curves on Figure IV point out clearly that the difference in weight distribution at curb weight between the two statistical groups is relatively small, and that the difference in the front weight distribution with the five passenger load amounts to nearly 1.5% quite uniformly through the greater part of the range.

PERCENT OF WEIGHT ON FRONT

FIG. IV

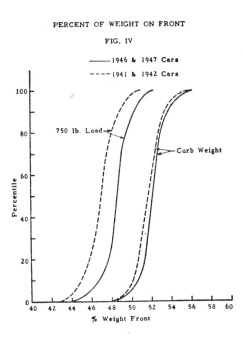

In PG-133 a factor called △ % front weight was used. This is simply the difference between the weight distribution in percent on the front wheels at curb weight and with the five passengers, 750 lb., load. It is a direct measure of the change in weight distribution as the passenger load is added. Since the center of gravity of the passenger load is to the rear of the middle of the car, the addition of the passenger load always decreases the proportion of the weight on the front wheels.

5

Figure V shows △ % front weight, or the change in weight distribution with the addition of passenger load, on the 1941-42 and the 1946-47 statistical groups. The mean value of the 1941-42 cars is 4.6%, which means that on these cars the percent weight distribution on the front is nearly 5% less with the passenger load than at curb weight. The mean of the 1946-47 group is only 3.4%, indicating that the addition of the five passenger load has a considerably smaller effect on change of weight distribution than was the case of the 1941-42 cars. This, of course, is to be expected since the center of gravity of the passenger load is farther forward in the 1946-47 cars.

The data on Figure V are given in percentile form on Figure VI. The curve for the 1947-47 cars is more nearly uniform and has a steeper slope in the central position, indicating that the distribution of this data on this group of cars has a narrower range and is somewhat more consistent than in the 1941-42 group.

△ % FRONT WEIGHT

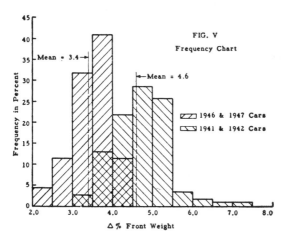

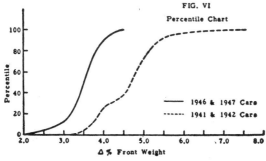

6

11

Using the Help of Others

A GREAT NUMBER of the projects upon which you report will be done entirely by yourself. Often, however, you will find that you have to call on someone else for help. Sometimes this help is given in person; sometimes it comes from the printed page.

When I was writing this book, for example, several people read the finished chapters. All of them made suggestions about things they thought I had left out, or about places where they thought I had not been clear. Similarly, when you do a project, you may find that people help you run tests, provide you with needed data, give suggestions that help you refine your procedures, and so on. Such help is personal.

In Chapter 4, I needed to use a term and concept that belonged to someone else—that of the three-level report. So I borrowed the idea from Messrs. Richards and Richardson, who had published it. Their idea gave me just as much help as if they had told me about it personally. In making an investigation, you too may have used methods which you borrowed from the report of someone else. Or in reporting information, you may have had to get some of your facts from someone else. You are just as indebted as if the help were personal, and you will want just as much to say "thanks."

The following chapter is concerned with such situations. It gives further reasons for making acknowledgments, evaluates some of the techniques most often used, and then deals with some other special problems that arise when material is borrowed.

WHY MAKE ACKNOWLEDGMENTS?

Making acknowledgments not only gives the thanks that any normal person feels for help given him. It may be legally necessary, it is an ethical obligation of any professional man, it may aid in establishing the authority of the writer, and it may provide valuable aid to the reader.

MEETING LEGAL OBLIGATIONS

The exact words or form in which things are presented is protected by both copyright and common law. So important is the right to ownership of expression that it was written into Section 8 of Article I of the Constitution of the United States. Copyright laws do not protect any *idea* as such. Doing so might be against the public interest, for it might slow down the spread of knowledge. But the way of *expressing* the idea is recognized as property. Thus authors are given a monetary incentive to publish their ideas—and again the public interest is advanced.

The law prevents us from duplicating the exact wording of an author without permission. Likewise, we cannot reproduce a table, picture, or other illustration. Doing so makes us liable to suit for damages. If we lose the suit, the court may not only assess damages against us but also punitive costs, sometimes to twice the amount of the judgment. Hence if it is desirable or necessary to use an author's exact expression, we must get permission of the copyright owner, and we must make proper acknowledgment. Details of how to get permission and use the material are given at the end of this chapter.

MEETING ETHICAL OBLIGATIONS

In order to advance the profession and themselves, professional men share their knowledge with great freedom. The man who shares good ideas helps his colleagues. In turn, he can reasonably expect his reputation in the field to advance. He gets important psychological compensation even where he may not get more money. If we use his ideas, the very least we can do is to tell whose they are.

This idea has a reverse twist too. If we thank people, they are likely to want to help us again when we need it. And the more that people share ideas, the more the profession advances—we along with it. In return, we can expect people to thank us when we earn the thanks.

In the long run professional ethics pay off. The man who steals another's ideas may win the immediate praise of his boss, but his colleagues know the ideas are stolen. And when the truth comes out, it hurts. It may mean your job. It always means that your colleagues will withhold information from you.

ESTABLISHING AUTHORITY

If someone knows that we have had the assistance of experts, he may have more confidence in our facts. This is true whether the assistance was given personally or in writing. For that reason we may want to support our own statement by citing an authority for it.

One caution is necessary here. The fact that a writer—even an authority—says that something is true does not make it so. Therefore we must evaluate critically—we cannot blame someone else for any mistakes. It is true that we may not be responsible directly for the mistaken fact or conclusion. But when we accepted it as true we showed bad judgment, and we are responsible for our mistakes in judgment.

AIDING THE READER

Another very important reason for making acknowledgments is that doing so may give a reader invaluable aid. We can tell him where he may go to find further information on the facts, ideas, or conclusions which we borrow.

He may want to check our sources for either of two reasons:

1. To get additional background information to help in interpreting the report.
2. To check on how the person we have cited as an authority arrived at the facts or conclusions which we borrowed.

HOW TO MAKE ACKNOWLEDGMENTS

Any method of making acknowledgments must fulfill our legal and ethical obligations. After that, what we acknowledge and where we acknowledge it depends on the same four guides we have used throughout this book. If the reader trusts us (the writer), there is no need for any method to facilitate his checking on us. If he is likely to be highly critical, he may want to use the acknowledgments to see how the borrowed facts were obtained. Then we must document fully and exactly. If little material is borrowed, we can use a simple method to document it. The following paragraphs evaluate the most common methods of making acknowledgments in terms of these guides.

Positions considered are the text itself, the prefatory positions, bibliographies, and footnotes.

THE TEXT ITSELF

Acknowledgments can be made in the text itself. That is, the acknowledgments are placed right in with the other material. One way does this in the course of a sentence, thus:

> In an article in the *Journal of Engineering Education* for December of 1953, C. J. Freund stressed the fact that . . .

Another way simply places the source of the data in parentheses after the material used.

The method has the advantage that the reader cannot overlook the acknowledgment. It has the disadvantage of taking up a great deal of text. And if there were many such references, the ideas of the text would get hopelessly confused by them.

In practice, then, direct reference to sources in the text itself is limited to reports which use only a few references. However, this position should be used if we want to be sure the reader sees the reference. For example, we may be criticizing a certain article, or talking about a man's theory as such, and we want the reader to know about whom we are talking.

Here a compromise is best. We can mention the man's name in the text, but give the rest of the information by footnote or in a bibliography.

THE PREFATORY POSITION

Chapter 5 pointed out that acknowledgments are often made in the prefatory position. Generally, those made there are personal. Acknowledgments for permission to quote also often go there.

The preface may also show the reader where to go to get substantiating data or further information, but it has severe limitations in doing so. For instance, if the report uses the borrowed information in "chunks," the preface can say:

> All data on composition and tensile characteristics of the various aluminum alloys were drawn from . . .

or

Chapters 9 and 10 are based upon . . .

But if many sources are used or if the material is used piecemeal, mixed with other material throughout the report, the method of acknowledgment becomes much too clumsy.

BIBLIOGRAPHIES

As used here, the term "bibliography" means a list of written items. Different techniques and their combinations will be discussed.

Alphabetized

DEFINITION AND DESCRIPTION. Some sort of alphabetical arrangement is used in all bibliographies. The simplest type merely runs all items into a single list, alphabetizing by the last name of the author. Where the author of an item is unknown, the first important word of the title is used to determine an item's placement in the list. No attention is paid to the nature of the item. The following brief bibliography, for example, successively lists an unsigned pamphlet, an unpublished report, a book, an unsigned magazine article, another book, and a signed magazine article:

Aero-Craft Lightweight Aluminum Boats (pamph.), St. Charles, Michigan: Harwill, Inc. [1953?].

Borchert, James P., *Examination of Accounts, the Nodu Company* [Unpublished], Pontiac, Michigan: Reynolds and Ryan (November 25, 1954).

Kelly, Walt, *The Pogo Papers,* New York: Simon and Schuster, 1953.

"Little Audrey," in *Esquire,* 41:88-89 (April, 1954).

Pinner, Max, and Benjamin F. Miller, eds., *When Doctors Are Patients,* New York: Norton, 1952.

Titus, Harold, "The Wide Missouri Gets Wider," in *Field and Stream,* 58:45-47; 99-101 (March, 1954).

AN ASIDE ON FORM. The individual items in the list above are in acceptable forms. There are many other forms equally acceptable, and you probably know one of them. If not, any handbook of English composition will show an acceptable one. Or you can adopt the standard form used in one of your professional magazines. Be sure to adopt a form which places the last name of authors first. For a book, the reason is that when someone goes to a library to find it, he goes first to the card catalog. The catalog always contains an "author card" in alphabetical order by last name.

Also be sure that the form you adopt tells the reader something about what each item is. Thus underlining of a title, or putting it all in capitals, shows that it is a complete and separate item. Quotation marks around a title show that it is part of some larger item. For example, the items in this bibliography would be decoded as follows:

An individually bound item titled Aero-Craft . . . , in pamphlet form, published at St. Charles, Michigan, by Harwill, Inc., probably in the year 1953.

This author wrote a report, not part of another report or of a series of reports. Its title was *Examination* . . . , and it was written for Reynolds and Ryan, of Pontiac, Michigan, on the date given. (This title makes clear it was a report. If it did not, the word "report" would be added after the title in brackets.)

Kelly wrote a book called *The Pogo Papers* which Simon and Schuster published in New York in 1953.

This article, which had no author given, appeared as part of this magazine in April of 1954. It was in volume 41 of the magazine and occupied the two pages given.

Pinner and Benjamin edited a book on doctors as patients. Norton published it in New York City in 1952.

Titus wrote an item on the Missouri River which appeared in the magazine called *Field and Stream* in March, 1954. It was in volume 58 of the magazine. The main part of the article covered pages 45 to 47. It was continued on pages 99 through 101.

A satisfactory form for any bibliographical item must do what the forms used have done. It must tell who wrote it, what the item is, who published it, and when. To find an article the reader needs also to know in what magazine he should look for it. Libraries catalog magazines by their names. They do not catalog articles. The volume number is valuable because some libraries bind magazines with the volume number on the back of the volume. The date gets the reader to the particular issue of the magazine. The page numbers get him to the page. With pamphlets and reports, especially "company" or unpublished ones, he also needs to know where to write to obtain a copy.

Any form which accomplishes these ends is satisfactory.

PLACEMENT. The simple alphabetized bibliography is placed at the end of the report. If the report has an appendix, it is placed there, as either the first or last item.

EVALUATION. The simple alphabetized bibliography does accomplish some things. It does give credit in a general way, and it does give the reader a list of things which he can consult if he wishes further information. It has these items gathered together in one place.

But such a bibliography gives credit in a general way *only*. All the reader knows is that the writer got some help from these authors. Somewhere in the report their works may have been used. To check on any fact he questions anywhere in the report, the reader has to go through all the items listed. If the items are many, the chore would be altogether too much. Even for a few items, it would be a job.

This type of bibliography also makes unnecessary work

for any reader who wishes to broaden his knowledge by consulting all the items. Libraries catalog books in one catalog file and magazines in another. He would have to sort the items mentally as he consulted each file.

In view of these limitations the only time that such a bibliography ought to be used is when

1. It contains very few items.
2. We are sure our readers will not want to check back particular facts to their sources.

Classified by Type of Item

DEFINITION AND DESCRIPTION. A second variety of bibliography classifies the written items used according to whether they are books, reports, pamphlets, magazine articles, unpublished manuscripts, and so on. Then within each of the classes, except magazine articles, items are listed alphabetically, exactly as in a simple alphabetical bibliography.

With magazine articles, another subclassification is often used. That is, under the heading of "magazines," the first listing is alphabetical by periodical. Under the name of the magazine are then listed all the articles from that magazine. The name of the magazine is then omitted from each item, though otherwise its form is the same as in the simple alphabetized bibliography. Listing under each magazine is usually alphabetical by author, though it may be done by number and date of the periodical when there are a great many articles from the same magazine.

EVALUATION. Such a bibliography has two strong advantages:

1. It clearly tells the reader exactly what each item is.
2. It is of greatest convenience to the reader who wishes to check the entire list of items.

The second of these advantages grows out of the way in which libraries are arranged. Books are cataloged in a card catalog by themselves. The reader takes the list of books and compares it with what the library has, as listed in the catalog, without having to sort out the items while he is doing so. He also finds periodicals in a separate catalog, listed by the name of the periodical, just as the bibliography is arranged.

Like the simple alphabetical bibliography, however, this bibliography shows the reader only in a general way what has been used in the report. If he wants to check a particular fact back to a particular source, he must go through every item in the bibliography. It will not do for the critical reader.

Classified by Subject Matter

DEFINITION AND DESCRIPTION. Another arrangement classifies the items in the bibliography according to the phase of the subject with which each deals. The items which deal with all phases are placed in a class called "General."

When this arrangement is used, it may be combined with a classification by type of item. Under each phase of the subject, items will be classified as to book, report, periodical, and so on.

PLACEMENT. A bibliography of this type is often placed at the end of a report, just as any other bibliography, but it is also frequently broken up. That is, after each developing section of the report, there will be placed the part of the bibliography which deals with the subject matter of that section. At the end of the report will appear the general items only. If it appears desirable to assemble the whole list in one place, items will appear both at the end of the appropriate section and in a composite list at the end of the report.

EVALUATION. When such a bibliography is subclassed by type of item, it retains most of the advantages of the first kind of classified bibliography. It also is helpful to the reader who wants to check on one phase of the subject only, or on one phase at a time. (That is why it is often used in textbooks or manuals, which the student studies in parts.) And if a critical reader wishes to run down the source of a particular fact, he has to go through only part of the total list.

The last sentence implies the major limitation of this type of bibliography—the reader who wishes to check on a specific fact or generalization cannot go directly to the one particular source.

Numbered

DEFINITION AND DESCRIPTION. To overcome the limitations of the bibliographies previously discussed, a numbered bibliography may be used. First of all, the items are arranged in any of the ways already described. Then the items are numbered progressively—1 to the first item, 2 to the second, and so on straight through the list. Each item in the bibliography then has its own identifying number.

Next, whenever the text uses anything from one of the items, the appropriate reference number is also used. If at a particular point in the text the number "22" appears, the reader knows that the material so marked is based upon the item numbered "22" in the bibliography.

PLACEMENT. The bibliography is placed in one of the locations already described. However, if it is broken up and placed at the end of sections, numbers may be assigned to the items at the end of each section independently. This practice is followed when there are so many items that the numbers would reach three or four figures, and when every item is referred to in one section only.

PLACEMENT OF REFERENCE NUMBER. The placement of the reference number in the text follows the same procedure as for footnoting. It is written as a superior number—which looks just like an exponent number—or it is placed in parentheses in the same line as the text. The exact placement varies with the situation.

As a general rule, the reference number appears right after the material used. If a fact in the middle of a sentence is borrowed, for example, the number appears right after the fact. But if the number appears at the end of a sentence, the situation is not so clear. Does the number include simply that sentence or several preceding sentences also?

One convention is that such reference numbers carry back either to the preceding reference number or to a paragraph break. That is, if no other number has appeared in a paragraph, it is assumed that all which preceded the reference number *in that paragraph* came from the same source.

The convention is useful in helping us distinguish our own material from that which has been borrowed—we can always make an artificial paragraph break. If we cannot do so smoothly, then we must employ phrasing which clearly shows when we have shifted from our own to borrowed material.

It follows that if three paragraphs in a row are all borrowed from the same source, the same reference number will appear at the end of each. This is different from footnoting practice, where a reference number is never repeated. With a numbered bibliography, the reference number is repeated as often as it is needed.

The number should not be repeated more often than is necessary. If a whole section or chapter comes from a single source, we can simply place the number after the section head. The same holds true for any subdivision which has a separate head. Or if most of a section comes from one source, we can place the number on the heading, and then add a footnote which says that, unless otherwise noted, all material is from this source.

On occasion, an introductory remark is followed by the reference number. For example, if a borrowed list or a long quotation is single spaced or put in a smaller type, the reference number would get "lost" typographically. If a formula is borrowed, the reference number might be mistaken for part of the formula. Placing the number after the introductory remark avoids these difficulties.

EVALUATION. A numbered bibliography obviously has all the advantages of whatever kind of bibliography is used as its base. In addition, whenever a reader wants to check on any item which we have borrowed, he can go directly to the one source from which it came. And not only does it show the exact authority for borrowed material; it also gives each author who helped us specific credit for his particular contribution. In addition, it does not have the formidable appearance of footnotes and is easy for a typist or printer to handle. Because of all of its advantages, the numbered bibliography is widely used, especially in scientific and technical writing.

It does have two limitations. Whether the first exists depends upon the length of the sources we have used. If each of the sources is short, the reader will not have to look through much material in order to find the information which he is seeking. But if any item is long, the reader may have to search through several pages. The second disadvantage will exist if any of our readers is very critical—he will be forced to keep turning from the text to the bibliography and back again.

Numbered, Plus Page Reference

To help the reader get to the exact page of any source,

some modified systems have been evolved. Three are particularly useful.

The first of these uses the numbered bibliography in the customary way, as described on page 146. Then, after each item in the bibliography, it places the page numbers which were used from the item, in the same order in which they are used in the report. This is helpful when some of the items are long, because the reader has a limited number of pages which he must check. But if many references are made to any one item, its usefulness disappears.

Hence a second variation. In it, the reference number in the text is immediately followed by a page number, thus: "22:103." This means that the material is drawn from page 103 of bibliographical item number 22. The practice is useful, but sometimes looks very clumsy on the typed or printed page. Imagine, for instance, a page containing a dozen references such as "117:278-92."

To minimize awkward references, there is a third variation in technique. First, it lists the exact page number references after each item of the bibliography in the same order in which they appear in the text. Then each page number is assigned a reference number. After each item, then, there appears a list something like this:

(1) 207, (2) 328-47, (3) 23, (4) 96-103

In the text, a double number is again used, only now the second number refers to the number after the appropriate bibliographical item. Thus "22:7" would mean "Go to item 22 of the bibliography. Refer to reference 7 after that item to find the page number from which I have taken this material."

With any of these methods the reader will know exactly where he can find the original presentation of the borrowed material. However, it remains true that if any reader wants to know *at once* the source of any item, he cannot do so without turning back in the report to the pages upon which the bibliography appears.

Annotated

Any of the types of bibliography so far discussed is sometimes annotated. That is, each item in the list is followed by a statement as to the nature of the information it contains or a critical evaluation of it. The practice is useful if the reader of the report is likely to want to do background reading to supplement the information presented in the report. He will have a better idea whether he wants to look up any item.

General

With any bibliography, it is helpful to tell the reader how it was built. How was the search for material conducted? Does it consist of the items referred to in the text only? Does it contain all the items examined in the course of getting ready to write this report? Does it consist of only the more useful items found? Is it complete for the area or period covered?

These questions can be answered either in the preface or in a headnote preceding the bibliography. The practice is not, it is true, a general one. But it ought to be.

FOOTNOTES

The final device for making acknowledgments is the footnote. In short papers, footnotes alone often are enough. In longer reports, footnotes are used in combination with some type of classified bibliography.

Definition and Description

Footnotes are so called because their traditional and usual placement is at the bottom or foot of the page. They can be used to give explanations or further information which it is felt some readers might want, but which would interfere with the development of the main idea of the text. Here, however, the main concern is with their other use—that of showing sources near the point of use.

Footnotes may take a wide variety of forms, none of which is preferred by all writers or readers. Roughly, the systems can be classified into the traditional Latinate and the short form.

THE TRADITIONAL LATINATE. The older form makes use of Latinate terms and abbreviations, unquestionably because it came into use when Latin was the language of scholarship. It is widely used in such fields as history, English literature, and similar traditional disciplines. In the sciences and technical fields, however, it is being displaced by a short form system or by a numbered bibliography. The reason is doubtless uncertainty on the part of both writers and readers as to how to use such Latinate forms as *ibid., loc. cit., op. cit., infra, passim,* and so on.

More or less detailed explanations of the system can be found in style books and in handbooks of English composition. The first time any bibliographic item is cited, full bibliographic information is given, plus the page number being cited. Later references make use of the Latin forms. Since full bibliographic information is given at the point of first citation, a bibliography is not absolutely essential. However, in order to gather all items in one place, a bibliography is used whenever more than a few sources are cited.

There is certainly no real objection to the system, and if used correctly, it does display the writer's erudition. However, a large number of readers will not understand it, and others will recoil from its scholarly look. Unless you are sure your reader is used to it, therefore, a short form is more desirable.

THE SHORT FORM. Like the Latinate form, the short form is often used along with a bibliography. When it is not, the first reference to any item must give full bibliographic information, plus the page number cited. Otherwise the system is very simple and cannot be misunderstood by the reader. In general, the note gives the last name of the author, plus the page number being cited—"Kelly, p. 38." Where more than one author has the same last name, the reference adds initials or first name—"Kelly, W. X., p. 38." If an author has written more than one item being used in the particular report, the first significant words of the title are added—"Kelly, *Brake Tests* . . . , p. 38."

This system has the advantage that the reader cannot misunderstand it. It does sometimes result in longer footnotes than necessary with the Latinate system.

Placement

Although by definition footnotes are notes coming at the bottom of the page, they actually are sometimes placed in other positions. Following are the ones used and the advantages and disadvantages of each.

FOOT OF PAGE. The customary position is at the foot of the page. The advantage is that the reader wishing to find out the source of a particular item has merely to glance to the bottom of the page. He does not have to keep turning back and forth in the report. It follows that when our reader is a professional man who will critically examine our work, the best footnote position is at the bottom of the page on which the citation is made.

Disadvantages of this placement are two. First, in typing and printing, some effort is required to get footnote and text to "come out right" on the page. Second, some readers seem to be allergic to footnotes—they equate footnotes and hard reading. The latter, however, will not be the critical professional readers who want to use footnotes.

AFTER TEXT REFERENCE. To avoid the difficulty in typing and printing from their manuscript, some writers place the footnote directly following the reference number in the text. The technique is to make a line all the way across the page, put in the footnote, make another line, and then continue with the text.

While this practice is helpful to the typist—or to a printer who specifies it—it tends to interrupt the reader. It should be avoided in the final presentation of any report.

AT THE END. Sometimes footnotes do not appear on the page on which the source is cited, but are gathered together at the end of the report. This practice makes for convenience in typing and printing. It has some advantages over the numbered bibliography in making clear exactly what comes from what sources. However, it does require the critical reader to turn back and forth in the report. And if several references are made to the same source, it takes up more space than a numbered bibliography. Moreover, if the reader is to have all sources in a form convenient for him to use in the library, it must be supplemented by a classified bibliography.

In long reports, a variation can be introduced—footnotes can be gathered at the end of the sections instead of at the end of the whole report.

Some people studying report techniques have difficulty in distinguishing the numbered bibliography from footnotes gathered at the end. The distinction is actually simple. When a numbered bibliography is used, the reference numbers in the text will not be in numerical sequence, but the items in the bibliography will be. When footnoting is used, both the reference numbers in the text and the items in the list at the end of the report or section will be in numerical sequence, but the items listed will have no other principle of order.

Use of Reference Numbers

The placement of reference numbers in the text is the same for footnotes as that already described for the numbered bibliography.

In using reference numbers for footnotes, there are some minor variations in practice. With short reports, the usual practice is to start with "1" and number the footnotes progressively throughout the report. With longer reports, the same practice may be followed. Sometimes, however, there are so many footnotes that if the report is numbered in sequence from beginning to end the numbers will run into three digits. Then the common practice is to begin over again at "1" with each new section or chapter.

The practice of beginning numbering anew with each page is just about obsolete. It gives too many problems in typing from manuscript, in retyping, and in setting in type. That is, unless the pages come out even in copying, the footnotes must be renumbered.

Some writers use printer's symbols such as * to designate footnotes. After a numerical item in a table, such a symbol must be used, to avoid confusing the number by an added number. Notes so identified always appear at the bottom of the page. Other writers use reference numbers for source footnotes and the printed symbols for explanatory footnotes. The practice has some advantages. The reader who will want to use the explanatory footnotes is likely to be one not fully acquainted with the field; the reader who uses the source footnotes is likely to be the professional reader. Each reader will know whether he will want to check the footnote. However, the system breaks down when the writer wants to give both an explanation and a source in the same footnote.

In any given situation, the simplest practice that will do the job is always the best. But if it is desirable to ascribe particular ideas to the people who contributed them, then either a numbered bibliography or footnotes must be used. The former is the easier, but footnotes at the bottom of the page have the advantage when most readers, or the most important reader, are likely to want to see at once the source of the borrowed ideas.

The advantage of not having to turn back and forth in the text is of course lost if footnotes are grouped at the end of the report or of sections of a report. And footnotes must be supplemented by a bibliography if it is desirable to group the items to facilitate the reader's doing his own background research. Otherwise footnotes most successfully do all the things that acknowledgments have to do.

HOW TO SOLVE RELATED PROBLEMS

Borrowing material from others creates four problems other than making acknowledgments:

1. When should material be quoted, and when should it be put in the writer's own words?
2. If material is to be quoted, how go about getting permission to use it?
3. If material is not quoted, what is the easiest way to make sure it is really put in our own words?
4. If material is to be ascribed to a specific source either through footnotes or a numbered bibliography, how decide what to give credit for?

1. WHAT TO QUOTE

It is never a good idea to quote another person directly unless there is a particularly good reason to do so. Most of the time what you need to borrow is the other person's idea, not his expression of it. If you quote a great many people directly, your report is likely to become a hodge-podge of different styles. Moreover, it is hard to weave the exact words of others into a unified pattern of development such as any report ought to have. Unless there is a good reason to quote, then, the best rule is not to do so.

Following are the good reasons for quoting.

First, you may want to introduce the writer's exact words as evidence. For example, you may be interpreting what he said, and you want your reader to see the exact grounds for your interpretation. This happens when you are going to take issue with a writer, when he is ambiguous or obscure, or when you think he has been generally misunderstood. Notice that here the quotation is the basis for a new contribution of your own.

Second, you may want to use the writer as an authority. You could say the same thing, in your own words, but he is in a better position to be believed. In Chapter 9, for example, I quoted Mr. Stonex. I simply wanted to reinforce my point by the direct testimony of someone who obviously would know about that point.

Third, it is both difficult and useless to do anything else with very exact formulations. Suppose, for instance, someone has worked out a new table, or a new formula, or a chart based on data he uncovered, or a listing of principles he has established. To change these would be difficult and might misrepresent them. Moreover, any change would be a forced one—obviously done simply to avoid quoting. Nothing is to be gained by struggling to make changes in things like these.

Fourth, the thing may have been so beautifully or so well said that it cannot be said better, even for the different purpose you have in mind in writing your own report. I think you will agree that such circumstances are practically nonexistent in technical writing.

Unless one of these four conditions holds, the best practice is to borrow the idea, but put it in your own words.

If you do decide to quote, the quotation must be exact. If it is desirable to quote material, but part of the passage is not needed, words can be omitted. To tell the reader where deletions have been made, three dots are used. If the deletion is at the end of a sentence, some writers use four dots.

Of course the omission should not change the sense of the original.

At other times it may be necessary to insert words of your own in the quotation in order for it to make full sense or to read clearly out of its context. These additions are inserted in square brackets. Parentheses cannot be substituted, as they would indicate a parenthetical remark of the original author.

2. HOW TO GET PERMISSION

When anything is borrowed exactly, it is a legal requirement to get permission. This includes not only wording but graphic material. Actually, there is one exception to this requirement. In practice, student papers quote sources freely without permission. But these are submitted for a single class and are not published in the usual sense. Moreover, it would burden publishers to correspond with every student who wanted to quote—in a term paper, for example!

Except for student papers submitted for class only, however, permission ought to be obtained. No difficulty is involved unless the request is clearly outrageous or silly— as when one man asked to reproduce practically half a book as part of his report. Publishers are very willing to give permission for any legitimate purpose, though they may charge a fee. So are most companies.

The procedure is to write to the publisher or company which issued the work from which you want to borrow.[1] If they do not own the copyright, they know who does, and they can act as agent or forward your request. Tell

[1] Government publications may be quoted without permission.

exactly what it is that you wish to quote, how the quotation will appear in your paper, and the probable distribution of your report. You can expect permission in a very few days.

If you do not give full details in your letter, the publisher will mail back a form on which you fill out the details. You might just as well give them to begin with.

One warning—if there will be a limited number of copies of your report, be sure to say so. Otherwise you are likely to get a reply which asks for a copy of your final report.

In borrowing material within your own organization or plant, it is not legally necessary to get permission—no one is likely to sue you. Nevertheless, it is good practice to clear the item. It makes the person who wrote the original think more of you, and it insures against your getting a reputation as a leech on other people.

3. HOW TO BE SURE TO USE YOUR OWN WORDS

Either because they do not know any better or because they are lazy, a few people try to avoid getting permission to quote by changing things very slightly. You don't want to be like them. In the first place, minor changes do not relieve you from legal responsibility. In the second, any competent person in the field will know exactly what you are doing and lose his respect for you as a professional man. But sometimes phrasing very close to the original is accidental. It results from writing directly from notes. The way to be sure you really get things in your own words is to master the material sufficiently that you can write independent of your notes. Place them aside, outline what you want to say, and write from the outline. Return to the notes only to fill in exact facts and figures and to supply annotation where it may be needed. Doing this will insure that you use your own organization and your own words.

4. WHAT SHOULD BE ANNOTATED

Whether a numbered bibliography or footnoting is used, the question sometimes comes up as to what things should be ascribed to sources. Actually there are two practices—the professional practice, and the one that is required of students.

A professional man who has been practicing a long while should not find much problem. Certain things are common knowledge in the field. Put it this way. If the generalization or statement of fact were questioned, the professional man could immediately bring instances and examples from his own experience to prove what he meant. The professional man, therefore, annotates only what clearly belongs to someone else. If when challenged, he would cite a particular study or theory of someone else, then he should have annotated the information. In other words, facts or theories known to be the work of some particular recent worker in the field are always acknowledged.

This is different from the practice you had to use in writing term papers when you were a freshman in college. Then your instructor told you to footnote everything you didn't know when you began doing reading on the project. One reason was to teach you to footnote. Another and better one ties in with professional practice. If as a student any of your material had been challenged, all you could have done was to say, "This book says so." You really needed to cite your authority.

Even in professional practice, look your work over carefully. If when you ask, "How do I know *that?*" you have to refer to the work of someone else, then it is a good idea to annotate the material.

PRACTICE SUGGESTIONS

1. Acknowledgments other than prefatory are made in the sample reports on pages 336, 384, 478, and 550.
2. The most elaborate uses of acknowledgments are in technical books and textbooks. Examine a few to see some of the variations used. Note both their weak and strong points in using the various techniques.
3. Examine magazines in your particular field of specialization to determine the methods they use. You may even want to make a study of the frequency of various methods.
4. Does your collection of reports make acknowledgments? What kind? In what form? Would you make any changes?

12

Writing and Checking

So FAR we have dealt with designing the report rather than with writing it. That is because it is the design of reports which primarily differentiates them from other kinds of expository writing. Nowhere, however, are the principles of good language more important than in reports. If the report is to your superior, he will not want to have to puzzle out what you mean—he does not have the time to do so. He will just stop reading the report. If you are writing to those on the same level in the organization or on a lower level, they may not stop reading, but they may misunderstand what you have written. You will not get the result that you want.

To be understood, you need a good, detailed plan consistently carried out and carefully checked. The longer the report, the more conscientiously systematic you must be. The shorter the report, the larger a minor inconsistency will seem.

This chapter reviews some of the points that a systematic approach must take into account. Points covered include:

    I. Using a Detailed Outline
    II. Determining and Maintaining a Point of View
    III. Writing for the Reader's Level
    IV. Planning and Checking the Paragraphs
    V. Choosing the Right Word
    VI. Writing Easy-to-Read Sentences

VII. Assisting the Reader by Means of Punctuation
VIII. Avoiding Confusion in Abbreviations and Numbers

I. USING A DETAILED OUTLINE [1]

By the time you are ready to do the actual writing of any report, the over-all plan will be clearly in mind. You will know the major points to be covered in the introduction, you will have decided on the main sections of the report, and you will know what the subsections are to be.

When you write these items down, you have an outline of the entire report. It will look something like this outline of a report on establishing standard data.[2]

I. *Introduction*
    A. Statement of Problem
    B. Assemblies Included
    C. Method of Attack
    D. Order of Reporting
II. *Conclusions and Recommendations*
III. *Change Bobbin*
    A. Establishing the Standard Value
    B. Establishing the Standard Minutes-Per-Piece Allowance for Any Length of Sew
    C. Determining the Standard Minutes-Per-Piece Allowance
    D. Interpreting the Data
IV. *Fix Thread Breakage*
    A. Determining Causes of Thread Breakage
    B. Determining the Minutes-Per-Sew-Inch Allowance
    C. Interpreting the Data

---

[1] In this chapter, sections and subsections are assigned numbers and letters to make it easy to refer to any section or subsection.

[2] The report itself is in the Appendix, page 281.

V. *Rip and Resew*
  A. Determining Causes of Rip and Resew
  B. Determining the Minutes-Per-Sew-Inch Allowance
  C. Interpreting the Data
VI. *Change Spool of Thread*
  A. Establishing the Minutes-Per-Change Allowance
  B. Establishing a Minutes-Per-Sew-Inch Allowance
  C. Grouping the Minutes-Per-Inch Values
  D. Interpreting the Data
VII. *Change Needle, Oil Machine, Snip Tie Cords, Reposition Material*
  A. Change Needle, Oil Machine
  B. Snip Tie Cord, Reposition Material

Now is a good time to look again at the over-all plan to consider alternatives. It is much easier to switch things around in an outline than after they have been written out in full. When the order seems the best possible, apply to the outline these checks:

A. CHECK MAIN HEADS TO SEE THAT THEY ARE PHRASED IN THE SAME WAY

All ought to be, except for the introduction and conclusions. The following are not consistently phrased:

> Tau Island Scheme
> From Silos to Plot 1
> Trucking from Ash Basin to Plot 1

Rephrased, they could become:

> Pumping to Tau Island
> Trucking from Silos to Plot 1
> Trucking from Ash Basin to Plot 1

This check for parallelism of expression is important because it shows whether a single principle was used to arrange the sections. If it was not, it will be next to impossible to phrase the heads in the same kind of language without getting a stilted and awkward effect. Try doing it with the following:

> Offices
> Salesroom
> Utility Rooms
> Hallways
> Carrying Out Changeover

Difficulty is encountered because the first four heads divide space according to function, the last is a step in a chronological plan.

B. MAKE THE SAME CHECK FOR THE SUBHEADS UNDER EACH MAIN HEAD

There is no need for the subheads under IV, say, to correspond to those under V, but all under IV should be consistent with each other.

C. CHECK FOR OVERLAP BETWEEN MAIN HEADS AND BETWEEN SUBHEADS UNDER THE SAME MAIN HEAD

Overlapping likewise shows that a single principle of order has not been used. In the following example method of operation and type of motion have both been used. An automatic machine could be either rotating or oscillating.

> Manually Operated
> Automatic
> Rotating
> Oscillating

D. CHECK MAIN HEADS TO SEE THAT NO MAIN POINT HAS BEEN LEFT OUT. NEXT, OR JUST BEFORE WRITING EACH SECTION, DO THE SAME FOR EACH SUBHEAD

The following leaves out a main point:

> Scrape Dishes
> Pile Dishes in Rack
> Close Door
> Turn Switch

The dishes probably will not get completely washed—no detergent was put in the machine.

These checks save mistakes in writing and time in revising. The outline will become the table of contents of the final report, and each head in the outline will also serve as a heading in the body of the report. If they are in good shape from the beginning, revision will not be needed.

From this point on, techniques vary. If you like, you can complete the outline in full detail. If you have been working on a project, sort together by section all of the data accumulated. If you are giving information from past experience, jot down on cards all of the points you believe ought to be made. Then progressively sort the data or cards into smaller groups until you are satisfied with the arrangement. The outline can then be "filled in" for the entire report before you begin the actual writing.

Personally, I find it easier not to go so far all at once. Instead, after sorting the data, I fill in the points of each subsection just before I write it.

Either procedure finally results in a fairly complete outline for every subsection. In a subsection of any length at all, recording the subpoints in an outline allows you to check for logical sequence before actually beginning to write. You can use the same checkpoints as for main sections.

II. DETERMINING AND MAINTAINING
A POINT OF VIEW

The next major step is to decide the point of view that you will take towards your material. The same facts can be expressed in different ways. For example,

> Two types of bobbins are used in the Cut and Sew Department.
> We use two types of bobbins in our Cut and Sew Department.
> You should use two types of bobbins in the Cut and Sew Department.
> Use two types of bobbins in the Cut and Sew Department.
> I use two types of bobbins in my Cut and Sew Department.

The first example uses an impersonal or objective point of view. Only the facts are reported. The other four are from personal points of view. The one which employs "we" is from the point of view of someone writing as representative of his organization. Those which use "you" or the imperative are from the point of view of someone giving orders or advice to someone else. The last one, which uses "I," suggests that the writer runs or owns the department concerned.

Any point of view can be correct. Which to use depends upon the relationship in which the reader, writer, and material stand, or on where the writer wants the reader's attention to be centered.

In what situations is each point of view suitable, and what are the advantages and drawbacks of each?

A. THE OBJECTIVE POINT OF VIEW

The objective point of view is used whenever we want the reader to center his attention on the facts. You or I may have studied the problem, determined the facts, and made the recommendations, but we don't want the emphasis on us. The impression that we want to give is factual. (Here was the problem—it existed just like this and anyone who looked at the situation would have seen it just this way. Here are the facts—they aren't just my opinions as to what is so; they *are* what is so. Any competent person would see them this way. Here are the recommendations—they aren't simply ideas I happened to dream up, but are logically inescapable once the facts are known.)

Of course everyone does know that "facts" and interpretations of them will vary according to the competence of the investigator. In this situation, however, we don't want the reader to be thinking of us and the possibility of human error on our part.

Some of the effectiveness of the objective point of view lies in the fact that objective writing reflects objective thinking. The man who keeps his feelings and his opinions out of his writing probably has not allowed them to color his facts or affect his method. At the very least, he has been able to distinguish fact from feeling before he has done the actual writing.

Because it places emphasis on the facts, the objective point of view is suitable for most scientific and technical writing. The more formal the situation and the more remote the relationship of reader and writer, the greater the chances that it will be appropriate.

Unless there is a very good reason for doing otherwise, then, use the objective point of view in any report that may possibly be seen by someone above your immediate superior. Make an exception only of prefatory material that appears separately, as in a preface or letter of transmittal. Since such material concerns the reader and writer, it can be as personal in tone as necessary to perform its function.

The objective point of view is characterized by the use of the third person and by wording with a minimum of emotional coloring.

1. *Third Person and Passive Voice*

"Third Person" means anyone or anything not me, you, or us. Third person does not require passive voice, but passive voice must sometimes be used with it.

Here are three guides to help in determining whether to use active or passive voice.

a. USE ACTIVE VOICE UNLESS THERE IS A GOOD REASON NOT TO DO SO.

Active voice *seems* more active. Something *does* something to something else. Hence a sentence in active voice seems more lively and is easier to read. For example, compare these two sentences:

Next the die strikes the metal sharply.
Next the metal is struck sharply by the die.

In the first sentence the subject is active—the die does the striking. In the second, the subject is passive—the metal simply lies there. The agent involved—the die—is buried in a phrase. In the first sentence, you picture the die, see it go into motion, and then imagine the moving die arriving at its object. In the second sentence, you first see the metal lying there. You then have to suspend any image of the striking until you know what did the striking.

b. USE PASSIVE VOICE IF THE AGENT INVOLVED IS NOT SIGNIFICANT TO YOUR PURPOSE.

If you had to describe the simple process of changing a tire, for example, you could write:

First the mechanic assembles the tools—a jack, a jack handle that also serves as a wrench, and two pieces of wood to use as blocks for one rear wheel. After making sure that the car is in gear and the brake is set, the mechanic places the blocks in position and the jack under the bumper. Next he moves a selector switch on the jack to the "up" position, and works the jack handle up and down.

If not by now, in a few more sentences the mechanic and "he" will become obtrusive. The reason is that the reader's attention is supposed to be centered in the process itself, not in the person who is doing it. A switch to the passive is desirable:

First the tools are assembled—a jack, a jack handle that also serves as a wrench, and two pieces of wood to be used as blocks for one rear wheel. After the car is placed in gear and the brakes set, the blocks are put in position and the jack placed under the bumper. Next a selector switch of the jack is moved to the "up" position and the jack handle worked up and down.

If you really wanted the reader to center his attention on the mechanic, you'd have to give him some guidance, like this:

The mechanic did the job simply and efficiently. First he assembled his tools—a jack, a jack handle that also served as a wrench, and two pieces of wood to use as blocks for one rear wheel . . .

Note the difference in emphasis—the process was described only as an illustration of the mechanic's efficiency, not for its own sake.

c. USE THE PASSIVE WHEN IT WILL HELP KEEP THE READER'S THOUGHT PATTERN MOVING STRAIGHT AHEAD.

The first example that follows is in active voice, but it causes back-tracking. The pattern is die to metal to finger, back to metal.

Next the die strikes the metal and shears it to shape. A mechanical finger then moves away the shaped metal and scrap.

Using passive voice once gives a straighter line of thought —die to metal to finger:

Next the die strikes the metal and shears it to shape. The shaped metal and scrap are then moved away by a mechanical finger.

The principle just discussed explains why the passive is so often used in breaking an idea into its parts. The large idea is named first, then its parts, and then each part is discussed in the order named.

The employes are classified as hourly-rated, nonexempt salaried, and exempt salaried.

NOT:

Hourly-rated, nonexempt salaried, and exempt salaried make up the classes of employes.

2. *Emotional Wording*

In objective writing, words and expressions that imply an emotional reaction on the part of the writer are not used. Advertising copy illustrates the nonobjective approach:

Crunchy, golden-brown, delicious, they tempt the most finicky appetite.
Glide like a breeze over even the choppiest wave.

In reports, this poetic tone is not likely to be found, but single phrases sometimes betray an emotional reaction:

these filthy conditions
failed to meet goals
delinquent accounts
splendid achievement
remarkable advance in styling
the operator was negligent in not stopping the machine before . . .

More objective phrasing would be:

conditions below standard

did not meet goals

past-due accounts

$12,000 decrease in maintenance costs

change in styling

operator did not observe the malfunctioning of the machine

in time to . . .

3. *Advantages and Drawbacks of Objective Point of View*

The great advantage of the objective point of view is that it gives the impression that what is being said is factual. It carries conviction. Its disadvantage is that its interest-level must be low. People are most interested in writing that contains active verbs, proper names, personal pronouns, and picturable words and phrases. Objective writing must often use the passive voice and cannot use the other devices and remain objective.

B. THE "WE" POINT OF VIEW

The "we" point of view can be effective. It can also be pompous, stilted, and offensive.

Sometimes "we" means *our company, our department,* or *our group.* The point of view is effective when communication is between people who feel closely identified with the organization. The report on page 322 occasionally uses this attitude:

A test garden has been started in the ash disposal basin to determine the ability of our fly ash to grow a plant or grass cover. If successful we will be able to use this ability to prevent erosion . . .

The following opening of a directive illustrates the same use:

On March first our department will make its long-awaited move to new quarters. The moving crew will be coming in shortly after 5:00 P.M. on Monday and will complete the job before 8:00 A.M. on Tuesday. We can facilitate their work and make sure nothing is lost or misplaced if we do the following:

In this example "we" means the members of the department or *you and I together.* "We" is used in the same sense in reports to stockholders:

Altogether, 1954 has been our most successful year so far. We have not only maintained our margin of profit but have strengthened our position through diversification of our products.

The "we" point of view is especially effective in taking the sting out of certain types of admonition:

These figures show that we have not been sufficiently effective in reducing absenteeism just before and just after holidays.

Substitute "you" and notice how much harsher the statement becomes.

The "we" point of view is stilted and offensive when used to mean *I*—the regal plural. In effect it says *me and God.* Note this opening from a memorandum:

We are pleased to learn that your department has completed another month without accidents, and we wish to express our congratulations.

It would have been better to have written:

Congratulations on another month entirely free from accidents.

Even when properly used, the "we" attitude cannot be sustained over more than a paragraph or two. It becomes monotonous and artificial. It must be relieved by either the objective or the "you" point of view.

C. THE "I" POINT OF VIEW

The least useful point of view is that of the first person

singular—"I." Even when it must be used, as in a letter of application or in some letters of transmittal, it ought to be minimized. Biggest offenders are executives "writing down" to their subordinates. They are the same people who use "we" to mean *me and God.* They write:

It gives me great pleasure . . .

OR

I have noted with concern . . .

The tone assumes that the superior expects his employe to be intimately interested in the superior's feelings.

If kept at a minimum, "I" can be used in prefatory material, as on page 411. It can also be used in identifying or intensifying an opinion or judgment. ("It is my belief that . . . ," or "I am fully convinced that . . .") Finally, it is suitable in telling of an incident which happened to oneself. The incident must not be told in a bragging tone, and the practice is most effective when it involves a joke on the writer.

D. THE "YOU" POINT OF VIEW

Used correctly, the "you" point of view is very effective. Used incorrectly, it can misfire catastrophically.

It is a desirable viewpoint in most letters, including letters of transmittal:

Here is the report you requested . . .

It is also desirable in giving information where the reader is directly involved, provided the points made are favorable to the reader or he actively wants the information:

In the Red Feather campaign just ended you have helped set a new record for your company and your community.

OR

This little booklet tells you of your new health insurance

plan. . . . Read it carefully and then put it away where it will be handy if you ever need it.

In giving directions the "you" viewpoint is convenient and neutral in effect. People do not resent directions from those who know what they are talking about and are supposed to give them. A department head would not resent a memorandum that began:

> To help relieve congested parking conditions, will you see that the following regulations are called to the attention of all in your department?

This memo continued with several rules, all stated in the imperative.

The directive just quoted used another device that takes the sting out of directions stated in the imperative—it gave a sensible reason for the directions. If no reason is given, resistance can be expected. How would you react to a directive that opened thus:

> You are to take the following steps at once.

If the imperative is sustained too long, it gives the effect of nagging. So does "you should." The solution is to list the directions whenever possible and to introduce the list with a neutral statement:

> The generator can be removed in the following steps:

The "you" point of view can be badly misused. The first misuse occurs when "you" does not obviously apply to the reader. No executive cares to be told how to operate a machine; he will be perfectly willing to learn how the machine is operated. Or consider the speaker who gave a canned lecture to a group of Boy Scouts, telling them, "You'll get greater cooperation from your children if you sign a *Dad-Daughter* or *Dad-Son* pledge."

A second misuse occurs when stupid or wrong conduct is imputed to the reader:

Follow these directions carefully. You cannot expect best results if you do not. (The implication—the reader won't follow the directions but then will be stupid enough to blame the poor results on poor directions.)

You have been negligent in turning in these reports.

As you can see, you are running in the red this month.

E. CONSISTENT AND MIXED POINTS OF VIEW

The over-all tone of any piece of writing ought to be consistent. In reports that go outside the department, no difficulty will be encountered if an objective point of view is used everywhere except in prefatory material. In less formal pieces of writing, complete consistency is not always a virtue. An excellent sample of a mixed point of view is on page 576. The principle employed is shown in the last two sentences of the first paragraph:

. . . First is your remarkable record of accomplishment for 1952. Second is the serious problem with which we are faced in view of the extremely high backlog of open suggestions.

The "you" viewpoint continues to be employed in talking about praiseworthy accomplishments. The problem is always spoken of in terms of what "we" (you and I) can do to correct it. "We" is also used in reviewing the facts.

Because they are all personal, the "we," "I," and "you" points of view are often mixed together like this. Any of them can also be mixed with the objective. Mixture of the three personal viewpoints will never be bad if "you" always means one explicit reader (not anyone in general), if "we" always means either the company or *you and I together* and if "I" always means the actual writer.

Notice that where the objective and personal are mixed, the personal viewpoint is the dominant one. Statements put objectively are mixed in to relieve the dominant viewpoint. If the objective point of view is dominant, it is not a good idea to mix in the personal. An exception has already been given—at certain points in describing a procedure, process, or mechanism it may be desirable to shift to the imperative. If so, the items in the imperative should be listed and introduced by a topic sentence.

A shift in point of view is objectionable if it is haphazard and unnecessary. A quick shift is especially confusing:

The tip-up is now set. First we dig a hole about a foot in diameter. Next get the reel ready. You must be sure that it runs free and the line is not tangled.

The writer of this sample would have avoided confusion if he had decided upon some point of view *before he began to write*. He would have revised the paragraph if he had consciously asked himself what point of view each sentence expressed.

To prevent ineffective and confusing shifts, the best plan is to write down who the reader is to be, the use he will make of the material, and how you stand in relation to him. Next record the operating rules for that piece of writing. An example might be:

READER—My boss (Labor Relations Director). He plans to show it to the Personnel Director.

USE—They want straight information to make a decision, the nature of which I don't know.

WRITER—I have access to the facts. This report is going up—there is no personal relationship. I'm a human fact-gathering and classifying mechanism.

VIEWPOINT—Objective in body of report. No *we, you, I*. No imperative.

III. WRITING FOR THE READER'S LEVEL

No one would expect a third-grader to understand a phrase like "the metaphysical postulates underlying Descartes' epistemology." We know that some writing can be too hard for some people. The trouble is that we tend to be too modest—we figure that if we know a word, everyone else must; or that if we can follow a complex statement, everyone else ought to be able to do the same. As a result, we write *at our own reading level.* That is, we write as if everyone were just as expert in the field as we, just as familiar with the idea we are expressing, and just as good in general reading ability.

The assumption is wrong. Few people who read your reports will be as expert in the field as you—they are not supposed to be. Hardly anyone will be as close to the facts as you. The executives who read your reports will vary as much in reading skill as do college students. Readers on lower organizational levels will almost always be less competent technically, less familiar with the situation, and less skillful in reading.

Writing is hard to understand if it contains hard words, hard sentences, or hard paragraphs. Hard words are ones that are too long, too technical, or too abstract. Hard sentences are ones that are too long or that do not make clear the relationships of the words that make them up. Paragraphs can consist of easy sentences, but they will still be hard if they are too long or if the relationships of the sentences are not clear. To really confuse a reader, all we need to do is to combine hard words, hard sentences, and hard paragraphs.

The level of difficulty of a piece of writing can be measured by techniques evolved by experts in "readability." Their formulas are based on sound principles. You should examine some of their books and pick out one of them as a guide in measuring your own writing. Some of them are listed at the end of this chapter. The formulas are not supposed to tell you how to write well, but they will tell you when your writing is too difficult.

All formulas take into account sentence length and word length, but they vary in other aspects. McElroy's,[1] a very simple one, counts each sentence separately, like this:

1. Count *one* for each word of one or two *pronounced* syllables.
2. Count three for each word of three or more *pronounced* syllables.
3. To get the grade-level of difficulty, divide the total of each sentence by two.

If a sentence counted twenty, for example, it should be intelligible to a man with a tenth-grade education. If it counted forty, even college graduates would have difficulty with it.

All formulas take many other factors into account. Mc-Elroy's, for example, counts a proper name as one, doesn't count the pronounced suffix of a plural noun. Devices such as parallelism and listing reduce fog count—and so on. The point is that many such formulas are available. You should investigate them and select the one you find easiest to use.

These formulas show you when revision is necessary. If, for example, you are writing to college graduates, you could theoretically write to a grade level of sixteen. Actually, you would do better to write to a level of ten or twelve— people can read faster and understand better several levels *below* their top capacity.

Don't try to apply one of these formulas bit by bit as you write. Do keep in mind the easy reading level of the people who must read your report. *Right at the beginning* picture the reader to yourself. Decide at what level of writing ability you should aim. Then write a paragraph or two about

[1] John McElroy, *How to Make Writing Communicate*, Columbus, Ohio: Readability Associates, 1949. (This is a photographically processed training manual on which much of the following discussion is based.)

some phase of your subject. Next apply a readability formula to what you have written. If it tests high, revise it till it tests at the level you have planned, or below.

Why do this *before* you set yourself to the business of continuous writing? Why not write everything first, then check back and revise?

Simply because you will find that a piece of writing seems to take on a *pattern of complexity.* If you start writing clearly enough it is easy to maintain that style. If you start with complicated phraseology and long words, you keep writing that way. It is just as when you talk to someone— once set, the tone of a given conversation is likely to remain the same.

The rest of this chapter concerns itself with how to obtain simplicity and clearness. The principles apply in first writing, in checking, and in revising. You will find them most valuable in checking and revising.

The material covered here is to be found in greater detail in any of the good college handbooks of English. It is not a substitute for them. If you do not now have such a book, get hold of one. Best for you will be the one that you used as a college freshman, because you will already have some familiarity with it.

The reason for reviewing certain points here is to give emphasis to them in terms of making ideas clear to the reader. The points selected are those which seem to me to give the most difficulty to mature writers.

The order of the discussion is arbitrary. Principles of paragraphing are discussed first because it seems to me that I am likely to have a fairly large idea-unit in mind as I write. Sentences fall into place in a particular way because of their relation to the other sentences in the paragraph. I am assuming that this is a common experience.

Second to be discussed is word choice. I find that if I think in "hard" words, my sentences seem to acquire a corresponding complexity of pattern. Third are considered points to check to make sure that sentence relationships are clear. Next comes punctuation, because it helps make such relationships clear. Last are some suggestions to insure that style in abbreviations and numbers will not confuse the reader.

IV. PLANNING AND CHECKING THE PARAGRAPHS

A paragraph that is easy to read is short, is focused on one phase of the subject, makes steady forward progress, and has clear relationships between sentence ideas.

A. LENGTH

A long paragraph is not necessarily *bad*. Neither is a short one necessarily *good*. Where to shift from one paragraph to another depends partly on the effect upon the reader and partly on the other three requirements just named.

The reaction of the reader is based upon his expectations. Unconsciously he expects each paragraph to be an important step forward in his task of understanding the report. He gets a certain satisfaction and relief from feeling that he has mastered another chunk of what we have to say. It follows that a long paragraph repels him—it looks as if he had a big job ahead of him.

A piece of writing in which the paragraphs are consistently only a sentence or two long looks easy to read. Shortly, however, the reader is conscious of a choppy effect. There are useless pauses while his eye spans vacant white space. Besides, the paragraph breaks had told him that the ideas were not extremely closely related. If he finds out that they are, he has to go back mentally to group the paragraphs that belong to a single unit. In effect, he has to do his own paragraphing.

Good paragraph length will come as a result of writing paragraphs that are good in other aspects. However, if even a good paragraph runs over a page of double-spaced type-written copy, break it up—a solid page of type looks hard to read. If instead several paragraphs in succession are very short, first look for the over-all relationship that made them come in logical sequence. Express this idea in a topic sentence and combine the short paragraphs into one.

B. UNITY

A paragraph focused on one phase of a topic has *unity*. That is, there is one central idea with which all the sentences in the paragraph are concerned.

If you outline, your paragraphs are almost certain to have unity in the sense that they cover just one thing. The title of the report, for example, is just one thing. So is the smallest unit shown in the outline. Either could in theory make a unified paragraph. A paragraph that really lacked unity could result only from throwing in something that did not belong in the part of the outline you picked for the paragraph.

But unity and the appearance of unity are two different things. A kangaroo, a whale, a squirrel, and a monkey have a common relationship, but it isn't an obvious one until it is pointed out. (They are all mammals.)

To check a paragraph for the appearance of unity, read it by itself. If you can immediately state the single basic idea with which it is concerned, it will have the appearance of unity. If you cannot, the unifying idea must be explicitly stated. In report writing, where the elements of suspense are not important, state the idea in the first sentence of the paragraph. In longer reports, this sentence can be reinforced by a paragraph heading. In short reports, where no section is over a paragraph in length, the paragraph heading can be used as a substitute for the topic sentence.

C. FORWARD PROGRESS

A reader likes to feel that he is getting somewhere. Theoretically, each sentence should give him the feeling that he has covered another step of the topic with which the paragraph is concerned. The following paragraph illustrates the principle. The first sentence states that the paragraph will deal with variations in a procedure according to type of oil. Each of the next three sentences tells him of the variations for one type of oil.

> This procedure varies according to which of three types of crude oil is being refined. Paraffin base oils are in the main distilled so as to carefully avoid cracking or decomposition by heat. Asphalt base oils may be run with steam to a fuel-oil residuum or to a heavy asphalt, or, if a high yield of light products such as gasoline or kerosene is desired, to a solid residuum or coke. Mixed base oils may be run with steam to a fuel oil residuum, but if the oil is suitable for the production of lubricants, it may be run with little or no steam to a dry residuum or coke.

If the paragraph is outlined, it is seen that each sentence concerns a subhead of the main topic, thus:

Variations according to type
1. With paraffin base oils
2. With asphalt base oils
3. With mixed base oils

All paragraphs ought to have the forward movement the reader expects. Rarely, however, is each sentence a full step forward as in the example above. Indeed, to get each sentence so that it took a complete step, the writer had to use sentences that are too long for easy reading. Since the pattern cannot often be followed, the writer needs to help the reader by words which show him the relationship of sentences to the over-all paragraph plan.

D. CLEAR RELATIONSHIP

The following paragraph on fuel economy illustrates the general principle of making the relationship of sentences clear. Here is a detailed outline of the paragraph:

Through more thorough vaporization
1. By using manifolds
   a. Type: small
   b. Purpose: to keep mixture velocity high
   c. Disadvantage: power reduced at high speeds
2. By using supercharger
   a. Method: mixture passes over rapidly moving vanes
   b. Result: gas globules chopped up
3. By introducing supersonics
   a. Method: sound waves break up particles
   b. Result: two miles per gallon increase

Here is the developed paragraph; each sentence has been numbered for identification:

(1) Since some of the fuel in the cylinder is "solid" that is, has not been vaporized, fuel economy can likewise be improved by more thorough vaporization. (2) One method depends upon small manifolds to keep the velocity of the mixture high. (3) However, this method reduces power at top speeds. (4) Another method uses a supercharger. (5) Here rapidly moving vanes chop up the gas globules as the mixture passes through. (6) A third method depends upon the introduction of supersonics into the manifold. (7) The sound waves break up the gas particles. (8) With this last method experimental engines show as much as two miles per gallon increase.

The paragraph opens with a sentence which states the topic idea of the paragraph—improvement through more thorough vaporization. (Incidentally, in the first part of the sentence a connection is also made with what has gone before, in two ways: "likewise" shows that this is an additional

way of gaining fuel economy; "since some of the fuel oil
. . . is solid" recalls an idea which had already been mentioned.)

The main forward-moving or developing ideas in the
paragraph are contained in sentences 2, 4, and 6. The reader
is told that they are the main ideas by the words *one
method, another method,* and *a third method.*

After sentence 2, the reader would normally expect another main step. The word "however" is used to show that
instead he will get a contrast, and "this method" shows
that the contrast will be to the idea of the preceding sentence.

Sentence 4, marked as a main forward step, is likewise
not followed by the next main step. The reader is therefore
told the relationship of sentence 5 by the word "here" (i.e.,
"in the supercharger").

Sentence 6 is marked as a main forward step (*a third
method*). Sentence 7 is not a main forward step but is not
marked as a lesser idea. It need not be, because by now the
reader does not expect each sentence to move forward, and
sentence 7 is an explanation of 6 in the same way that 5
was an explanation of 4.

The last sentence, 8, opens with a phrase that shows the
sentence will not be a main step and that it relates to the
idea of sentence 6. Incidentally, notice that the sentence
ends on the idea of *increase,* which recalls to the reader the
whole topic idea of the paragraph.

How should the principle of marking the relationships of
sentences be applied? No one can be expected to outline in
the detail shown. Certainly no one will look at such an outline and then, in virtue of the relationships shown in it,
consciously insert relating words as he goes along. Writing
is not that stereotyped and mechanical. However, when
the first draft is checked, certain paragraphs may not seem
to "hang together." If you find any like that, check them

first for unity, second to see if the main forward steps in the development are clearly marked, and third to see if the relationship of lesser sentences is clearly indicated to the reader.

V. CHOOSING THE RIGHT WORD

In the discussion of reading level, it was seen that long words make for difficult reading. Words which don't fit the tone of the context also give trouble—they pull the reader up short. Another type of difficulty comes from words which are vague or abstract—they do not carry a clear meaning. In most reports, therefore, it is best to prefer the short word, the formal word, and the concrete word.

A. LENGTH

Long words are harder to understand than short ones. Which, for example, is easier here?

His visual deficiency is a psychosomatic disturbance.
His poor eyesight is all in his mind.

Short words are not necessarily *better* words. In the example given, the word "psychosomatic" is a technical term that has a great deal of meaning to a psychologist. It recalls to him an entire complex of knowledge about how the mind may affect the body. Most technical terms are like this one—they are a shorthand for people in a specialized field. If you are writing for a technical person, you ought to use such terms. On the other hand, people outside the field are not likely to understand them.

Here are three guides that aid in selecting the word of the right level of difficulty:

1. *Generally choose the simpler word.*
2. *In writing to a technical man, use any helpful techni-*

cal terms in his own specialty (NOT YOURS). For all ex-cept technical words, continue to prefer the simpler ones.

If one reader will be in the technical specialty but others may not, don't use technical terms in the introduction, the conclusions, or the opening, closing and organizational parts of the sections. If the technical word is absolutely necessary for exactness, use it even in these places, but explain it immediately.

B. FORMALITY

By association, words acquire different levels of formality. "Juvenile delinquent" and "hood" mean the same, but the former came to us from social science, the latter from the underworld.

The actual words in a phrase may be neutral or formal, but in combination become informal—"Get on the ball." In addition, grammatical completeness and exactness are suitable to the formal situation. ("We knew he'd be there" *vs.* "We knew that he would be there.")

When you talk to somebody, you automatically adopt the proper formality in tone and word choice. To take advantage of the fact when writing, just think of the particular person who will read the report. Keep a mental picture of him in front of you all the time, and once in a while stop and take an especially good look at that mental picture.

C. CONCRETENESS

The more concrete a word is, the less chance there is for misunderstanding. That is to say, the more specific the thing for which the word stands, the clearer picture the word gives:

> person (any human)
> man (any human male)
> employe (anyone who works)

male employe (any man who works for someone else)
George McGuiness (one particular man)

These sentences might mean the same fact:

A person threw an object at another person.
George McGuiness threw the dish at Mabel.

Obviously the second sentence gives the clearer picture and is more exact.

In report writing, or any writing where you wish to be understood, use as concrete words as you reasonably can. Leave the abstract and general words to politicians and others who want to mean all things to all people—to sound as if they were saying something when they are not.

VI. WRITING EASY-TO-READ SENTENCES

Although all the words in a sentence may be clear, it may still be hard to understand. It may be too long, or the relationships of the sentence parts may not be clear.

Here is a sentence that is too long:

Information about customer orders, schedules, and shipments is entered to loose-leaf records maintained in ring binders which contain, arranged in classification by part number of the item, complete records for each particular part ordered by the customer, the number of binders being needed for each customer depending upon the total number of items ordered by that customer.

Whenever a sentence looks too long, it should be checked by one of the readability formulas discussed on page 176. If it is over the easy-reading level you have determined for your reader, it should be broken into several sentences. The example could become:

Information about customer orders, shipments, and schedules is entered to records maintained in loose-leaf binders. At least one binder is used for each customer, more being added if necessary. In the binder the complete information for each item ordered is classified by the part number of the item.

The relationship of sentence parts will be clear if

Related words are kept close together
Ideas are in a natural order
Relationships are expressed exactly.

A. RELATED WORDS

In English there are no endings to show whether a noun is subject or object, or to show what adjective goes with what noun. Word order is therefore very important. There is a world of difference between

John hit the ball.

AND

The ball hit John.

Clear sentences keep related words as close together as possible. "Related words" are those such as subject-verb, verb-object, modifier-word modified, parts of a verb, and parts of a verbal phrase. Here are some examples that show what happens when the principle is violated.

The time, if one-color assemblies are run, will be greatly reduced.
(If one-color assemblies are run, the time will be greatly reduced.)

The brush removed in a matter of minutes all accumulated sludge.
(In a matter of minutes the brush removed all accumulated sludge.)

There have been gathered changes to be made in the text under the heading of "Errata."
(Changes to be made in the text have been gathered under

the heading of "Errata." Under the heading of "Errata" have been gathered changes to be made in the text.)

The subject is asked to select the picture on each card that he likes the best.
(The subject is asked to select on each card the picture that he likes best.)

Flood waters have in many instances damaged the towers.
(In many instances flood waters have damaged the towers.)

If we wish to in the future continue this practice, certain changes are needed.
(If we wish to continue this practice in the future, certain changes are needed.)

Some of the examples used above show that all related words cannot always be placed exactly together. Placing some words together forces other related words *apart*. Judgment has to be used. Take for example the sample sentence that we looked at last:

If we wish to in the future continue this practice, certain changes are needed.

Here the phrase "to continue" is split by "in the future." If we move the latter as we did, it is no longer next to *continue*, which it modifies:

If we wish to continue this practice in the future, certain changes are needed.

Suppose we try an alternate position next to "continue."

If we wish to continue in the future this practice, certain changes are needed.

Here splitting "continue" from its object "this practice" is worse than splitting it from the modifying phrase—we choose the least evil.

Now try putting the phrase *just before* the verbal it modifies:

> If we wish in the future to continue this practice . . .

Here "in the future" stands between a verb and a verbal. It could modify either. Does the sentence mean "wish in the future," or "continue in the future"? This position is therefore inacceptable.

Next try the phrase after "we." There it splits subject and verb and clearly modifies "wish" instead of "to continue." If that is what the writer means, he can get the same effect by placing the phrase at the first of the sentence, and so avoid splitting "we" from "wish."

> In the future, if we wish to continue this practice . . .

Now however the emphasis has been changed—"in the future" seems more dominant, the condition less important. If the writer wants the new meaning he now has, plus emphasis on the *if* clause, he'll have to write:

> If in the future we wish to continue this practice . . .

The experiment with the sentence shows that the principle is not a hard and fast rule. It is a guide to be employed with good horse sense.

B. NATURAL ORDER

Keeping related words together gets them in a logical order so far as meaning is concerned. But even a logical order is annoying if a natural order is violated. The following is an example:

> One finished gear was tested. Microstructure of the case and core was examined after they had been checked for hardness.

In the second sentence time order has been violated. The sentences should read:

One finished gear was tested. After the case and core had been checked for hardness, they were examined for microstructure.

If the tests were of equal importance, a better revision would be:

The case and core were tested for hardness and for microstructure.

In addition to having the confusing time order, the original sentence was weak—the strongest position in a sentence, the end, ought generally to be reserved for the main clause.

Unless there is a good reason not to do so, natural order should be maintained. Besides time order, some other orders to watch are these:

CONDITION—consequence (If . . . , then . . .)
CAUSE—effect (Because . . . , . . .)
REASON—result (Since . . . , . . .), (so that . . . , . . .),
            (In order that . . . , . . .)
EXCEPTION—generalization (Although . . . , . . .), Un-
            less . . . , . . .)

What is a good reason not to follow the suggestion? First is the content of the preceding or following sentences. If a sentence following a cause-effect relation went on to explain or illustrate the *cause,* the cause should come last in the sentence in question. Second is the emphasis desired.

Because he did not believe in charity, he refused to contribute.

He refused to contribute because he did not believe in charity.

C. EXACT RELATIONSHIPS

Inexact expression of relationships in a sentence always confuses a reader. Inexactness comes from vague, false, or deceptive expression.

1. *Vague Relationships*

If a word or phrase has nothing to which to attach itself, or if it appears that it could attach itself equally well to more than one thing, the reader has to stop to figure out what is meant. Vagueness is likely to result from pronouns that have no clear antecedent, from phrases with nothing to modify, or from groups of words that can modify two things. Some examples follow.

a. PRONOUNS

Here is an *it* without clear antecedent:

When a new employe violates a rule, it should be corrected at once.

The "rule" certainly is not the referent of "it." Possibly the unexpressed word "violation" is intended. The writer could mean, "When a new employe violates a rule, he should be corrected at once." Or, "When a new employe violates a rule, it should be explained to him at once."

Every pronoun does not have to have a specific noun for its antecedent. A reference like that in the following sentence is all right:

Women stated that they do not prefer the washer and drier combined in a single unit. This came as no surprise to the investigators.

Here it is perfectly clear that the idea to which "this" refers is the preference of the women. However, it should not be casually assumed that all similar references will be clear. The surest way to be clear is to check pronouns for a specific antecedent. Unless the tone of the writing is informal, the reference should be made explicit: "This preference came as no surprise . . ."

b. Unattached or ambiguously attached phrases.

The reader will try to attach an unattached phrase to the wrong idea sooner than see it dangle unattached:

While still glowing intensely, plunge the steel into the quench.

The sentence sounds as if the operator *you* might have the glow on. It takes a moment to see that the steel is meant. Try "while it is . . ." or better, change the last part of the sentence to "the steel is plunged . . ."

To see the fish in their natural surroundings, the aquarium had glass portholes in the walls.

Change this one to

So that the fish could be seen in their natural surroundings, . . .

If the two ideas to which a phrase can attach are actually expressed in a sentence, the phrase can almost always be moved to a clear position:

I never realized why we had so many retail outlets before I made this investigation.
(Before I made this investigation, I had never realized why we had so many retail outlets.)

2. *False Relationships*

Sometimes ideas belong together but the wrong relationship is expressed. Check especially the connective "and." In a first draft writers are likely to use it as a substitute for almost any connective:

He is only thirty and he is already general manager.

Depending on the emphasis wanted, this sentence should become:

He is only thirty, but he is already general manager.
Although he is only thirty, he is already general manager.

Sometimes a sentence needs more drastic revision to eliminate the false "and." Here the ideas joined are clearly unequal:

The storm broke at eleven o'clock at night, and it caused severe electrical disturbance.
(The storm, which broke at eleven o'clock at night, caused severe electrical disturbance).

The stop is a simple type and consists of a hole located in the stripper.
(The stop is a simple type that consists of a hole located in the stripper. The stop, a simple type, consists of a hole located in the stripper.)

Other connectives joining main ideas should also be checked to see that the right idea is emphasized:

Fertilizer was applied because the grass was deep green.

Depending on what is meant, this sentence should become:

Because fertilizer had been applied, the grass was deep green.
The fact that the grass was deep green indicated that fertilizer had been applied.

3. *Deceptive Relationships*

Sometimes the expression of a sentence idea is not really vague or false but simply deceptive. After a moment's thought the reader can tell what was meant, but for a while he was on the wrong track. This situation occurs when we shift unnecessarily from one construction to another. Particularly deceptive are shifts in number, in structure of coordinated elements, and in sentence pattern.

a. SHIFTS IN NUMBER

In a first draft, even the most careful writer will make errors in number or "accord" of subjects and verb or of pronoun and antecedent. As a result either the reader is temporarily confused as to whether *one* or *several* is meant, or he has trouble connecting the right subject and verb, pronoun and antecedent.

Between subject and verb. A subject and verb normally come close together in a sentence, and we automatically make both singular or both plural. Lack of agreement comes when we forget what the subject is or are no longer sure what it is. Following are instances when problems may come up in agreement of subject and verb:

(1). *Other words that come between subject and verb contain a word of a different number.*

Volume *sales,* the goal of every business, *depends* primarily on loyal customers.

The writer began to say "Volume sales depend . . ." By the time he got to the last of the sentence he was thinking "every business depends."

(2). *Two singular subjects are joined by "and."*

If the two subjects joined by "and" are clearly two or more separate things, the verb will be plural:

A statement and a duplicate have already been sent.

If the two subjects clearly merge to a single idea, so that both you and the reader will think of just one thing, the verb will be singular—it will agree with the "psychological" rather than with the "grammatical" subject. The classic example is:

Bread and butter are foods.
Bread and butter is plain but good.

In the first sentence bread and butter are thought of as two different foods. In the second, they are thought of in combination—one bite gets both.

Less obvious are these:

Both time and money *have* been wasted.
Much time and money *has* been wasted.

In the first, time and money are clearly thought of as two things, as indicated by the word "both." A plural verb follows. In the second "have" would be correct enough, and would have agreed with the plural subject. However, the word "much" indicates that the writer was thinking of the two as a single amount or expenditure. Because his psychological subject was singular, he used a singular verb.

When this problem comes up, just make sure you are clear in your own mind whether you want the reader to think of a single amount or unit. Decide on that basis. If still in doubt, play it safe and use the grammatical subject.

(3). *Two subjects are joined by "or."*

Here the general rule is that each subject is thought of by itself. Consequently, if two singular subjects are used, the verb will be singular.

Mr. Sully or Mr. Boyle *makes* a test to determine if the defect has been satisfactorily repaired.

The idea is that Mr. Sully makes the test, or Mr. Boyle makes it. In actual fact, in any one instance they do not *both* make the test. The verb must be singular.

Where one subject is singular and the other plural, the one nearest the verb is last in our minds, so we make the verb agree with it. In practice, writers arrange their sentences so that the plural comes last and hence dominates the verb clearly.

The service manager or mechanics call the defect to the customer's attention.

(4). *The subject is followed by words other than "and" which add something to it.*

Such words are ones like "as well as," "together with," "in addition to." These expressions are parenthetical, as shown by the fact that they have no fixed place in the sentence—they and the phrase they introduce can be moved. They do not affect the number of the verb.

This information, in addition to my own experiences, is summarized here.

(Note the phrase could have been moved: "In addition to my own experiences, this information is summarized here.")

(5). *The subject is singular in form but includes several individuals.*

("Army," "management," "number," "department," "company," "corporation," "crew.") British practice treats them as plural. In America we theoretically regard them as singular if they have a plural form (army—armies). Yet if the idea of several is reinforced by an intervening plural idea, we often treat them as plural:

The management consists of a president and a secretary-treasurer.

BUT:

A number of people *are* going.

A shift between the two practices is not bad if it is made only once. A shift back and forth is always bad. Here is a sample of a shift that will not be objected to by most people:

The sales department handles all customer contacts and sales. Their activities include locating prospects, making sales, and follow-up.

(6). *The subject follows the verb.*

The change in position never should affect agreement.

There *are* usually a few low *spots*.
Across the field *run rows* of lights.

(7). *Plurals of Latin extraction are used.*

Words which particularly give trouble are "data," "phenomena," and "criteria." Typical confusions are:

This *data shows* that a change is needed.
This *phenomena is* an unusual one.
The best *criteria is* how much he saved.

Actually all three words are plural. The singulars are "datum," "phenomenon," and "criterion." The sentences should therefore read, "This datum shows . . ." (or "This piece of data shows" or "These data show"), "This phenomenon is . . . ," "The best criterion is . . ."

Data has been used as a singular so often that the usage has been accepted by some compilers of dictionaries. Nevertheless, many people still follow the strict usage. I advise you to do so—no one will be offended if "datum" is used as a singular; some will be if "data" is so used.

The use of "phenomena" and "criteria" as singulars is not accepted anywhere.

Between pronoun and antecedent. Pronoun and antecedent give trouble when the pronoun is singular in form but contains the idea of more than one. These pronouns are "everyone," "everybody," "nobody," "anyone," "anybody," "neither," "either." Their usage resembles that of collective nouns or of subjects joined by "and" in that the idea in the mind of the writer tends to determine agreement. If words emphasizing plurality come between them and their verb, the verb may be plural. So pronouns that refer to these pronouns also tend to become plural:

Everyone bring his own tools.

Anyone releases a part for work when it is badly needed. They do not have to wait for routine approval.

b. Shifts with coordinate elements.

When two ideas are joined, a reader expects them to be in like form, or *parallel*. If the form is shifted, he expects a change in idea. Keeping the forms similar reinforces the similarity of the ideas.

You wouldn't write:

He liked to spade the garden and preparing the hotbed.

Obviously the sentence should read "to spade . . . and prepare" or "spading . . . and preparing." Here are some other examples of such deceptive constructions:

This machine is light, smooth-running, and won't stain.
(This machine is light, smooth-running, and stainless.)

It is a question of reducing our overhead, or we must find more outlets for our product.
(It is a question of reducing our overhead or finding more outlets for our product.)

Having the money, and because he wished to make a safe investment, he invested in these bonds.
(Having . . . and wishing . . . , or Because he had the money and because . . .)

c. Shifts in sentence pattern

Deceptive shifts occur in sentences because by the end

of the sentence we forget the way in which we started to express the idea. Either of two ways may be good, but the mixture keeps the reader jumping from one point of view to another. Here are some examples:

> We knew it was going to rain; you could tell by the way the wind had changed and by the smell of the air.
> (Shifts point of view—change "you" to "we.")

> The reason for the decline in employment is because defense contracts have been curtailed.
> (The reason . . . is that . . . , or The decline . . . is caused by the curtailment of defense contracts.)

> The department contains many new faces every week, all of whom soon learn to operate these machines.
> ("Faces," a part, was used to stand for the whole employe. The image was forgotten, and the sentence ended with a disembodied face operating a machine.)

VII. ASSISTING THE READER
BY MEANS OF PUNCTUATION

One of the last items to check is punctuation. Punctuation is important primarily because it aids the reader in interpreting sentences.

Punctuation marks are of two kinds:

1. Those used to show the importance or relationship of ideas.
2. Those purely arbitrary or conventional.

Those in the first group clarify or change meanings. Those in the second are purely matters of custom.

The following sentence illustrates the first class:

> Three ships were afire, two sinking and one beaching.

Some readers might interpret the total number of ships

as six, others as three. A colon makes the sentence clear, because it has the definite meaning that whatever follows it explains whatever preceded it:

Three ships were afire: two sinking and one beaching.

The above colon shows the relationship of ideas. But in the expression "11:15" it simply serves to separate hours from minutes. Except that the use of the colon is customary, any other mark would have served just as well.

Marks showing the relationship of ideas fall roughly into five groups—"roughly," because the groups overlap.

These groups are:

A. Punctuation denoting a sentence idea and how the reader is to interpret it.
B. Punctuation denoting relationships of sentence ideas.
C. Punctuation within a sentence to show the degree of connection between ideas.
D. Punctuation to show departure from normal word order, or departure and return, or to prevent false joining of ideas.
E. Special and optional punctuation.

They will be discussed first and then:

F. Arbitrary or conventional punctuation.

A. PUNCTUATION DENOTING A SENTENCE IDEA AND HOW THE READER IS TO INTERPRET IT

Certain punctuation marks distinguish sentence ideas from lesser ideas. They also tell the reader how he is to interpret the sentence, just as voice stress pattern and intonation do when we are talking.

1. If a sentence is a statement of fact or opinion, use a *period*. Most sentences are of this sort.

2. If a sentence is a question, use a *question mark*. The mark tells the reader to expect an answer or to supply one himself.

   a. Sentences which ask questions frequently do not have an expressed subject or verb: Why?, What for?

   b. Indirect questions are not really questions. They are a statement of what the reader said. Use a period to close them:

George asked Caledonia how many would be at the party.

3. If a sentence is to be interpreted as expressing a marked reaction on your part or on the part of a person you are quoting, use an *exclamation point:*

Such a conclusion is impossible!
Come here!

B. PUNCTUATION DENOTING RELATIONSHIPS OF SENTENCE IDEAS, OR A LIKE RELATIONSHIP BETWEEN A SENTENCE AND LESSER IDEA

Sometimes two sentences are more closely related to each other than they are to the surrounding sentences. The relation can always be shown by function words such as *but* or *therefore,* but it can sometimes be shown by punctuation alone. The same specific relation can also be shown between a complete sentence and a lesser language element. These marks are the *colon,* the *dash,* and the *semicolon.*

1. If the second sentence or element explains, specifies, or is an example of the first, use a colon or a dash. The marks mean the same thing in this usage. Either is correct, but the colon is more formal.

The machine grinder works somewhat on the principle of the lathe: the work revolves while the grindstone is fed into it.

One thing is certain—research will continue to give the world new discoveries.

In the first of these examples, the sentence following the colon explains the idea "somewhat on the principle of a lathe." In the second example, the sentence following the dash specifies what the *one thing* is.

The principle does not change if the material following the punctuation is a question or even a single word. The material that follows makes explicit an idea contained in the introducing sentence:

This report was written with but one thing in mind: what have I learned about piston and connecting rod assembly?

There was only one thing that he really wanted—sleep.

In this use the colon or dash means *namely, that is, to be exact*, or *for example*. It is redundant and unnecessary to use both these phrases and the equivalent mark.

2. If the second sentence or element is closely coordinate with the first, use a *semicolon*. Make an exception if "and," "but," "for," or "or" is used, except as specified in item VII-E-3 on page 215. The semicolon shows that the two sentences are more closely connected than other sentences. If desirable, the exact nature of the relationship may be made clear by means of a sentence modifier or conjunctive adverb.

An architect designs a building; a draftsman only prepares the blueprints.

If the part is approved, the die is put back on the production line; otherwise it must be further repaired.

When tested under service conditions, commercial greases show a marked variation in stability: some break down into thin oils and tend to cause excessive leakage; others are highly sensitive to temperature changes.

An error sometimes made is to substitute a comma for a semicolon. A comma cannot substitute unless the second sentence starts with a coordinating conjunction. Here are the three ways in which sentence ideas are joined by connecting words, and how to tell what punctuation to use:

a. By relating words which are *not* conjunctions. They are words like "therefore," "hence," "consequently," "also," and "for example." There is no need to try to remember a list, because there is a simple test for these words; when they are used, a semicolon is needed. The sentences come under the principle explained in item VII-B-2, page 203. Here is an example and how to test it:

The snow looks very deep and heavy; nevertheless, I think we should try to get through.

Notice that in its own sentence—the words following the semicolon—the word "nevertheless" may be moved.

I nevertheless think we should try to get through.

At the same time, the sentences as they stand could not be written out of order and mean the same thing:

Nevertheless, I think we should try to get through; the snow is very deep and heavy.

If a relating word meets both these tests, it is not a conjunction, and a semicolon is required.

b. By coordinating conjunctions. When such conjunctions join sentence ideas, a comma is used before the conjunction. Here is the procedure for testing:

The snow looks very deep and heavy, but I think we should try to get through.

In its own sentence—the group of words following the

comma—"but" cannot be moved. Try the test we made with "nevertheless":

I but think we should try to get through.

Experiment here to see the number of positions to which "nevertheless" can be moved. Each time, try the same move with "but." The difference will be readily apparent. Now try the second test—write the two groups of words out of order, leaving "but" with its own group.

But I think we should try to get through, the snow looks very deep and heavy.

The "but" no longer contrasts with the other group of words, but with something which came before—and the comma is quite evidently wrong. If a relating word behaves like this, put a comma before it.

   c. By subordinating conjunctions. Again there is no rea-
      son to remember a list—a test tells what the relating
      word is. If it behaves as in the following example, it
      is a subordinating conjunction and a comma is prob-
      ably required as shown. (Check Item VII-C to de-
      termine if a comma or nothing should be used.)

Although the snow looks very deep and heavy, I think we should try to get through.

Here only one test is necessary—the one group of words can be moved without any change in meaning—only in emphasis:

I think we should try to get through, although the snow looks very deep and heavy.

C. PUNCTUATION WITHIN THE SENTENCE TO SHOW THE DEGREE OF CONNECTION BETWEEN IDEAS

Words may combine to form a single idea, whether they are written solid or not. In the sentence "The dark blue suit was sold," the words "dark blue" denote a single color. In the sentence "He owned a large alarm clock," "alarm" and "clock" join as surely as if they were written as the one word "alarmclock." In the sentence "People who are criminals should be jailed," the words "who are criminals" join with the word "people." It is only "people-who-are-criminals" that should be jailed, not all people.

Items are joined or are separate in different degrees. Degrees of joining (closeness of connection) are shown by writing words solid, by hyphenating them, or by placing them near each other. Degrees of separation are shown by a pair of commas, a pair of parentheses, or a pair of dashes.

Since degrees or graduations are involved, and since there are no really sharply marked stages, this principle is the hardest to apply by means of following set rules. Yet once the general idea is grasped, the principle is really easy to use. Think of all the examples and directions that follow as simply illustrations of the application of the principle.

1. When two or more words join to make one idea, they are usually written separately. A dictionary will show which should be joined by a hyphen and which are written solid. In general

   a. Words that have been said together so often that they seem a single word are written solid. So are words intentionally made from two words, as when a word is coined for something new: "forehead," "blackboard," "automobile," "airplane."

   b. Words that might be mispronounced if written solid retain the hyphen a long time. So do ones which would give an un-English combination of letters. Eventually, even some of these will combine solidly. Examples are "worn-out clothes,"

"well-known man," "so-called lady," "forty-eight,"
but "cooperate."

c. In some situations a hyphen can be used when it
normally would not need to be, in order to show
the right degrees of joining:

There were three hundred-man groups.

2. If groups of words ought to be separate, they are set
off with two parentheses, two dashes, or two commas,
one at the beginning and one at the end of the separated element.

a. If the element is felt to be sharply separate in
thought, set it off with parentheses or dashes.
The parentheses are formal, the dashes less so.

One of the most common cutting tools—perhaps the most
common—is the drill.

b. If the element itself contains commas, then dashes
or parentheses *must* be used.

Each type of machining—the plain cylindrical, the internal,
the tool and cutter, and the centerless—has its definite place
in the grinding of metal.

Tin and lead cause excessive dimensional changes (warping,
swelling, and cracking) accompanied by loss of tensile
strength.

c. If the element is not very sharply separate in
thought, but must not join, a pair of commas is
used. Commas serve in the vast majority of instances.

The choice that must most frequently be made is whether
an item really is separate or not. Should commas be used
or nothing at all? The most reliable test is to see if the idea
in question can be expressed in a separate sentence without

altering the *exact* sense of the original. Here is how the test works:

> Stories which deal with murder should not be told to little children.

The item in question is "which deal with murder." Try putting it in a separate sentence:

> Stories should not be told to little children.
> Stories deal with murder.

The idea has clearly changed. The revision implies that no stories should be told to children and that all stories deal with murder. The item should not be set off.

Now try this one:

> Testing, which is the last operation, is done on an ordinary bench.

The two-sentence test results in

> Testing is done on an ordinary bench. It is the last operation.

The test works with all elements, regardless of any grammatical terminology. Try the two-sentence test on the following properly punctuated samples:

ADJECTIVE CLAUSES

Her eyes, which were dark, flashed angrily.

Union leaders who are racketeers should be removed.

APPOSITIVES

Jackson, a brilliant administrator, will do the job well.

I have three brothers. My brother Donald teaches in an engineering college.

INSERTED OR TRANSPOSED ELEMENTS

The old plant, windowless and shattered, was not worth repairing.

The paint, even though peeling and cracked, still retained its color.

Fenton Lake, or Long Lake, is fourteen miles from here.

(Notice that each of these can either be placed in a separate sentence or in an adjective clause: "Fenton Lake, which is also called Long Lake, is fourteen miles from here.")

PARTICIPLES

(Some of the following elements come at the beginning or end of a sentence. When that occurs with *any* joining element, one of the commas is superseded. The same applies to dashes, but not to parentheses.)

George, running for life, finally got across Saginaw Street.

The type of flow existing in the circuit may thus be determined.

Running for life, George finally got across Saginaw Street.

The time limit being up, we turned in our catch.

ADVERBIAL ELEMENTS

(Most adverbial elements are not set off. Very loosely added ones, however, fall under the same principle. See Items VII-D-4 and VII-E-6 for other punctuated adverbial elements.)

He stayed till Monday, when he left.

(He stayed till Monday. Then he left.)

We can't play tennis when it rains this hard.

He always goes to Canada, where he finds the best hunting.

He always goes where he finds the best hunting.

D. PUNCTUATION TO SHOW DEPARTURE FROM NORMAL WORD ORDER OR DEPARTURE AND RETURN, OR TO PREVENT FALSE JOINING OF IDEAS

The parts of an English sentence have a regular pattern or word order. When we hear one type of word we expect to hear another type immediately. If someone says "John" we expect him to go on. If he stops, we ask, "What about

John?" We are waiting for a verb. If someone says "The black . . ." and stops, we'll ask him "The black what?" We are expecting a noun. A typical order we expect is this:

		NOUN			
		ONE	OR PRONOUN		
ARTICLE	ADJECTIVE	SUBJECT	VERB	ARTICLE	OBJECT
The	brilliant	light	hurt	the	plants.

Possessive or demonstrative pronouns substitute freely for articles. Adverbs that modify a verb can be put in just before or after the verb—or almost anywhere else, since the verb is the dominant idea of the sentence. An adjective is expected to come just before its noun and an adverb modifying an adjective just before its adjective.

To illustrate, consider the following modifications in the sample sentence.

The brilliant light hurt the plants.
The brilliant light quickly hurt the plants.
The extremely brilliant light hurt the plants.

If there is an indirect object, it comes between the verb and the object.

George threw Jack the ball.

Except where a word or word group joins closely, commas are used to signal a departure from this normal word order, a return to it, or a departure and return. If you look back to item VII-C above, you will see that the elements set off with commas break this normal word order. Hence a comma is placed at the beginning to signal a departure, and at the end to signal a return. The only reason item VII-C was set ahead of this discussion is that the exception could not be explained until the idea of close joining was explained.

The rest of this discussion, item D, shows the variety of ways in which this principle is applied.

1. Closely related words are NOT punctuated:

ARTICLE—NOUN (the light)
POSSESSIVE PRONOUN—NOUN (his plants)
DEMONSTRATIVE—NOUN (that light)
SUBJECT—VERB (light hurt)
VERB—OBJECT (hurt the plants)
VERB—INDIRECT OBJECT—OBJECT (threw Jack the ball)
VERB—ADVERB (unfortunately hurt; ran quickly)
ADVERB—ADJECTIVE (extremely brilliant)
ADJECTIVE—NOUN (brilliant light)
VERBAL—OBJECT (to hit the ball)

2. Prepositional phrases should be considered as "joining modifiers" as long as they are close as possible to the element they modify. Adjective phrases are usually closely joining elements placed immediately after the noun: "a man *of the people.*" Since adverbs modify verbs, adjectives or other adverbs, they appear in many places in sentences and the reader has no firm expectation about them. There is no *departure* to indicate. Such phrases, therefore, are punctuated only in special circumstances that will be pointed out later.

3. When an element is not followed by the expected succeeding element, but by another coordinate element, the fact is signalled by a comma. If only two such items are joined, a coordinating conjunction can substitute for the comma. If three or more items are joined, the coordinating conjunction can substitute for the last comma also. However, the combined signal can also be used: both comma and conjunction.

In this practice, the comma is warning the reader that the expected element is not yet going to appear. No comma is used after the last item in the series because the expected item appears.

> Convenience, cleanliness, and comfort are the chief advantages of an oil burner. (The commas signalled that the verb was not yet coming.)
>
> He was a quiet, timid person. (The comma signalled that the noun was not yet to follow the adjective "quiet.")
>
> The waves were wild, tricky, and dangerous. (The expected period did not follow "wild.")
>
> The man got up slowly, laboriously, painfully.
>
> This is a government of the people, by the people, and for the people.

4. The next illustration of the principle suggests that either conjunctions or readers are lazy. It is usually expected that a conjunction will join the smallest elements possible. If one appears at the end of a sentence, we expect it to join a coordinate word or other small element. When two sentence ideas are being joined, therefore, a comma is used to signal that fact.

   a. Before "and" or "or" the comma prevents the reader from joining the *object* noun which so often ends a sentence idea to the *subject* noun which will start the next sentence idea.

Fakers are taking advantage of the sympathy of the American people, and legitimate business organizations are going to suffer. (The comma prevents the misjoining that would cause the reader to believe the sentence was "Fakers are taking advantage of the American people and legitimate business men.")

The contesting parties will have to abide by such decisions, or laws will have to be passed to insure that they do. (Prevents "such decisions or laws.")

   b. Before "for" or "but" the comma warns readers not to take the subject of the second clause as the *object* of "for" or as coordinate with a simple sentence element that "but" might be contrasting.

The copper is seldom tested, for its chemical purity is not important in this instance. (Prevents "The copper is seldom tested for its chemical purity.")

The trip was dangerous, but thrilling events made up his life. (Not "dangerous but thrilling.")

No enemies were there, but men still stood guard. (Not "No enemies were there but men.")

5. Long adverbial elements may precede the subject. A comma at the end of such an element does two things. It signals that the long-awaited subject is about to appear, and it prevents the misreading of the subject as an object. Where the element is short and does not tend to "grab" the subject, no punctuation is needed. But if even a short element ends with a verb, a verbal, or preposition, it must be punctuated, for these are sure to grab the subject.

As the road narrows, the trees shut out more and more light.

As the motor is gradually heating, the resistance of the motor unit is decreasing.

After the jacket has been pressed on, the unit is clamped to a conveyor.

Even if an element looks as if it might grab, it is not punctuated if the subject and verb are inverted—the comma would be a sign that the subject was about to appear.

In summing up, his error appears. (NORMAL)

In summing up appears his error. (INVERTED)

6. If a connective has both a strict and a loose meaning, the reader expects the stricter one. He is warned when the connective is used as the loose equivalent of another.

He whistles as he works. ("As" denotes continuing time.)

He did as he was told. ("As" indicates manner.)

He ought to like the work, as he did it himself. ("As" is used as a loose equivalent of "because.")

He hasn't been home early since he bought his new car. ("Since" means time.)

I won't be home early, since I want to try out my new car. ("Since" used loosely as "because.")

They get math easily, while I have to work at it. ("While" used loosely for "but.")

Watchmen do their work while others are sleeping. ("While" denotes time.)

E. SPECIAL AND OPTIONAL PUNCTUATION

1. As we saw earlier (VII-D-3) in a series of three or more items in which the last item is preceded by a coordinating conjunction, the comma is optional. If the sentence also contains a conjunction to connect more important sentence elements, the comma in the minor element is dropped—it is not really needed anyway.

Located on the controller drum are all of lighting, heating and defrosting switches, the exciter field switch, and various other control buttons.

An alternative solution is to retain the comma in the minor series and *step up* the commas in the larger series to semicolons.

Located on the controller drum are all of the lighting, heating, and defroster switches; the exciter field switch; and various other control buttons.

2. Where items in a series contain other items which themselves must be punctuated, the more important commas become semicolons, just as in the second alternative above.

This procedure is done in a regular order: first, the left rear; second, the front left; third, the right rear; and last, the right front.

3. For the reason just given, the comma before a co-ordinating conjunction joining two sentence ideas may be replaced by a semicolon. It may also be replaced by a semicolon if greater separation is wanted. In informal writing, it may even be replaced by a period. A dash likewise can increase separation. The slight differences in emphasis, rhythm, and formality can be seen by trying all in the same sentence:

They claim to be training management, and they go to great lengths to get good material.

They claim to be training management; and they go to great lengths to get good material.

They claim to be training management. And they go to great lengths to get material.

They claim to be training management—and they go to great lengths to get material.

4. The same variation works before a conjunction connecting parts of a compound predicate. Normally no punctuation is used, but we could write:

They closed their books at the end of the unusually long hour, and quickly went out the door.

This variation cannot be used, however, if the sentence is begun with a modifier intended to apply to both of the elements joined. The comma would reduce the strength of the modifier, and make it seem to apply to the first element only. So we write:

At the end of the unusually long hour, they closed their books and quickly went out the door.

5. Some adverbial words seem to affect the whole sen-

tence rather than a single word: they tell how the sentence is related to a preceding sentence. They are set off with commas unless they "split" the parts of a verb. Then punctuation is optional. (Obviously, if they appear at the first or last of a sentence, they need just the one comma to separate them from the rest of the sentence.)

The work, however, is more than one man can do.
They felt, for example, the need of further directions.

These employes have therefore been up-graded.
These employes have, therefore, been up-graded.

6. Punctuation for emphasis is also sometimes used with simple adverbs.

The brilliant lights unfortunately hurt the plants.
The brilliant lights, unfortunately, hurt the plants.

Unfortunately the brilliant light hurt the plants.
Unfortunately, the brilliant light hurt the plants.

F. ARBITRARY OR CONVENTIONAL PUNCTUATION

The remaining discussion deals with arbitrary uses of marks of punctuation. They have only a minimum of meaning. They do not stand in the same close relationship to thought that the preceding ones did. The following list contains those that will be most commonly used.

1. Some abbreviations are followed by a period: Mr.
2. Disconnected thought or a break-off in thought may be shown by a dash or by a series of dots.

"I don't know," he said. "The trouble is . . ." He hesitated a moment.

3. Omission of words from a direct quotation is shown by three dots.

Omission of words . . . is shown by three dots.

4. Numerals or letters used in a list or outline may be written in many ways. In one piece of writing only one method should be used.

1   1.   (1).   (1)   1).   1)   -1-   1-

5. In expressions of time, references to the Bible, and other instances where numbers must be grouped, the colon is used. The comma, point (period), parentheses, and brackets are also used in grouping numbers, as in mathematics.

1:15 PM   Luke 7:18   2(a — b)   0.112 $2.85

6. The salutation of a letter is followed by a colon, comma, or nothing at all. In general, the colon is used in formal business communications, the comma in less formal letters and friendly letters, and no mark at all only when extremely open punctuation is used throughout the letter.

Dear Sir: Dear Mr. Jones: Dear Mr. Jones, Dear George, Dear Sir

7. In letters, both dates and addresses are set off with commas within lines. Ends of lines may or may not be punctuated.

411 Redwood Avenue   411 Redwood Avenue,
Dayton 5, Ohio   Dayton 5, Ohio,
June 7, 1954   June 7, 1954.

8. Within a sentence, the parts of dates and addresses are set off by commas.

On June 10, 1954, he left Miami, Florida, and returned home.

9. Initials, titles, and Jr. following a name are set off with commas.

Jones, A. J.

Clifford Cliffside, Jr., is a patient of A. J. Jones, M.D., the well-known surgeon.

10. Directly quoted words are put in quotation marks. Single quotation marks are used to show a quotation within a quotation. Commas set off any introductory words when conversation is reported, but commas are not used before other quotations.

"Quite true," he said, "though the shout 'Yoicks' was somewhat confusing."

All people agree that other people should "love thy neighbor as thyself."

11. Titles of books, magazines, and other separately bound items should be in italics (underlined). Titles of articles in magazines and chapters in books are put in quotation marks:

"Milling Machine Construction" in *Machine Tool Operation*

12. Words or letters to be discussed as such are put in single or double quotes, or in italics. If the item is to be made plural, 's is used.

All his *i*'s look like *e*'s.
The word "you" gave trouble.

13. Foreign words are put in italics until "naturalized."
14. Italics are sometimes used for emphasis.
15. An apostrophe can show omission of letters in a contraction: "don't, doesn't."
16. An apostrophe differentiates the possessive case of nouns.
    a. To form any singular possessive, add 's: "a dog's life."
    b. To form a plural possessive, first form the plural. If the plural ends in s, use the apostrophe only:

"dogs' lives." If the plural does not end in s, add 's: "men's number."

17. If a figure must be repeated for accuracy, as in a quotation of prices, the figure is placed in parentheses.

The total cost will be fifty dollars ($50.00).

18. Editorial comment is put in brackets: [. . .]

19. To show a syllable break at the end of a line, a hyphen is used. Words of one syllable are not broken, nor are words broken so as to change their pronunciation.

VIII. AVOIDING CONFUSION IN NUMBERS AND ABBREVIATIONS

Numbers and abbreviations are both used extensively in report writing. They can cause the reader confusion. In one report, for example, the following abbreviations appeared for pounds per square inch:

> lbs. per sq. in.
> lbs/in²
> P.S.I.
> psi
> lbs. per in. sq.

No practice of using abbreviations is of itself good or bad. But the practice selected ought to be one that the reader can understand, and it ought to be consistent.

The same is true in the writing of numbers—when should figures be used, when words?

In the interests of consistency, certain organizations are now doing fine work in setting up recommended standard practices. Two standards have been selected for reproducing here. If a professional organization in your field has also produced standards, get hold of them and follow them.

A. RECOMMENDED PRACTICE FOR WRITING NUMBERS

This style sheet[1] presents a recommended practice for the writing of numbers.

The general rule is to use figures whenever possible. In addition, the style sheet incorporates the "rule of ten" for isolated numbers, instead of the language rule of writing out numbers that can be expressed in not more than three words. (See Numbers, Rule 5.)

The rules, accompanied by examples, are the following:

Numbers

1. *If a sentence begins with a number, the number should be expressed in words:* This rule is used when the sentence cannot be effectively revised.

   CORRECT: Fifty applicants were interviewed for the position.

2. *When a number standing first in the sentence is followed by another number to form an approximation, both should be in words:*

   CORRECT: Fifty or sixty will be enough.

Note: *It is undesirable to begin a sentence with a number:* The best practice is to place the number within or at the end of the sentence.

   CORRECT: The confirmation request was answered by 559 businesses.

3. *When a sentence contains one series of numbers, all members of the series should be expressed in figures:*

   CORRECT: There were 25 applicants from Arkansas, 15 applicants from Texas, and 10 applicants from Oklahoma.

---

[1] Adapted from "Numbers Style Sheet," *American Business Writing Association Bulletin,* April 1953. Used by permission.

4. *When a sentence contains two series of numbers, the members of one series should be expressed in words and those of the other series should be expressed in figures:* If this rule is not followed, confusion results because of too many groups of numbers.

> CORRECT: Five students scored 95 points; seventeen students scored 80 points; and eleven scored 75 points.
>
> CORRECT: Three senior accountants made $50 a day; two semi-seniors made $40 a day; and five junior accountants made $35 a day.

Note: More than two series of numbers should be tabulated for clarity.

NAME OF ACCOUNTANT	DAILY RATE	ESTIMATED WORKING DAYS	TOTAL ESTIMATED EARNINGS
Barlow, Helen	$50	3	$150
Dickinson, Al	35	2	70
Oman, Charles	40	1	40

5. *When an isolated number is ten or below, it should be expressed in words:* This rule does not apply to exact dimensions.

> CORRECT: He hired 56 women employees.
>
> CORRECT: The new salesman sold eight refrigerators last month.

6. *When numbers are expressed in words, as at the beginning of a sentence, a hyphen should be used to join the compound numbers, twenty-one through ninety-nine.*

> CORRECT: Fifty-six; twenty-one; ninety-three.

7. *When one number immediately precedes another number of different context, one number should be expressed in words; the other, in figures:*

CORRECT: The specifications call for twenty-five 2 by 4's.
CORRECT: The deposit slip listed four 5's as the only currency.
CORRECT: You ordered 275 three-inch bolts.

8. *When a numerical quantity contains more than four digits, each group of three digits (starting at the right) should be set off by a comma:* Obviously, this rule does not apply to dates, street numbers, serial numbers, and page numbers.

> CORRECT: 1000; 1021; 5280
> ALSO CORRECT: 1,000; 1,021; 5,280
> CORRECT: 1,000,000; 1,253,878; 35,000; 43,120

9. *When large numbers (more than three digits) are to be tabulated, special care should be taken to align them properly:* In a tabulation the right or last digit of the longest number should be used as the main guide. Consequently, the longest number is found and the plan made accordingly.

CORRECT:	
	1,150
	1,000
	25,150
	500
	325,200
	25
	1,250,000
	5
Total	1,603,030

Money

1. *When several amounts are written close together, all should be expressed in figures:*

> CORRECT: The assets were $17,000; the liabilities were $3,000; and the net worth was $14,000.

2. *When an amount of money consists of dollars and cents, the amount should always be expressed in figures:* The dollar sign should precede the amount (unless in a tabulated column).

> CORRECT: The invoice total was $50.51.
> CORRECT: The bonds were sold at $999.50 each.

3. *When an amount of money consists only of dollars, it should not be followed by a decimal point and a double zero:* The double zero is not necessary, unless the amount is tabulated in a column which includes both dollars and cents.

> CORRECT: The invoice total was $150.
> CORRECT: $ 250.80
> 200.00
> 312.70
> 286.50
> ────────
> $1,050.00

> a. When a series of money amounts contains mixed figures, all even figures should include zero for consistency.

> CORRECT: The committee raised amounts of $15.00, $33.75, and $75.00 in the three rummage sales.

4. *An amount should not be written in both figures and words:* This procedure is acceptable only in legal documents and financial documents.

> CORRECT: The check was for $57.
> CORRECT: The total assets are $23,000.

5. *An isolated amount of money of more than ten cents but less than one dollar should be expressed in figures:*

CORRECT: The piggy bank yielded $.57.
CORRECT: The piggy bank yielded 57¢
CORRECT: The piggy bank yielded 57 cents.
CORRECT: The piggy bank yielded nine cents.

6. *An isolated amount of money in even dollars should be written in figures. When the even amount is ten dollars or less, it should be written in words.*

> CORRECT: The check was for $57.
> CORRECT: The other check was for five dollars. (Assuming an isolated amount.)

7. *When amounts of money are to be tabulated, care should be taken to align the numbers correctly:* The right-hand digit of the largest amount governs the tabulation. All decimals, commas, and dollar signs should be aligned properly. A dollar sign should be used both at the beginning of a column and at the end of a column after the underline. It should be set far enough to the left to take care of the largest amount.

CORRECT:	$ 50.00	CORRECT:	$1,000.50
	100.90		$5,000.00
	1,100.10		475.00
	10,133.10		
	————		————
	$11,384.10		5,475.00
			————
			$6,475.50
			1.00
			35.00
			————
			$6,511.50

Miscellaneous

The following numbers should be expressed in figures.

1. *Dates:*

CORRECT: October 10, 1951
tenth of October

CORRECT: 10 October 1951
Your letter of October 10 was most welcome.

Do not use *st, nd,* or *th* with the day of the month.

2. *Street numbers:*

CORRECT: 1503 Garland Street

3. *Numerical names of streets:*

CORRECT: 110 First Street*
110 69th Street

CORRECT: 110 110th Street
110 110 Street

4. *Numbered items such as page numbers, chapter numbers, figure numbers, table numbers, chart numbers, serial numbers, and telephone numbers:*

CORRECT: Page 10
Chapter 10

Chapter X

Figure 8
Fig. 8
Table X
Table 10
Chart 10

CORRECT: Chart X
Service Serial No. 01845283
Policy No. V9109815
Claim No. 13189756
Telephone 757-W
Telephone CA-7175
Model No. 3223

5. *Decimals:*

CORRECT: 10.25
3.1414
0.3535

---

* All numerical street names under ten should be spelled out in accordance with general rule of ten.

6. *Dimensions:*

CORRECT: 8½ by 11 inches   CORRECT: 2 by 4 inches

7. *Time:*

CORRECT: 7 P.M.
7 a.m.
seven
o'clock

CORRECT: 7:35 P.M.
7:35 p.m.
seven in the morn-
ing

8. *Percentages:*

CORRECT: 6 per cent

six per cent
("isolated"
figure
only)

CORRECT ONLY IN
TABLES OR CHARTS: 35%
99.99%
0.09%

9. *Fractions:*

CORRECT:
1/32
3/64
25/64
25/100 or
0.25

one-half   110 1/5
two-thirds
one-fourth   or

three-fourths   110.2

B. AMERICAN STANDARD ABBREVIATIONS FOR SCIENTIFIC AND ENGINEERING TERMS [1]

Introductory Notes

SCOPE AND PURPOSE

1. The Executive Committee of the Sectional Committee on Scientific and Engineering Symbols and Abbreviations

---

[1] Extracted from American Standard Abbreviations for Scientific and Engineering Terms, Z10. 1-1941, with the permission of the publisher, the American Society of Mechanical Engineers, 29 West 39th St., New York 18, N. Y.

has made the following distinction between symbols and abbreviations: Letter symbols are letters used to represent magnitudes of physical quantities in equations and mathematical formulas. Abbreviations are shortened forms of names or expressions employed in texts and tabulations, and should not be used in equations.

FUNDAMENTAL RULES

2. Abbreviations should be used sparingly in text and with due regard to the context and to the training of the reader. Terms denoting units of measurement should be abbreviated in the text only when preceded by the amounts indicated in numerals; thus "several inches," "one inch," "12 in." in tabular matter, specifications, maps, drawings, and texts for special purposes, the use of abbreviations should be governed only by the desirability of conserving space.

3. Short words such as ton, day, and mile should be spelled out.

4. Abbreviations should not be used where the meaning will not be clear. In case of doubt, spell out.

5. The same abbreviation is used for both singular and plural, as "bbl" for barrel and barrels.

6. The use of conventional signs for abbreviations in text is not recommended; thus "per," not /; "lb," not #; "in.," not ″. Such signs may be used sparingly in tables and similar places for conserving space.

7. The period should be omitted except in cases where the omission would result in confusion.

8. The letters of such abbreviations as ASA should not be spaced (not A S A).

9. The use in text of exponents for the abbreviations of square and cube and of the negative exponents for terms involving "per" is not recommended. The superior figures are usually not available on the keyboards of typesetting

and linotype machines and composition is therefore delayed. There is also the likelihood of confusion with footnote reference numbers. These shorter forms are permissible in tables and are sometimes difficult to avoid in text.

10. A sentence should not begin with a numeral followed by an abbreviation. Abbreviations for names of units are to be used only after numerical values, such as 25 ft or 110 v.

ABBREVIATIONS*

absolute . . . . .abs	Baumé .Bé
acre . . . . spell out	board feet (feet board
acre-foot . . . . .acre-ft	measure) . . . . .fbm
air horsepower . . . . .air hp	boiler pressure . . . . .spell out
alternating-current (as ad-	boiling point . . . . .bp
jective) . . . . .a-c	brake horsepower . . . . .bhp
ampere . . . . .amp	brake horsepower-hour. . .bhp-hr
ampere-hour . . . . .amp-hr	Brinell hardness number . . .Bhn
amplitude, an elliptic	British thermal unit[1] . .Btu or B
function . . . . .am.	bushel .bu
Angstrom unit . . . . .A	
antilogarithm . . . . .antilog	calorie . . . . .cal
atmosphere . . . . .atm	candle c
atomic weight . . . . .at. wt	candle-hour . . . . .c-hr
average . . . . .avg	candlepower . . . . .cp
avoirdupois . . . . .avdp	cent . . . . .c or ¢
azimuth . . . . .az or α	center to center . . . . .c to c
	centigram . . . . .cg
barometer . . . . .bar.	centiliter cl
barrel .bbl	centimeter . . . . .cm

* These forms are recommended for readers whose familiarity with the terms used makes possible a maximum of abbreviations. For other classes of readers editors may wish to use less contracted combinations made up from this list. For example, the list gives the abbreviation of the term "feet per second" as "fps." To some readers ft per sec will be more easily understood.

[1] Abbreviation recommended by the A.S.M.E. Power Test Codes Committee. B = 1 Btu, kB = 1000 Btu, mB = 1,000,000 Btu. The A.S.H.&V.E. recommends the use of Mb = 1000 Btu and Mbh = 1000 Btu per hr.

centimeter-gram-second
(system) ....cgs
chemical ....chem
chemically pure ....cp
circular ....cir
circular mils ....cir mils
coefficient ....coef
cologarithm ....colog
concentrate ....conc
conductivity ....cond
constant ....const
continental horsepower ..cont hp
cord ....cd
cosecant ....csc
cosine ....cos
cosine of the amplitude, an
elliptic function ....cn
cost, insurance, and freight ..cif
cotangent ....cot
coulomb ....spell out
counter electromotive
force ....cemf
cubic ....cu
cubic centimeter ....cu cm, cm³
(liquid, meaning milliliter, ml)
cubic foot ....cu ft
cubic feet per minute ......cfm
cubic feet per second ....cfs
cubic inch ....cu in.
cubic meter ....cu m or m³
cubic micron cu μ or cu mu or μ^3
cubic millimeter ..cu mm or mm³
cubic yard ....cu yd
current density ....spell out

cycles per second ..spell out or c
cylinder ....cyl

day ....spell out
decibel ....db
degree² ....deg or °
degree centigrade C
degree Fahrenheit ....F
degree Kelvin ....K
degree Réaumur ....R
delta amplitude, an elliptic
function ....dn
diameter ....diam
direct-current (as adjective) d-c
dollar ....$
dozen ....doz
dram ....dr

efficiency ....eff
electric ....elec
electromotive force ....emf
elevation ....el
equation ....eq
external ....ext

farad ....spell out or f
feet board measure (board
feet) ....fbm
feet per minute ....fpm
feet per second ....fps
fluid ....fl
foot ....ft
foot-candle ....ft-c
foot-Lambert ....ft-L

² There are circumstances under which one or the other of these forms is preferred. In general the sign ° is used where space conditions make it necessary, as in tabular matter, and when abbreviations are cumbersome, as in some angular measurements, i.e., 59° 23′ 42″. In the interest of simplicity and clarity the Committee has recommended that the abbreviation for the temperature scale, F, C, K, etc., always be included in expressions for numerical temperatures, but, wherever feasible, the abbreviations for "degree" be omitted; as 69 F.

foot-pound ....ft-lb
foot-pound-second
 (system) ....fps
foot-second (see cubic feet
 per second)
franc ....fr
free aboard ship ....spell out
free alongside ship ....spell out
free on board ....fob
freezing point ....fp
frequency ....spell out
fusion point ....fnp

gallon ....gal
gallons per minute ....gpm
gallons per second ....gps
grain ....spell out
gram ....g
gram-calorie ....g-cal
greatest common divisor ....gcd

haversine ....hav
hectare ....ha
henry ....h
high-pressure (adjective) ...h-p
hogshead ....hhd
horsepower ....hp
horsepower-hour ....hp-hr
hour ....hr
hour (in astronomical
 tables) ....h
hundred C
hundredweight (112 lb) ....cwt
hyperbolic cosine ....cosh
hyperbolic sine ....sinh
hyperbolic tangent ....tanh

inch ....in.
inch-pound ....in-lb

inches per second ....ips
indicated horsepower ......ihp
indicated horsepower-
 hour ....ihp-hr
inside diameter ....ID
intermediate-pressure (adjective) ....i-p
internal ....int

joule ....j

kilocalorie ....kcal
kilocycles per second ....kc
kilogram ....kg
kilogram-calorie ....kg-cal
kilogram-meter ....kg-m
kilograms per cubic
 meter ..kg per cu m or kg/m³
kilograms per second ......kgps
kiloliter ....kl
kilometer ....km
kilometers per second .....kmps
kilovolt ....kv
kilovolt-ampere ....kva
kilowatt ....kw
kilowatthour ....kwhr

lambert L
latitude ....late or φ
least common multiple ......lcm
linear foot ....lin ft
liquid ....iq
lira ....spell out
liter l
logarithm (common) ....log
logarithm (natural) ...log. or ln
longitude ....long or λ
low-pressure (as adjective) ..l-p

lumen ....l*
lumen-hour ....l-hr*
lumens per watt ....lpw

mass ....spell out
mathematics (ical) ......math
maximum ....max
mean effective pressure ....mep
mean horizontal candle-
    power ....mhcp
megacycle ....spell out
megohm ....spell out
melting point ....mp
meter ....m
meter-kilogram ....m-kg
mho ....spell out
microampere ......μa or mu a
microfarad ....μf
microinch ....μin.
micromicrofarad ....μμf
micromicron ......μμ or mu mu
micron ....μ or mu
microvolt ....μv
microwatt ....μw or mu w
mile ....spell out
miles per hour ....mph
miles per hour per
    second ....mphps
milliampere ....ma
milligram ....mg
millihenry ....mh
millilambert ....mL
milliliter ....ml
millimeter ....mm
millimicron ....mμ or m mu

million ....spell out
million gallons per day ....mgd
millivolt ....mv
minimum ....min
minute ....min
minute (angular measure) ....'
minute (time) (in astro-
    nomical tables) ....m
mole ....spell out
molecular weight ......mol. wt
month ....spell out

National Electrical Code ..NEC

ohm ....spell out or Ω
ohm-centimeter ....ohm-cm
ounce ....oz
ounce-foot ....oz-ft
ounce-inch ....oz-in.
outside diameter ....OD

parts per million ....ppm
peck ....pk
penny (pence) ....d
pennyweight ....dwt
per ..(See Fundamental Rules)
peso ....spell out
pint ....pt
potential ....spell out
potential difference ....spell out
pound ....lb
pound-foot ....lb-ft
pound-inch ....lb-in.
pound sterling ....£
pounds per brake horse-
    power-hour ....lb per bhp-hr

---

* The International Commission on Illumination has changed the symbol for lumen to lm, and the symbol for lumen-hour to lm-hr. This nomenclature is used in American Standard for Illuminating Engineering Nomenclature and Photometric Standards (ASA-Z7.1-1942).

pounds per cubic
    foot ....lb per cu ft
pounds per square foot ......psf
pounds per square inch .....psi
pounds per square inch
    absolute ....psia
power factor .....spell out or pf

quart ....qt

radian ....spell out
reactive kilovolt-ampere ...kvar
reactive volt-ampere ....var
revolutions per minute .....rpm
revolutions per second ......rps
rod ....spell out
root mean square ....rms

secant ....sec
second ....sec
second (angular measure) ...."
second-foot (see cubic feet per
    second)
second (time) (in astronomical
    tables) ....s
shaft horsepower ....shp
shilling ....s
sine ....sin
sine of the amplitude, an ellip-
    tic function ....sn
specific gravity ....sp gr
specific heat ....sp ht
spherical candle power .....scp
square ....sq

square centimeter ..sq cm or cm²
square foot ....sq ft
square inch ....sq in.
square kilometer ..sq km or km²
square meter ....sq m or m²
square
    micron ...sq μ or sq mu or μ²
square
    millimeter ....sq mm or mm²
square root of mean square ..rms
standard ....std
stere ....s

tangent ....tan
temperature ....temp
tensile strength ....ts
thousand ....M
thousand foot-pounds ....kip-ft
thousand pound ....kip
ton ....spell out
ton-mile ....spell out

versed sine ....vers
volt v
volt-ampere ....va
volt-coulomb ....spell out

watt ....w
watthour ....whr
watts per candle ....wpc
week ....spell out
weight ....wt

yard ....yd
year ....yr

IX. CONCLUSION

This chapter is by no means complete—it cannot substitute for complete books which deal with particular phases of writing. It has not even said anything about spelling.

Perhaps it should. Misspellings are unfavorably noticed by people who recognize no other mistakes in writing. If you don't know how to spell, you'd better learn. Your secretary won't be able to help you—she's the girl who sat next to you in high school and got even worse grades than you did.

If you feel in the least unsure about spelling, or about any of the other phases of writing that this chapter has covered, consult one of the following types of book. They should be at the desk of anyone who writes reports:

1. A handbook of composition
2. A book on making writing easy to read
3. A good dictionary

These will be useful friends.

PRACTICE SUGGESTIONS

1. Examine one or more of the following books. Then take samples of your own writing and test them for readability.

   FLESCH, Rudolf
   > *The Art of Plain Talk,* New York: Harpers, 1946
   > *The Art of Readable Writing,* New York: Harpers, 1949
   > *The Art of Clear Thinking,* New York: Harpers, 1951
   > *How to Test Readability,* New York: Harpers, 1951

   GUNNING, Robert
   > *The Technique of Clear Writing,* New York: McGraw-Hill, 1952

   SHIDLE, Norman G.
   > *Clear Writing for Easy Reading,* New York: McGraw-Hill, 1951

2. Rewrite the portions you found too difficult.
3. If you are working in a class or group, ask your instructor or group leader to analyze your writing for its major weaknesses. Then get your English handbook out and review these areas. He will tell you on which you should concentrate first.

13

Helping the Reader by Good Format

When the actual writing of the report is done, the final step is to put it in the format that will be easiest for the reader to use. And more is involved. A business-like, competent-looking report makes a good impression at first glance. A sloppy, cheap, or careless looking report doesn't. It gets the whole thing off to a poor start. Moreover, our reports represent us, and some people know us largely through our reports. If any person is worth reporting to, he is worth making a good impression on.

In most organizations, a report of a given nature is expected to follow certain local conventions. They are helpful—you know what to do, the reader knows what to expect, and he gets it.

With less routine reports, none of the formats conventional to your organization may display the material in the most usable way. The format has to be specifically designed to fit the report situation.

This chapter gives general guides for adapting formal elements to particular situations. The discussion assumes that the report will be typed, not printed. If it is to be set in type, and you furnish the printer good, clean copy, he will do the rest.

COVER

Short reports which will be used once and then filed do not need a cover. But if the report is longer than half a dozen pages, if it will be used by several readers, if it will get hard or repeated use, or if it deals with an important situation, a cover is needed. Standard covers are available in all materials from heavy paper to imitation leather, and all of them can be bound by various methods.

A cover provides protection in use. It holds the pages of the report firmly in place—the outer pages are not likely to be torn loose, as with a report stapled in the upper left corner. The cover keeps grease and dirt off the pages. It resists wear. Finally, it gives a finished appearance to the job—the report looks more impressive.

The cover is not intended to *hide* what it contains. Someone looking at the outside of the report should have an idea of what is in it. Consequently, the cover always ought to provide at least the title and the writer's name. Other data may be added if thought useful—the name of the person to whom the report is submitted, the name of the company, the date, and an identifying file or project number.

TITLE PAGE INFORMATION

The title of any report is intended to identify it and give a preliminary idea of what it is about. In some kinds of writing, it is also intended to attract the reader's interest. In a report, the reader wants to get a clear statement of the subject and then be allowed to judge for himself whether he needs to read the report.

Most report titles represent a compromise between brevity and exactness. If a title is too brief, it doesn't give sufficient idea of what the report is about. For example, take the title:

PLASTIC MODELS

This title might apply to anything from shop window dummies to ashtrays. But if the title is too long, it both looks clumsy and fails to give quick identification:

DATA RESULTING FROM VARIOUS APPLICATIONS OF THERMOSETTING AND THERMOPLASTIC MATERIALS TO THE MANUFACTURE, TESTING, AND USE OF SELECTED EXPERIMENTAL MODELS OF CERTAIN OF THE COMPONENTS OF THE 195X DELTALATOR

Here the writer tried to state his entire problem in the title. A compromise might be:

PRACTICABILITY OF USING PLASTICS
TO MAKE EXPERIMENTAL PARTS

The last is probably what the reader really wants to know anyway—can plastics be used to make experimental parts?

The longer the report, the more likely it is to have the title on a separate title page. Customary information is the title (underlined or in capitals, or both, in the middle of the page), the person or people to whom the report is submitted, the name of the author, the company name, and the date. The words "a report on" can be placed above the title, and "submitted to" and "by" or similar phrases can precede the appropriate names. Sometimes other items are added: "authorized by _____," "tests run by _____," "approved by _____," "Report number _____," and so on. The exact location of these items is unimportant so long as they do not distract from the title and are placed so as to balance well on the page.

Shorter reports use other ways of accomplishing the same

result. Some start with the title centered at the top of the first page. The names of the recipient and writer appear just beneath. Some use business letter form, with the addition of a subject line to show the title. (The inside address and the signature show the reader and writer.) A large number take some sort of memorandum form. The so-called "inter-organization" letterhead is used, or the word MEMORANDUM at the top of the page. "Subject," "to," "from," and "date" come next, in almost any order or balanced arrangement. If information as to "authorized," "run by," and so on is needed, it can come here too. But often, to prevent cluttering the top of the page, the latter information is put at the bottom of the first page or at the end of the report.

One side issue might as well be taken care of here— should reports be signed, and where? All reports need some sort of identification. Even routine "form" reports usually carry a place for initials. Initialling or signing fixes responsibility—and credit. Usually, only the original needs the signature.

Reports which have a letter of transmittal or a preface are signed at the end of the letter or preface. Writers of short memorandum reports use any of three places. Some prefer to sign right after the statement of conclusion. Others sign after the developing sections, but before appended data. Some prefer to sign at the very end. If you have no personal preference, do what your boss does. Routine reports of course have a place for signature already established by custom or by a space that is provided.

TABLE OF CONTENTS

One value of a table of contents is that it shows what topics a report takes up. But this is secondary. Its primary function is to serve as a finding list. The reader uses it to get to the particular part of the report in which he is interested. It is frequently used after the report has been read, when the reader wants to return to a part. For any report, the right table of contents is the one which gets the reader where he wants to go.

Any report long enough or important enough to need a cover also needs a table of contents. And as we will see, such an aid helps even short reports, when properly handled.

Any table of contents shows at least the main developing sections of the report. If the reader is likely to want to check a subsection of the report, it also shows the subsections. How fine a breakdown is given depends on what the reader is likely to look up, and whether it will be easier for him to find it in a table of contents or in an index. There is no sense in carrying the divisions too far—the reader will not know the report well enough to guess in what major section you handled some minor subpoint.

The most common form of table of contents is simply an outline of the heads of the report. The wording is exactly the same in the heads and in the table. If numbers and letters are used with the heads in the text, they are used in the table; otherwise not. After each heading in the table, on the right-hand margin, is the page number on which the heading appears in the text. If there is an appendix, its contents are shown at the end, under the heading of "Appendix."

Another type of table of contents lists the main heads only and gives page numbers for them. Then, set in under each main head is a running list of the subheads. For them page numbers are not usually given.

The first type is preferable. The second does give a kind of review of what is in the section and the approximate order, but it requires the reader to hunt through several pages to find what he wants.

Another practice is to give main heads only on the main table of contents, and then to give a detailed table of contents at the head of each section. The practice has advantages in some manuals and textbooks where the sections will be used by themselves—often by different people—but has no advantage in most reports.

Reports as short as three pages can also make effective use of a table of contents that shows page numbers. Then it appears right under the title, right under the subject line, or in a centered list just above the opening sentence.

In most short reports, listing the order of discussion at the end of the introduction serves the same purpose. Knowing what topics are taken up, the reader can glance down the page and over the next one to pick out the heading in which he is interested. For merely a couple of pages, of course, he doesn't need page numbers.

In very routine or stereotyped reports no table of contents or substitute for it is needed. The reader knows exactly what to expect, in what order, and looks right away for the heading he wants.

LIST OF ILLUSTRATIONS

If a report has many illustrations, or has some to which the reader may want to refer individually, it ought to have a list of illustrations. If the list is short, it can be put on the same page as the last part of the table of contents—under its own heading, of course. If it is longer, it should be placed on a separate page. The titles of the illustrations as listed exactly correspond in wording to the captions on the illustrations themselves. Page numbers are shown.

The list can be subdivided into parts labeled tables, graphs, photographs, and so on. That practice is good where there are large numbers of each type, or where the illustrations are given the various labels.

Short reports rarely need a list of illustrations.

HEADINGS

The discussion of the table of contents assumed that the report has headings in the text. It should, even if it is no more than a page in length. Heads help the reader get to the part of the report that he wants to use.

On a typewriter, heads can be made to stand out from the text and be differentiated as to importance by capitals, underlining, and position.

In order of importance, the following are the combinations of capitals and underlining:

<u>CAPS UNDERLINED</u>

JUST CAPS
<u>Lower case underlined</u>

Unless necessary, I avoid underlining capitals—they make extra work for the typist, and underlining may cut through carbons. For the same reason, most typists, given a choice, use plain caps in preference to underlined lower case.

Differences in importance indicated by *position* are the following:

1. Centered (on a separate line, of course).
2. Indented halfway between the left margin and the regular paragraph indentation, and on a separate line. Equally good is flush with the left margin and on a separate line. Don't use both ways in the same report.
3. Regular paragraph indentation, followed by a period or dash, and then, on the same line, by the text.

In each instance the heads may be either capped or underlined. But in no case should a head in a more important *position* be given less important *type*.

Occasionally, with short reports, the so-called hanging

or reverse indentation is employed for main heads. The head is set farther to the left than is the left-hand margin of the lines of type. The practice makes the heads stand out sharply, so it is useful in memorandums where no table of contents is given.

In reports where the sections are of some length, each section head is placed at the top center of a new page.

All heads of the same order should be consistent with each other throughout any section. Preferably, they should be consistent throughout the report.

Whether heads are given Roman numerals, letters, numbers, or other designations is mostly a matter of local practice and the writer's preference. However, if the text makes back-and-forth reference to the heads, assigning an identifying symbol makes reference easier. It is simpler to refer to Section V than to have to give the whole heading of the section.

INDEXES

Most reports do not need indexes. The criteria are (1) that the report will be referred to after the original reading, and (2) that the report be so long that the table of contents cannot do the job. If the report will be a reference, and the reader will refer to it for isolated items rather than in "chunks," an index is required.

The index is usually the very last item in the report. Occasionally it is substituted in manuals for a table of contents, and placed in that position.

One way used to actually make an index is to read through a copy of the report, marking what should be indexed. The items are then copied off on cards with the appropriate page number, and then like items are sorted together. The whole is then alphabetized, subindexed if desirable, and typed up.

PAGE NUMBERING

In any report, number pages with arabic numerals, with the first page of the introduction as "1." The same sequence keeps on right through the appendix. If any pages come before the introduction, they are numbered in lower case Roman. Pages numbered in Roman are usually numbered at the bottom center. Anywhere in a report, if a page number would spoil an illustration or otherwise mar the looks of a page, leave the number off. But be sure to count the page in the numbering system.

In bound reports, whenever the practice is to start a new page with each new main section, those pages are numbered bottom center. Other pages are numbered in the upper corner farthest from the bound edge. This is the same practice as is followed in most books. It makes it easy to riffle through the corners of the pages to find the one you want. Also, the effect of the white space around main headings is not spoiled.

Short reports should also have the pages numbered. In what position does not matter so much, as no one will have to look through very many pages. So let your typist have her way, as she probably will anyway. She will probably number them either bottom or top center.

WHITE SPACE

Within limits of common sense, the more generous you are in the use of white space, the better your report will look. Use plenty of margin—an inch and a quarter on the inside edge—an extra quarter inch or so if the report will be bound. On other margins leave at least an inch. In planning tables and drawings, set them up so that they will have plenty of margin and so that the reader will not have to peer into the binding of the report to read them.

Do not "prettify" the report, but spare no pains to make it look readable. That will make a good first impression. And if you give the reader the help he needs in getting at the content, he will be favorably disposed toward that content.

In the final analysis, that is what the last fourteen chapters have been getting at—how to present the content in the best light—how to win the best consideration for your ideas.

PRACTICE SUGGESTIONS

1. Look at the samples of what may go on a cover—pages 281, 323, 367, 391, 435, 471, 489 and 533.
2. Sample tables of contents are on pages 287, 325, 372, 443, and 477. Compare the heads with those in the report text.
3. Lists of illustrations are on pages 291, 325, 373, and 445.
4. Use of heads in longer reports is shown on pages 281, 322, 366, and 390. Examine the remaining reports to see practices in other situations.
5. A good business letter form, without letterhead, is shown on page 535.
6. Various acceptable memorandum forms are on pages 348, 358, and 414.
7. Examine the entire format of your own sample reports. Would you recommend any changes?
8. At this point you have finished the discussion of reports. And ever since Chapter 4 you have been looking at different aspects of reports. Meanwhile, you have been studying the report samples in Part II in fragments. Now would be a good time to put these reports together. It will make a good review of the whole picture of how reports are written.

   Turn to Part II. For each report, read the analysis. Then glance over the report itself. You needn't *analyze* it again, except at points where you are doubtful. As you do this, I believe that the principles and applications will be clear in your mind. Good luck from now on in writing exactly the right report for every report situation you encounter!

14

Using Available Resources

THIS AND the next chapter do not directly concern how to write reports. Instead they concern techniques of finding out what is going on in your field, and of making sure that the information is readily usable by you.

Many men in business and industry waste a good deal of time doing things they don't need to do. The things have already been done. Or they waste time and money using outworn techniques. Or they start from scratch in solving a problem when good methods have already been worked out for similar problems, and all that is needed is a little modification or refining to suit particular circumstances.

In other words, we don't take enough advantage of what other people can do for us.

I think that depending too much on ourselves and our immediate colleagues is probably a bad habit that we develop from our first jobs. We are anxious to make good, and we concentrate hard on the particular job we are doing, which is likely to be a routine one that doesn't call for new insights. When we get more confidence, we begin to learn from older men and from our supervisors. Because we respect our colleagues, we come to respect our organization as a whole. Then, because we know it is a leader in many things, we tend to assume that it is ahead in everything. The notion grows that *our* team does everything best—and first.

This attitude is a healthy one. You ought to think that

your organization is the best in the world, and you ought to work hard to keep it so. But just a little reflection shows that no one person or no one organization is better at everything than everyone else. We all have competitors who are still in business and are making a profit. We all know men in our own specialization who are almost as good as we are, and one or two who are better.

Neither we nor our organization will stay at the top of the heap, or near it, if we don't use all the resources at our disposal as efficiently as we can.

This chapter does not deal with your personal resources or with what you have in the way of technical resources from past education and experience. You ought to know what these are; and you are surely working at developing and improving them, or you would not have read this book this far. Instead, it concerns some professional and printed resources that we sometimes neglect.

VALUES

Not all of these resources are equally good for the same things. Each has uses for which it is especially good. But taken altogether, they should help us do the following things:

1. KEEP UP IN THE FIELD

Knowledge is not static. Much of what we learn in school is obsolete or becoming so even as we learn it. The frontiers of our knowledge and accomplishments keep moving ahead. A process that was in the laboratory yesterday is in production today.

None of us can keep up with everything, but if when some new idea or application comes to our field we are aware of it early, we are so much ahead. When a problem or situation comes up in our office or plant, we may already know the answer—we know how someone else met a similar situation.

2. SOLVE PARTICULAR PROBLEMS

If we do not know the answer already, we know where to look for help. Hardly any problem in the world is unique. Somewhere, someone has run into something like it—at least enough like it to give us leads for attacking it.

3. FIND NEEDED FACTS OR INFORMATION

No one can or should keep in his head all the facts he may sometime need. Normally he will remember exactly only those things that he uses all the time. And we are always needing standard information which we have not needed before. Unless we know how to get it efficiently, we waste time.

HOW FAR THE SPECIALIST CAN HELP

For certain information, we call on the specialist. One of the most important things to learn is to use the organization. There is no sense in working out cost figures when someone else can do it much more quickly, and it is part of his regular job. There is no sense in our doing clerical work, when someone who is paid much less can do it just as well. But in our specialization, *we* are the specialists.

Even in respect to printed sources, we are the specialists. A librarian is not. A librarian can help us get started and can help us find what we ask for. But that is about all. No librarian can be expected to know as much about our field as we should. And even if the librarian could get us to the right reference, he could not know what topics were related to the problem we were investigating. Even knowing that, would he know how to pick out exactly the material we wanted, or to evaluate its worth?

These truths will become more apparent as we look at how to use some of the items we will discuss below—it takes a specialist—us—to use them effectively.

PROFESSIONAL AND BUSINESS ASSOCIATIONS

After colleagues in your own organization, the most fruitful source of help will be other colleagues in your own field. Science has known this a long time. Alchemists kept what they did secret—they and they alone wanted the gold for which they were seeking. But scientists, eager in curiosity and anxious to learn more, shared their common discoveries with their fellows.

Professions like medicine have inherited and followed this tradition of sharing. Modern business and industry have done the same—they have moved out of the area of alchemy, of the "trade secret." If new developments are kept secret at all, it is only for a short time. This is especially true of new methods. The reason is simple. If *you* know something that *I* don't know, and *I* know something that *you* don't know, and then we share it, we *each* know more than we did before. Obviously, we both are better off. We both go on from there, instead of spending time and effort finding out for ourselves what the other already knew.

One of the best ways to receive the benefit of this exchange is through professional and business organizations. There is one in practically every field, and in many there are several. Typical are the American Management Association, the American Society of Mechanical Engineers, the National Association of Cost Accountants, and the American Society of Tool Engineers.

Much new work is first publicly revealed at the meetings of these organizations—most of which have state or local chapters as well as national. In addition, when men in the same field get together, they like to talk shop. They tell what they are doing, or talk about the problems they have. They exchange help and suggestions—often far beyond what comes out of the formal meetings. Lasting associations of value are formed.

If you haven't done so yet, check up on the particular societies in your field, and remember that joining them will also usually give you a leading publication in your field.

PERIODICALS

The most recent information is almost always gained by personal contact. Not very far behind are the contributions which are printed in various periodicals. But you cannot rely simply upon the journal of your professional society—much valuable information may appear in journals of related fields, or even in nonspecialized magazines.

Fortunately we don't have to look through all these periodicals—or even through their indexes, if they happen to publish one each year. There are other indexes which record in a single collection articles which have appeared in a wide number of magazines.

These appear at various intervals. Each month, for example, they will index the articles which appeared the preceding month. The arrangement of items is always by subject or topic. Sometimes it is also by author and title.

If you wish to know what has been published that month, you simply go to the library, ask for the indexes which index the periodicals in your field, and look under the topics in which you are interested. Since cross-indexing is not always adequate, and since some indexes are not cross-indexed, you have to know your field to use them. If, for example, you ask a librarian about the latest articles on fixtures, he could look under that head for you, but the topic might not be productive. You would know enough—if you were in the field—to check also the topic of "jigs" and the main topic of "machine tools." You would find a number of articles that you would have missed if you had depended on him.

As you use the indexes, you will become acquainted with the topics which particular ones use for material in your field. Until then it is a good idea to jot down on a card all the topics under which the information might possibly be listed. As you come to cross-references, these can be added to the list and checked also. I find it useful to jot down on one axis of a chart the applicable topics. On the other I put the abbreviation for the index and the dates of each volume consulted. Then as I check each topic I place a plus in the proper column if I find an article listed, and a minus if I do not. After I use any index a few times, this record shows which are the productive topics in that index.

Fortunately, it is not necessary to use a separate index for each month. At intervals (usually of three or six months) all the articles are combined in a single volume. Then at the end of each year, all items are again gathered in a single volume. Hence checking the topics in one volume will tell what was published in that particular year.

To keep up in the field, these indexes can be checked periodically (once a year—or oftener, if the field is developing rapidly). Then the articles whose titles look promising can be noted and read later. The practice prevents falling behind the times. You will not do as did a gentleman of my acquaintance—he was spending a great deal of time and money having his engineers go through a long testing procedure when an empirical formula for doing the same thing had been developed and published two years before. Nor will you do as another did. He spent half a year on a project, only to discover that someone else had done the same thing before—and had published the results.

If a particular problem arises on which you need help, don't be content with checking the last volume of an index. Check back a number of years.

Such a check takes very little time, once you learn to use the indexes. Even reading the articles will not take long. With most of them, you can tell at a glance whether they will be of value, and there will be few that you will want to read very carefully. But one good one will be well worth the time spent.

Some of the indexes are described below. The list is by no means complete—I have simply selected some that are helpful. A good way to be sure that you know those most valuable in your own field is to go to the reference section of a large library. Usually these indexes will be shelved in one area. You can then look over any with promising titles. Or you can use the books described below under the head of *Guides to Reference Books.*

Industrial Arts Index, New York: H. W. Wilson, 1912 on.

This index lists more articles in the field of business and industry than does any other. It also lists many in the field of engineering. It comes out once a month and finally cumulates in an annual issue. It also lists some pamphlets, government publications, and so on. Like all of these indexes, it gives in the front section the magazines it indexes. Also in the front is an explanation of the abbreviations used. The annual edition carries further information on its contents and use. It lists by subject and author.

Engineering Index, New York: Engineering Index, Inc., 1884 on.

This index duplicates some of the entries in the *Industrial Arts Index,* but by no means all. The title is in one sense deceptive—many articles that concern related fields are also indexed there. Examples are accounting, industrial relations, personnel management, safety, and materials control. In addition, it lists papers, reports, society transactions, and books. The items listed are just the ones that have been acquired by the Engineering Societies Library. Note that the *Engineering Index* does not list all the articles in the magazines it indexes—it picks out the pertinent ones.

It is arranged by topic in the main part of the book, but contains an author index in the back. Check both back and front pages for other things it contains. The index comes out once a year only. However, it is supplemented throughout the year by a card service.

Both the *Engineering Index* and the *Industrial Arts Index* are essential. Each covers some things the other does not. The *Engineering Index* gives more help in one way—it tells what is in each item by means of a short abstract following the entry.

Special services provided by its publisher include translating and photostating.

International Index, New York: H. W. Wilson, 1907 on.

Check this one just to be sure. While it specializes in periodicals in the "scholarly" areas—pure science and the humanities—these include psychology, law, mathematics, economics, political science, physics, and so on. Try going through it for things in your field—more and more things of direct interest to business and industry are appearing in these publications.

It is indexed by subject and author, comes out six times a year, and then cumulates in the usual annual edition.

Reader's Guide to Periodical Literature, New York: H. W. Wilson, 1901 on.

This one will not be so productive as the first two listed because it handles general magazines such as *Life, Saturday Evening Post, Harpers,* etc. But it also catches such publications as *Science, Science News Letter, Foreign Policy Bulletin,* and *American Economic Review.* Besides, the general magazines sometimes give a good lead. It comes out monthly, cumulates at six months, and then again yearly.

Accountants Index, 1912 on.

This comes out only at three-year intervals, so it must be supplemented by other sources. Beside those above, the monthly bibliographies and reviews in the *Journal of Accountancy* must be used. This journal also indexes books and a variety of other publications.

There are numerous other specialized indexes. Examples are the *Education Index* and the *Agricultural Index*.

BOOKS

As a rule, books will not give as recent information as magazine articles, but more detailed discussions and new syntheses of material can be found in them. Books, therefore, ought to be checked regularly along with the periodicals. Though some of the indexes listed above do list books, the one best place to go to find them is the *Cumulative Book Index*, New York: H. W. Wilson, 1928 on.

It is arranged by subject, title, and author. It comes out monthly and cumulates every six months and annually. Five volumes, each covering several years, combine listings from 1928 to 1954.

All books published in the United States, and foreign books in English, are indexed in it, in addition to other material. Prices current at the time, publishers' addresses, and other information can also be found. Directions for using it are in the front pages of the annual volumes, just as with the periodical indexes.

PAMPHLETS AND BOOKLETS

Sometimes valuable information can be found in pamphlets and booklets. However, no really complete index of them exists. The Wilson Company is making a valiant effort in the field, and has produced an index of pamphlets which is worth checking:

The Vertical File Service Catalog, New York: H. W. Wilson, 1932 on.

It includes leaflets and mimeographed matter also. Unlike the others, it is now a thin little book, but it gets increasingly more valuable.

Most companies publish pamphlets and booklets. Many of these contain valuable information concerning developments in their field, as well as in their own product. Unfortunately, there is no generally distributed index of these as yet. Help can be obtained from some of the items listed below under the head of *Catalogs*. In their advertisements there, companies sometimes describe booklets or bulletins which are available.

GOVERNMENT PUBLICATIONS

The United States Government issues publications in many fields. Every two years these are catalogued in the *Catalog of Public Documents* . . . Washington: Superintendent of Documents, 1893 on. It is arranged by subject and author. Each month is issued the *United States Government Publications, Monthly Catalog*. This is superseded at two-year intervals. Since 1946, the government has also issued the *Bibliography of Scientific and Technical Reports*, Washington: U. S. Office of Technical Services.

These are worth looking into. It is surprising to find the amount of information published by the government in almost every area.

INDEXES OF OTHER PUBLICATIONS

Two other indexes sometimes give valuable information. *Doctoral Dissertations Accepted by American Universi-*

ties, published annually by the Association of Research Libraries, helps occasionally, though it is not always convenient to get hold of the items it lists. And since 1900, another Wilson Index, *Essay and General Literature Index,* has catalogued "works of a composite nature." That is, if a valuable item appeared in a collection along with others, you may find it indexed there.

BACKGROUND SOURCES

There are times when you need information in an area in which you have not done very intensive work before. You may even have been shifted to a new area. Or you may have been assigned to a project which requires that you do some extensive background reading before you can handle it. Before searching through all the sources listed above, you can check to see if someone has already compiled a satisfactory list of basic writings in the area. The place to do this is in another Wilson publication, published regularly since 1937, called the *Bibliographic Index.* It records books, articles, and other publications which contain such lists. It comes out monthly and annually. It does not itself contain the bibliographies—it lists the places where they can be found.

Quicker preliminary reviews can be obtained from two other types of reference work—yearbooks and encyclopedias.

The yearbooks give a quick view of developments in the field over the preceding year, and are actually special issues of particular magazines. The standard magazines in your specialty should be checked for such issues whenever you want a quick summary of the year. Some examples are:

American Machinist: Annual Review Number (January).
Automotive Industries: Annual Statistical Issue (March).

Heating, Piping and Air Conditioning: Directory and Show Number (January).

Industrial Marketing: Industrial Market Data Book Number (September).

Iron Age: Metal Show Issue (October).

National Safety News: Annual Safety Equipment Issue (March).

Printers' Ink: Weekly Magazine of Advertising, Management, and Sales (May).

Sales Management: Magazine of Marketing (May).

Steel: Magazine of Metal Working and Metal Producing (January).

The encyclopedias give a view over a longer period of time and make a good place to start in a field with which you are not familiar. They also can serve as dictionaries to define standard items, and they review standard processes. Examples are:

Jones, Franklin D., *Engineering Encyclopedia,* (2 volumes) New York: The Industrial Press, 1943.

Kingzett, Charles T., *Chemical Encyclopedia,* Seventh Edition, New York: Van Nostrand, 1946.

Motor Service's New Automotive Encyclopedia, Chicago: Goodhart-Wilcox, 1954.

Van Nostrand's Scientific Encyclopedia, New York: D. Van Nostrand Company, 1947.

Watkins Cyclopedia of the Steel Industry, Pittsburgh: Steel Publications, Inc., 1947.

SOURCES OF STANDARD FACTS

When an isolated piece of information is needed, such as a particular formula or fact, or when standard processes or procedures are wanted, special reference books can be consulted. Here are some of the types and the kind of information they list.

DICTIONARIES

Dictionaries overlap with encyclopedias. The latter may give definitions, and the former often give a very extended discussion of the term they are defining. There are special dictionaries in almost every field. Here are some of them:

Baughman, Harold E., *Baughman's Aviation Dictionary and Reference Guide,* First Edition, Glendale: California, 1940.

Beadnell, Charles M., *Dictionary of Scientific Terms Used in the Various Sciences,* London: Watts, 1942.

Brown, V. J. and D. G. Runner, *Engineering Terminology,* Second Edition, Chicago: Gillette Publishing Company, 1939.

Gardner, William, *Chemical Synonyms and Trade Names,* Fourth Edition, London: Technical Press, Ltd., 1936.

Trade Names Index, New York: Special Libraries Association, 1941.

Tweney, C. F. and L. E. C. Hughes, ed., *Chambers' Technical Dictionary,* New York: Macmillan, 1940.

United States Employment Service, *Dictionary of Occupational Titles,* Washington: United States Government Printing Office, 1939, 1943, and 1949.

HANDBOOKS

All sorts of standard information can be found in handbooks. Almost any field has several. Some are revised every year, as the *Tool Engineers' Handbook, Sales Manager's Handbook, Machinery's Handbook, Accountant's Handbook.* There are also general handbooks such as the *World Almanac.*

CATALOGS

Often we want to know who makes a particular product, or to identify a trade name, or to know to whom we should write to get particular information about a process or material. Information of this sort is contained in a group of reference books which can be described as catalogs. Some of them are exactly that; that is, catalogs of a large number of companies in a particular field have been bound together in a single book. The book is then indexed as to companies, products, trade names, materials, processes, and so on. The one with the widest coverage, *Thomas' Register of Manufacturers,* simply lists information. The next most general, *Sweet's File,* shows what look like regular advertisements, many of which give considerable detail, including rather complete descriptions and specifications. Others of the sort are *MacRae's Blue Book,* the *Modern Packaging Encyclopedia, Wadman's Diesel Catalog,* the *ASME Mechanical Catalog* and *Directory,* the *Modern Plastics Cyclopedia,* and *Wright's Material Handling Cyclopedia.*

FINANCIAL SOURCES

Facts concerning the operation and financial aspects of particular companies are found in such works as *Moody's Manual of Investments, Standard Corporation Descriptions,* and the *Dun and Bradstreet Reference Book.*

Investment prospects, earnings, history, and practically all information about companies to be found in their various annual reports can be located in these references.

BIOGRAPHY

Sometimes it is desirable to find information about a particular person. There are many biographical compilations which give this. Some are unreliable, since they list practically everyone who promises to buy a copy of the book, but many are reputable standbys. It should be remembered, however, that the people listed usually supply the information themselves, so relative length of an entry should not be considered. Some good ones are *Who's Who, Who's Who in America, Who's Who in Commerce and Industry,* and *Who's Who in Engineering.*

STATISTICS

The most generally valuable source of any sort of statistics about production or business in general is the *Statistical Abstract of the United States*, Washington: U. S. Department of Commerce.

GUIDES TO REFERENCE BOOKS

In using the various reference books, you may not find exactly what you want. If so, you can find help as to where to look by referring to guides to reference books. Some are general, and some deal with specific fields. For the field of engineering, a fine job has been done by Blanche H. Dalton in her *Sources of Engineering Information*, Berkeley and Los Angeles: University of California Press, 1948. Edwin T. Coman's *Sources of Business Information*, New York: Prentice-Hall, 1949, is helpful, and H. W. Johnson and S. W. McFarland's *How to Use a Business Library*, Cincinnati: Southwestern, 1951, is a convenient little pamphlet.

The classic general works are Isadore Mudge's *Guide to Reference Books*, Chicago: American Library Association, with its early supplement, and the supplements by Constance Winchell, which have appeared regularly since Mudge's work.

GETTING HOLD OF MATERIAL

After you have located the names of the books and magazine articles which have appeared upon a topic with which you are concerned, there is sometimes a problem in finding them. The first step is of course to go to the card catalog in the library, to see which of the books it has. Next you consult its catalog or index of periodical holdings. Often, however, you will find that it does not have all the items that you believe you want.

The next step is to consult abstracts. Some of the indexes mentioned at the first of the chapter have abstracts. You will find abstracts of books elsewhere. Valuable collections of abstracts are in the *Technical Book Review Index,* the *Book Review Digest,* the *Engineer's Digest,* and the *Engineering Experiment Station Record.* From them you may be able to determine if you really want some of the items.

Next you must get the assistance of the librarian. At your request, he will consult lists, called "union lists," which show the periodical holdings of other libraries; and he can order books for you from the Library of Congress and other libraries. Almost anything can be obtained in one of these ways, either directly or by having photostats or microfilms made. Some expense is usually involved.

SUMMARY

Once you have gone through the process of using the resources of libraries, you will find that it is much easier and takes much less time than it would appear. Summarized, the procedure is simply this:

1. To find what is going on in the field, or to find answers to a particular problem that is new to you, consult the periodical and book indexes.
2. For background information, consult the *Bibliographic Index,* yearbooks, and encyclopedias.
3. For standard definitions, facts, procedures, and processes, consult dictionaries, handbooks, collections of catalogs, financial reference books, biographical compilations, or statistical abstracts.
4. If you don't find what you want, go to guides to reference books for help.
5. To find what your library has, go to the local card catalog and periodical index. Ask the librarian for help in getting material not in the local library.

PRACTICE SUGGESTIONS

1. This first suggestion is to get you acquainted with the indexes you will need to use to keep up in your field or to find what has been written on any particular phase of your field. You should learn both what these indexes are like, and what topics are valuable ones to check.

    a. Select some *limited* topic in your field. (If you take a broad area, you'll end up doing a lot of unproductive copying of titles. A topic that produces only a few items will serve just as well—and save time. If on examining indexes you find you are getting too much material, limit the topic further yet.)

    b. Make a list of the indexes you should consult. This will include those listed on pages 248 to 254, plus any other specialized ones in your field.

    c. Go to the library and check these indexes for the last fully indexed year, to see what you can find. If on examination one of the indexes proves not to concern your area, cross it off your list. (But *don't* cross off any of the general indexes.)

    d. Make up a list of all the subject heads under which the information you are seeking might be classified. Use the recording system suggested on page 249.

    e. Record the items found.

2. If you are working in a class or group with others, your instructor or group leader may suggest problems to help you get acquainted with other references. If not, you can work with a friend and set up quiz problems for each other. (One man first goes to the reference books and makes out the questions, then gives them to the other.)

Keep a record of your steps, including missteps.

Questions you might ask are ones like those listed below. Go to the library and try them. Then check your answers against those on page 585.

A. A book on the history of the Western Reserve was published in 1949.
   - (a) Who wrote it?
   - (b) Who published it?
   - (c) Where was it published?
   - (d) How much did it sell for?

B. John Steinbeck is a co-author of a book on marine biology. Who is the other author, what is the title of the book, and when was it published?

C. Three men—Trent, Carter, Bateman—published an article on "High Temperature Alloys Based on Titanium Carbide" in the British periodical *Metallurgia* in August, 1950. (Volume 42, No. 250, pp. 111-115). You need to know whether it discusses fatigue strength and if so how you can get a copy of it.

D. Eggs seem like a funny thing to get from a slot machine, but I hear they're doing it. Someone told me last Christmas (1953) that he read an article about it. What was the article? When did it appear?

E. A friend tells you that an article he read recently, titled "Work Analysis Cuts Fatigue," should be useful to your research, but he can't remember anything else about it. Can you locate the article?—Author, periodical, issue, pages?

F. For a building expansion program at your plant you have been commissioned to prepare a detailed plan for installing electromagnets to handle shipments of nonferrous material. You have learned of a pamphlet which describes the design of such a device. How can you find it?

G. You have been assigned the project of preparing a paper on "Fire Prevention" at the meeting of your safety department. Where can you find a prepared list of source materials for your talk?

H. What is the Kraemer-Sarnow test?

I. Your boss has suggested you hire a "slub-picker." What's that?

J. What are two companies in Ohio that make baseballs?

K. Did the government issue any information on titanium in 1953? What branch of the government published it? Who wrote it? How much did it cost?

L. What amount of money was lent to members of credit unions in Montana in 1949?

Keeping Notes

GOOD RECORDS can make keeping up with your field easier and more fruitful. They can prevent your having to waste time doing over again something which you have already done once. And when you have to organize data from your records into a report, they can help you do so with a minimum of unproductive labor.

This chapter will cover some of the standard record-keeping techniques which have been found useful to professional men.

BIBLIOGRAPHIC INFORMATION

Knowledge that there is new information in your field will come to you in several ways. Someone may tell you of something he has just read, or you may come across a reference in your reading, or you may learn about it as the result of systematic search. The latter will occur whenever you do background reading toward solving a particular problem, or when you make a periodic check to see what has recently been happening in your field.

Whenever you learn of a new item, you ought to make a permanent record of it. It may save you hours of search and checking back later. Even if the item is no good, a note about it will prevent your checking it a second time.

MATERIALS

The easiest way to keep bibliographic information is on cards, one item to a card. Cards are more durable than slips of paper, and if each item is separate, the system is flexible. You can sort by author, topic, type of publication, and so on. The standard size of card is three-by-five. If you use that size for bibliographic information only, you can easily distinguish it from other notes.

Personally, I like the cards that have a hole in them at the bottom center. They can be held firmly in a file, or slipped in a ring of a notebook.

Instead of three-by-five cards, some of my friends use cards which can be key-punched for an office machine-recording system. Such a system is ideal if you can set it up so you can handle it yourself, or if you have mechanical sorting equipment available to you.

The simple system used by most people will be described here first, and then the more efficient—but expensive— variations. All systems record the same basic information.

PROCEDURE

Whenever you run across a new item, record it on the card. So that you won't have to waste time revising the cards later, select the standard order you prefer, as suggested in Chapter 11, and stick consistently to it. Don't simply copy the entry found in one of the standard indexes. They each use special nonstandard abbreviations to make the entry as brief as possible.

If any bibliographic information is missing—the date, for example—leave a space to be filled in after you have inspected the item itself.

I also like to put on the card a light pencil notation as to where I first learned of the item. If I can't find such an item when I go to look for it, the notation helps in checking back. Once the item is located, the note can be erased or ignored.

If you plan to check on a number of items at a time, sort the cards so that those for books are in one stack, those for magazine articles in another. Sort the cards for books by author, those for magazine articles by periodical. Then in the library you can check on the items in sequence. The convenience lies in the fact that books and magazines are cataloged and located in different places in the library.

When you have found an item in the library files, make a note of the library and of the "call number" assigned to the item. This number identifies the item and shows where it is shelved in that library. It will vary from library to library, but probably most of the time you will be using the library most available to you.

After you have examined the item itself, add to the card a note as to the topic or topics with which it deals, and a note as to its worth. The latter should be very brief, because if the item is any good you will want to take full notes on it as described later in this chapter. The idea is simply to remind you of what the item is like.

The cards may be set up in a variety of ways, but the same type of information should always go to the same relative position on each card, to facilitate sorting. One possible arrangement is this:

Library and call number   Topic
    Bibliographic data—in a standard form and order.
    Notes as to general content and worth.
                   Where you learned of the item

FILING AND KEEPING UP-TO-DATE

All bibliography cards should be filed permanently. Thus you will have a fairly full bibliography on any subject you've already looked up or on which you regularly try to keep up-to-date. For most people the convenient way to keep the file is by topic and subtopic, then subclassified by author. Using your file will soon tell you the most convenient arrangement for you. Once a bibliography on any subject has been built, it can easily be kept up-to-date. Whenever you make periodic checks of indexes, simply add any new items that you find.

VARIANT SYSTEMS

The punched card systems mentioned above record the same information. But the cards are then coded by punching to allow sorting by author, topic, type of material, and so on.

NOTE-TAKING

You are bound to take notes as a personal record of information of all sorts. Such a collection grows almost automatically, but often it is so chaotic that it is useless. Whenever you work on a project of your own, you record procedures, data, interpretations, and other ideas that concern the project. It is even a good idea to record preliminary guesses and hypotheses so you won't forget them. Unless the project is a "one-shot" affair on a routine matter, it is a good idea to keep the complete notes—they are likely to be useful for other things besides the final report of the project.

Notes may also come from background reading. And in the course of keeping up in the field, notes should be taken and added to what you already have on any subject.

Is such note-taking and keeping files of notes worthwhile? I have known of no one who has done so who has not found it valuable. One of my friends, for example, is famous throughout his organization for his ability to find answers quickly. When people get stuck they call on him.

One day he let me in on his secret. Actually, he often

doesn't know the answer—but his files usually do. Within a very short time he comes up with suggestions as to what to do to solve the problem at hand. His systematic notes regularly keep him up-to-date. The result is that he has achieved an outstanding reputation in his field throughout his organization. (Of course much of the time he doesn't find the specific answers, but he finds leads or suggestions which give him an approach to the problem.)

I asked him if he didn't spend a lot of time with his note-taking. His answer was "no." Once he had caught up in an area, he explained, very little that was really new came out in any given year. He guessed that he kept up on the entire system with perhaps one week's work per year.

Efficient note-taking systems are variations of one of three types: The conventional card system, the manual-punched card system, and the machine-punched card system. The rest of the chapter explains these systems.

THE CONVENTIONAL CARD SYSTEM

Principle and Materials

The conventional card system was devised to avoid the difficulties of the primitive and unusable "notebook" system of taking notes. It grew out of the fact that in practice hardly anyone uses items as he takes them. Whether from direct observation or reading, notes are used by being sorted to get like ideas together. This has to be done if they are to be easily compared. And the "notebook" method is unbelievably cumbersome.

I learned this to my sorrow as a young graduate student working on a thesis. With an application I still can't quite believe, I read everything I could find that John Dewey had written. And I took most copious notes—volume by volume, article by article. Since I had hardly any money—it was in the depression of the thirties—I not only took the notes continuously, but took them on both sides of the paper. Finally it was time to look over the store of riches, to sort, compare, digest, and interpret. A typical problem was the development of his interpretation of conscience—I found the appropriate passages scattered through a half dozen fat notebooks. It took me hours to locate them all, more hours to try to sort them together.

In desperation I called on a friend. The friend proceeded to type one side of each page of the notes so that everything was on one side. I then went through and labeled all passages as to the topic they concerned and as to the source, took a pair of scissors, and trimmed the notes apart. Then I was able to sort things together, even though they were in a hodgepodge of light slips of all sizes, susceptible to every summer breeze, and very awkward to handle. (I should add that I forgot to label some slips and never could identify them again.)

The card system protects its user from such troubles. It is based upon the idea of putting one note on a single card. That is, the note on a single card will never fall into two classifications of the most minor topical division the note-taker believes he will use. Each card is labeled with the suitable topic.

The card system is flexible—it permits sorting by topic or back to the original article. The notes are uniform in size and easy to handle. And the cards are durable and easy to store. The size of cards doesn't matter, but it should be different from that of the bibliography cards. Since the next size larger is four-by-six, I use that. I again prefer cards with holes.

Procedure

The note is taken in the briefest possible form that will preserve its sense. Generally, only the idea should be recorded, without following the wording of the original.

Abbreviations are used—standard and invented. (But if you invent any, keep a record of them until they become second nature with you—you may forget what they mean.)

Whenever a page is turned, the page number is noted on the card—this helps in future footnoting. Each card is given a topic label (often in breakdown form, so the topic head classifies the card to the main topic, the subtopic, and the sub-subtopic, and so on, as far as is useful). Finally a brief source notation is added, such as the author's last name and a key word of the title—just enough to give a guide to the author card in the bibliography, where full source information can be found.

A typical setup has the topic at the top of the card, the note in the center (with page number at the end of the note or where the note shifted to another page), and the source at the bottom. If the source of the note is ourselves—if it is our data or our guess or interpretation—it is so labeled.

For greatest usefulness, it is necessary to get a consistent system of topic notation. Sometimes an outline can be made out before the project or reading starts (the so-called directive outline). Standard texts in an area can often give a good base here. Other times the outline emerges as the notes are taken. Then it is sometimes necessary to go back and relabel when the final arrangement becomes clear.

Using and Filing

The system is valuable on a project of our own, for recording background reading on a problem, or for permanent notes. In actual fact, permanent notes grow through keeping notes used in specific areas, and then adding to them as you keep up in the field.

Notes of this sort are best filed by topic, then subtopic, and so on. Generally you want to recall the information in that way. But if you wish, you can recover the sequence of the original by sorting first by author, then by article (or whatever it is), and finally by page number within the article.

Advantages and Disadvantages

The system obviously has advantages over the notebook system. The notes are uniform in size, durable, and flexible. They permit storage in the most usable way.

But the system has imperfections. To get an original article back together is a tedious process, involving long hand sorting. Moreover, the actual note-taking itself is exacting and time-consuming. It is a useful system, but it is far from perfect.

THE MANUAL-PUNCHED CARD SYSTEM

Principle and Materials

The manual punch card system was, to my knowledge, first worked out in the field of metallurgy. The two basic articles describing it are:

Guy, A. G., and Geisler, A. H., "A Punch Card Filing System for Metallurgical Literature," in *Metal Progress* (Dec., 1947), 52:993-1000.

Westbrook, J. H., and DeWald, L. H., "A Modified Punch Card . . . System . . . ," in *Metal Progress* (Sept., 1948), 54:324-27.

Shortly after these appeared, the system became available through the American Society for Metals.

However, the system is not limited to any field, and several people are now using it in widely varied areas.

The essential idea is to use a card with holes punched all around the edges. These cards are bought ready-punched. Each hole is coded. Topics, subtopics, and so on, are assigned code numbers. When a topic appears on a card, a wedge-like cut is made from the edge of the card to the appropriate hole, with the apex at the hole. To sort a group of cards for a single topic, a long wire "needle" is thrust through the appropriate hole and the cards are given a shake. The cut cards drop out; those with the hole intact remain on the needle.

Procedure

Since a large number of code combinations can be punched on a single card, it is not necessary to take notes minor topic by minor topic, as with the conventional system. Notes for an entire article can be taken on one card. For a book, as many cards as are needed can be used in sequence. Whole articles can be clipped out and simply pasted to the card.

After the note is taken or the article is clipped to the cards, marginal notes should be made to show which parts of the note are classed in which categories. Page numbers and a source reference must also be supplied. The edge is then processed, and the note is ready for the files. A variation keeps the bibliographical information on the same card as the notes, and keys the edge to author and item as well as to topic.

Using and Filing

By use of the sorting needle, large quantities of cards can be sorted in a relatively short time. If the breakdown by subtopic is a fine one, all the material in the files that concerns even a minor point can be quickly located. Filing can be by topic or by author and article. Sorting is so easy that it doesn't much matter.

Advantages and Disadvantages

The system is much less clumsy than the conventional card system. Articles and other items can be recorded as a whole rather than piecemeal. In the conventional system each item has to be classed as the note is taken—in order to decide when to change note cards. In the manual punched card system, the classifying job can be done all at once after the notes are taken. And information is easy to locate, even if the files should get mixed up.

The system has two disadvantages. First, it is much more expensive. Second, a complete outline of the field is needed for making a systematic classification before the cards are punched.

THE MACHINE-PUNCHED CARD SYSTEM

The machine-punched card system is an offshoot of the manual. Notes are taken on the back of the cards used in standard machine accounting or recording systems. The notes can be taken in sequence, but in the system I saw in use, only one note was put on a card. The cards are punched to denote the topic and its subdivisions. Each card can also be coded to the bibliographic source, or the entire information punched on each card.

Cards are sorted by machine. In a short time a large group can be sorted to the most minute subtopic. If author and title are coded, a sort for either can be made equally quickly. Indeed, the types of sorts possible depend only on the ingenuity with which the code is worked out.

The system allows for quicker sorting than any other. This is its one great advantage. Its disadvantages are few. It does not, for example, allow an entire article to be clipped to a card—the card could not go through the sorter. Moreover, if a card becomes damaged, it must be redone. Finally, and this is the critical disadvantage—it can only be used by those to whom the machinery is available.

If I had to make a recommendation from among the systems, I believe it would be this: the young man starting out should use the conventional system until he has worked out a good system of classification of the areas in which he will have a permanent interest. Then, I think, he will find the manual-punched card system most efficient. The man already able to make a detailed classification will probably want to use that system at once.

The main thing, however, is not which system is used. It is to get some method that will systematically preserve vital information so that it is available when needed. And even if such a system is not used to keep up in the field professionally, it will be valuable for keeping notes for any project, and will make organizing the final report on it that much easier. For the more flexible the recording system, the easier it will be to arrange and rearrange the material until it is in the order most useful to both you and your reader.

PRACTICE SUGGESTIONS

After reading Chapter 14 you checked what was published last year on a specific topic. Now do these things:

1. Read the items, taking notes in one of the forms suggested (probably the conventional one).
2. Write a report reviewing what was written during the year. Don't review article by article, but by *subject matter covered*. Write as if you were reviewing for a written report to your colleagues.
3. Annotate the report by using a suitable kind of numbered bibliography or by footnotes.
4. Take the page that uses the *most references*. If you used footnotes, number the items in the bibliography, and redo the page in the style suitable to a numbered bibliography. If you used a bibliography, redo the page using footnotes.

PART II

Applications

16

Reports Showing How the Basic Patterns Are Modified

THIS CHAPTER contains two groups of sample reports. The first group consists of reports resulting from investigations; the second group of reports giving information.

Each group has the same internal arrangement. It begins with a report which uses a full "three-level" pattern. In the succeeding reports, as the report situation becomes more and more routine, the functional parts are simpler or disappear.

To avoid confusion, some of the reports have been modified to conform exactly with the material presented in the text. Variations are analyzed separately in Chapter 17.

All material identifying the source of the reports has been altered. Thus names of Greek letters have been substituted for names of companies. Other names are fictitious.

Some of the reports are actual reproductions. They had to be reduced photographically and consequently have smaller type. To save your eyes, the other reports have been printed in a type resembling typewriter type of normal size. Obviously, in the original reports the lines would be longer than they now are, for the pages of this book are not wide enough to carry a full line. As a result, the original reports took fewer pages. The actual number of the pages in the original is therefore given at the last of the material under "Report Situation."

Some of the reports that are shown single-spaced were

double-spaced in the original. The change was made to keep this book a handy size. Such changes are noted under the head of "Format."

In each sample, just after a functional part is discussed, a page reference is given to get you to the same part of the next report. Thus when you are studying "Prefatory Material," you can turn at once to the prefatory material of the next report. An exception is made if you need to turn forward only three or four pages.

Sometimes you will turn to the next report only to learn that it does not use the functional part under discussion. If so, be sure to read the "Report Situation" and examine the report to see why that part was unnecessary.

Because each functional part is influenced by the report situation, be very sure to read the material under that head each time you go through the reports. To help you, page references to it are given under the discussion of each functional part of each report.

Though the original reports were typed on one side only, after their first few pages they are reproduced here on both sides, in order to make a more compact book.

Group One
Reports of Investigations

STANDARD DATA FOR NONSTANDARD
ELEMENTS

REPORT SITUATION

THIS REPORT was written in a department concerned with fabricating the interiors of automobiles. It is an elaborate "three-level" report that closely follows the base pattern for reports of an investigation. It was written by an engineer still under supervision, who received advice from the Chief Time Study Analyst. The report then went to the supervisor of the department to whom it is addressed. A plant project committee next reviewed it. Since the division has several plants which perform the same operations, the report also had to be capable of being transmitted to them, through the central organization. The potential readership, therefore, included both technical people within the department and people who did not have an intimate acquaintance with the details of operation. Notice how the organization, the cross references, the specific diction and objectivity of the language combine to give the impression that great care was exercised, even though raw data are given only in a single sample. (Total pages of original report—100.)

The situation of the next report is described on page 322.

FORMAT

The format of this report was elaborate. It was sewed and bound in a hard cloth cover which had on it the information shown on page 281. It had a standard title page. A detailed table of contents and list of illustrations were used to facilitate finding specific items. (Note also how the Table of

Contents is an outline of the report, and how its headings correspond with those in the body of the report.)

In position and typography, heads follow the practices discussed in Chapter 14. The letter was single-spaced, as here; the rest of the material was double-spaced.

The format of the next report is described on page 322.

[*This page represents the cover*]

STANDARD DATA FOR NON-STANDARD ELEMENTS
OF
MAJOR CUT AND SEW FOUNDATION ASSEMBLIES

ALFRED A. BILL
ALPHA DIVISION

Report on

STANDARD DATA FOR NON-STANDARD ELEMENTS
OF
MAJOR CUT AND SEW FOUNDATION ASSEMBLIES

Submitted to
R. P. SANDRUM
LABOR STANDARDS DEPARTMENT
ALPHA DIVISION

By
Alfred A. Bill
August 1, 195X

PREFATORY MATERIAL

Except for identification of the author on the cover and title page, all prefatory material is in a letter of transmittal. Here memorandum form is used, since the report was transmitted within the organization.

The letter is not as elaborate as one which would go to an outside organization. The letter tells us that the occasion was a situation that needed correction. It was also an assignment of a project committee on suggestion of a department supervisor. This occasion evolved into this project because the data that were originally to be used were not satisfactory. A new and limited project was agreed upon—only part of the project could be performed.

The letter closes with the names of people who helped, and the type of aid they gave.

The prefatory material of the next report is described on page 324, the report situation on page 322.

THE ALPHA DIVISION

Labor Standards Department

To: Mr. Robert P. Sandrum   August 1, 195X
    Supervisor, Labor Standards Department

The non-standard elements existing in foundation sew operations have created a serious problem for the Labor Standards personnel. Because of the varying nature of non-standard elements, it has been difficult to set accurate and consistent work standards. The plant project committee, therefore, agreed that a definite need existed for standard data for foundation sew operations.

As originally assigned to me, the scope of the project included all operations of all assemblies manufactured in the Cut and Sew Department. However, it was soon discovered that information taken from the Labor Standards file could not be used to compile standard data. Consequently, it was agreed that I should observe the operations and record the times they occurred. The time involved in this process necessitated limiting the project to its present scope -- sewed foundation assemblies.

Sincere appreciation is due to Mr. Donald R. Carrold, the now retired Supervisor of the Labor Standards Department, who suggested the project and assisted in determining the approach.

Mr. Claude Jennifer, Chief Labor Standards Analyst, proved to be a most competent advisor in the project. His knowledge of Cut and Sew operations was very helpful and rates a special, "thank you."

The best of cooperation was received from the many production supervisors contacted. Mr. Donald Arntrip, Mr. Samuel P. Johnson, and Mr. Ralph O. Dikes, Superintendent and Assistant Superintendent of the Cut and Sew Department, respectively, were instrumental in obtaining this cooperation.

Alfred A. Bill

Alfred A. Bill

TABLE OF CONTENTS

LIST OF ILLUSTRATIONS

INTRODUCTION

The first two paragraphs are devoted to background. The first assumes the importance of a fair and equitable standard and moves to a brief basic theoretical discussion, showing where the subject fits into the general area. The second paragraph is specific definition.

The third paragraph gives a general statement of the importance of the area of non-standards. The next paragraphs give the area in which the problem arose and further describe it. The subsection ends with the very specific statement of the problem or final objective of the project.

The next paragraph limits the problem by telling what it will not include and by giving a breakdown into four specific areas that it will.

Next, under "method of attack," comes the account of the general procedure. Notice that there is no attempt to go into detail.

The final subsection gives a clear idea of what will be found in the rest of the report. Both the conclusions and the appendix are accounted for.

Though the report deals with a technical subject, the language is clear and simple. While you may not know exactly what a rear quarter or a bobbin is, you do have a good general idea of what the author was trying to do.

The introduction of the next report is described on page 326, the report situation on page 322.

STANDARD DATA FOR NON-STANDARD ELEMENTS
OF
MAJOR CUT AND SEW FOUNDATION ASSEMBLIES

I. INTRODUCTION

Statement of the Problem

The primary duty of a Labor Standards man
is to set a fair and equitable standard. To
perform this duty satisfactorily, it is
recognized that the facts of the operation
being studied must be accurate and complete.
These facts include not only the amount of
time required to perform the actual cycle of
the operation, but other facts such as engineering specifications, prevailing conditions and the work performed outside of the
normal cycle of the operation. The last
mentioned item takes form in delays or non-
standard elements. The evaluation of the
time allowed to perform these necessary
tasks is most influential in the ultimate
time value assigned to an operation.

A non-standard element is the performance
of an avoidable or unavoidable delay outside
of the regular work cycle. From this definition it is evident that two types of non-
standard elements are possible: those elements which must be performed to successfully complete the job, and those elements
which have no effect on the final content or
appearance of the job. Included in this
latter category are such items as fumbles,
talking, waits for stock from the previous
operation, etc. These items may exist in an
operator's performance during the course of

1

2

the day, but they cannot be allowed, as they
definitely are not part of the job content.

Non-standards are of such a nature that
they can cause great inaccuracy when setting
a work standard. Some of them may occur
very frequently during the period of a
study, and others may occur very infre-
quently or not at all. It is this inconsistency of occurrence that makes non-
standard elements so unstable and difficult
to evaluate.

In Cut and Sew foundation sew operations
there are many non-standards which must be
performed. Most frequent are change bobbin,
thread breakage, change needle, rip and
resew, change spool of thread, oil machine,
snip tie cords, and reposition material.
The Labor Standards Department has set time
values for change bobbin, thread breakage,
and change needle. However, these values
have been set only by common agreement between the parties involved in setting work
standards. The non-standard elements have
no set values, therefore, and times allowed
vary from study to study, depending upon
operator performance and conditions prevailing when the study was taken.

Because of the indetermined values of the
above non-standards the setting of work
standards up to this time has been a very
difficult and often trying responsibility.
Time study men have assigned allowed times
to these non-standards even though they have
had no yardstick by which to determine
whether a value was correct. They have re-
lied on past experience and on facts that

were found in past studies of similar operations. It has consequently been possible
that the value assigned to the non-standard
element was incorrect because of a mistake
made in determining the value originally
used in the past study. There is no greater
source of error than that of carrying over
time values from previous years without having proof of their validity.

Since evaluation was based on experience,
a new man in the department could not possibly evaluate non-standards because of his
lack of experience. He has had to rely on
the experience of other men in the department to assist him in setting a work standard. Therefore, a new man has been a handicap to the department because of the delay
in his development caused by waiting until
he too could evaluate non-standards with
some degree of accuracy.

This study was undertaken to eliminate the
problems so far discussed, by evolving accurate time values. The values were to result
from recording and analyzing actual times.
The final objective was to obtain standard
data for non-standard elements, in order to
eliminate inconsistency in work standards.

Assemblies Included

The study included all sewed foundation
assemblies made at the plant with the exception of genuine leather assemblies. Because
of the low volume schedule of genuine
leather assemblies, it would have been very
difficult to obtain enough readings to war-

4

rant any conclusions. A breakdown of the
other assemblies is as follows:

1.   Front Doors
2.   Rear Doors
3.   Rear Quarters
4.   Compartment Tops

Method of Attack

The problem of obtaining a sufficient number of readings to accurately set standard
time values was solved by actually observing
operations and recording the non-standards
which occurred. Past studies and records
proved to be of no value because of the lack
of supplementary information which was
needed to properly evaluate the recorded
times.

The observations were recorded on Form
No. 30361-A, the standard time study sheet.
Any pertinent information that would be
needed to help evaluate the times was also
recorded. This information in turn was
transferred to standard data work sheets to
allow grouping and analysis of like operations. A sample sheet of this form is in
the Appendix on page 78.

Order of Reporting

Following the conclusions and recommendations, this report is divided into five sections. The first four sections present the
standard data developed for the following
non-standard elements:

5

1. Change Bobbin
2. Thread Breakage
3. Rip and Resew
4. Change Spool of Thread

The fifth section deals with the non-standards for which no conclusive values could be developed. They are:

1. Change Needle
2. Oil Machine
3. Snip Tie Cords
4. Reposition Material

Following the main body of the report, in an Appendix section, all calculations are presented as proof of the standard data. The actual time readings are not included in the Appendix because of the large number of readings obtained. These data are on file in the Labor Standards Department.

CONCLUSION

Taken with the introduction, the conclusions give a good idea of the outcome of the project. These features are noteworthy.

1. The section opens with a formal topic sentence.
2. The five general conclusions are placed first. They tell us that the problem was solved. Standard data were evolved, and they did eliminate the specific difficulties mentioned in the introduction. The reader immediately knows the outcome.
3. A reader who wants more details on the exact values evolved can next read the specific conclusions, which give concrete values.
4. If the reader wants to find the method used to get a particular value, he can turn to specific pages—the conclusions are keyed to the body by page number.
5. Recommendations follow the conclusions. In this instance, the position is good, as shown by the easy transition from the last specific conclusion. On some occasions, however, and perhaps even here, it might be more effective to place general recommendations right after the general conclusions.
6. As often happens, some incidental recommendations of value resulted. But these are kept in proportion by their position at the end of the section.

Obviously, the writer kept clearly in mind the fact that he should put first what most readers will need or want. Likewise, he has made it easy for the reader to find further information on any point he wishes to.

The conclusion of the next report is described on page 328, the report situation on page 322.

II.   CONCLUSIONS AND RECOMMENDATIONS

Investigation of the non-standard elements present in foundation sewing resulted in the following conclusions and recommendations.

General Conclusions

Standard Data Curves. The standard data curves found at the end of each of the third, fourth, fifth, and sixth chapters will allow direct calculation of minutes per piece values. The use of these curves will result in the following advantages:

1. Reduce time required to compute allowances
2. Obtain values which are comparable to similar operations
3. Obtain accurate and reliable allowances
4. Allow inexperienced observer to set allowances
5. Aid in the estimating of work standards

Specific Conclusions

Change Bobbin. The data obtained support values of .400 minutes per change for a small bobbin, and .580 minutes for a large bobbin. These values result from the analysis presented on pages 13 and 14. Minutes per sew inch values for the various types of operations are presented on pages 80 to 84 of the Appendix. Minutes per piece curves are on pages 22 to 38.

7

Thread Breakage. The data obtained support minutes per sew inch allowances for the
following operations:

Type of Sew	Minutes per Inch
Riser to foundation sewing	
1. Top and bottom line sewing	.000137
Compartment top sewing	
2. Cloth to riser sewing (design line)	.0000819
3. Imitation leather to riser sewing (design line)	.0000702
4. Cloth and imitation leather to riser sewing	.000135

The analysis used to arrive at the above
figures can be found on pages 44 to 46.
Minutes per piece curves are presented on
page 48.

Rip and Resew. Minutes per inch values
for the rip and resew non-standard element
are as follows:

Type of Sew	Minutes per Inch
1. Riser to foundation sewing	
Top and bottom line sewing	
Compartment top sewing	.0000595
2. Cloth to riser (design line)	.0000819
Imitation leather to riser (design line)	.0000500
3. Cloth and imitation leather to riser	.0000420

8

The procedure used to develop the above values can be found on pages 52 and 53. Minutes per piece curves are presented on page 55.

Change Spool of Thread. The data obtained support a value of .700 minutes per spool change. The development of this value can be found on page 57. Minutes per inch values for the various types of per piece curves are presented on pages 62 to 71.

Change Needle; Oil Machine; Snip Tie Cords; and Reposition Material. Investigation of the data recorded for the four non-standards resulted in the conclusion that no final standard data could be developed. However, indications of true values are presented on pages 73 and 74. A plan to obtain sufficient readings to establish standard data is in the general recommendations which follow.

General Recommendations

It is recommended that the standard values in this report be checked at the beginning of each model year. Also, changes in production methods will necessitate revising the data to keep them up to date. For example, the 195X door foundation of the 1200 series door assemblies is different from the foundation being used on the 195Y model. This foundation may influence the factors discussed on page 14 of Chapter III, and cause a change in the values developed in the chapter for the change bobbin non-standard.

9

A separate file for standard data should
be maintained in the Labor Standards office.
Non-standard element times, as observed during a time study, should be analyzed and
recorded on the standard data work sheets
used in this investigation (shown on page 78
of the Appendix). In this manner, additional readings can be built up for use as
standard data. Standard data can then be
developed for the four non-standard elements
discussed in Chapter VII.

It is strongly recommended that work in
the field of standard data for non-standard
elements be continued. The advantages of
the data for foundation sewing, as outlined
in the conclusions, show that this type of
data is applicable. It follows that similar
data can be developed for:

1. Headlining assemblies
2. Cushions, backs, and back of back
   assemblies
3. Sunshade assemblies
4. Weather cord assemblies

Specific Recommendations

The following recommendations incidentally
evolved from this study.

Change Bobbin. Only Beta thread should be
used as bobbin thread. This thread allows
more thread to be wound on a bobbin and consequently results in less time allowance per
bobbin change (see page 16).

Instructions in the correct method to be
used to change the bobbin should be given to

operators not following the general method
presented on page 12. This would help the
operators meet the allowances presented in
Chapter III.

Change Spool of Thread. An attempt should
be made to schedule color runs of assemblies
in such a manner that the least number of
changes of thread will be necessary (see
page 58). If all one color assemblies could
be run for an entire day, the allowed time
for operations requiring color changes could
be reduced to the values found on the first
curves on the graphs on pages 62 to 66.

DEVELOPING SECTIONS

The Table of Contents shows that division into major sections is made according to the operations studied, a functional principle. The sequence is arbitrary, since no natural relation demands a set sequence. The operations where positive results were obtained come first. The Appendix is used for supplementary data. From the Table of Contents and List of Illustrations can be gathered the principle used in determining what should be in the Appendix. The curves included in the body of the report are the processed data which led to the conclusions. The Appendix materials consist of samples and basic factors that were used in preliminary stages of evolving the curves.

The subsections of Sections III to VI follow a consistent general pattern, but modifications are made to suit the specific situation. Section VII varies because no standard data were evolved and hence the same subsection heads were inapplicable.

Section III, reproduced here in full, shows that the sequence within sections is based on the chronological order in which steps have to be performed. Other points to notice are

1. The section is opened with an introduction that states these things: phase of problem considered, order of discussion, importance of this phase of the problem, specific statement of the problem, and a description of the method being studied. The latter sets the preliminary conditions under which the problem was worked out. It is a kind of background—even though it is a result of a study, the study was preliminary to the main issue.

2. The first subsection also opens by a division of the area under discussion.

3. The section ends with general conclusions. As the List of Illustrations shows, these were followed by the

III. CHANGE BOBBIN

In this section, standard data are developed for the change bobbin non-standard element. The first portion of the section discusses the background of the problem, and the problem itself. The solution of the problem is then discussed in the following phases:

1. Establishing the Standard Value
2. Establishing the Standard Minutes Per Piece Allowance for Any Length of Sew
3. Determining the Standard Minutes Per Piece Allowance
4. Interpreting the Data

The conclusions reached from the discussions of the above sections are then presented. Following the conclusions are the standard data curves.

The change bobbin non-standard element has the highest frequency of occurrence of all the non-standard elements present in foundation sewing. Because of this, the time value assigned to it can be very influential in determining the production per hour attainable.

In the past, the plant has used an allowance of .500 minutes for an operator to change a small or large bobbin. This allowance was not proven by data, and was only a figure assumed by the Labor Standards personnel to be correct. This value was thought to be "too loose," but no change curves evolved—the specific findings of the investigation of the bobbin phase. The curves, here not shown, took up eighteen pages.

The developing sections of the next report are described on page 334, the report situation on page 322.

DATA

The handling of procedure in this report clearly demonstrates how significant it is felt to be. (General procedure is of course given in the introduction.) In the text of each section, as in Section III, procedure is the dominating factor. For each phase we are told how the data were obtained, the number of observations (330), how taken, including elimination of disturbing factors, how they were processed, and how results were calculated. At every point the significance of each step is explained. Finally the method of interpreting the data is discussed with a specific example. The data themselves are given in processed form in the eighteen pages of curves at the end of the section. But the Appendix contains a sample of how they appeared on the original worksheets. The entire mass of data is not reported. As the introduction tells us, they are on file in the Labor Standards Department. They were too extensive to include.

The presentation of data in the next report is described on page 334, the report situation on page 322.

ILLUSTRATIONS

Illustrations, which are omitted here, are used for orienting the reader to the part discussed, as in the drawing of the rear door, or for condensing data into usable form, as in the curves. The drawings are referred to in the text, and what they show is highlighted. The curves condensing data are interpreted to show their use.

12

could be made without proof to substantiate
it. The establishing of a new value based
on facts was therefore the problem.

In order to establish a sound value, it
was necessary to determine the method which
was considered to be the best for performing
the changing of the bobbin. Of course, not
all the operators used the same method, but
the pattern was generally the same. The
following breakdown shows the method most
used by the operators. It is considered to
be satisfactory:

Left Hand	Right Hand
Wait	Open bobbin case
Wait	Release bobbin clamp
Remove empty bobbin	Remove full bobbin from spindle
Place empty bobbin on spindle	Wait
Wait	Wind thread on empty bobbin
Place thread in position	Place bobbin in chamber
Close case	Wait

Small deviations from this pattern were
allowed, but any great difference was noted
and the time value labeled and not accepted.
Of the 351 observations of small bobbin
changes 330 were accepted as satisfactory.
Fifteen observations of large bobbin changes
were recorded, and all were satisfactory.

Establishing the Standard Value

There are two types of bobbins in use in
the Cut and Sew Department. They are dif-

The location of illustrations depends on where they will be most useful. The orienting ones faced the appropriate text. The curves are to be used in future calculations, so they are placed in a convenient group at the end of the applicable chapter. Preliminary and supplementary illustrations are in the Appendix.

The illustrations of the next report are described on page 336, the report situation on page 322.

ACKNOWLEDGMENTS

The only acknowledgments are the prefatory ones at the end of the letter. No more are needed, as this is a primary study that did not depend on written source material.

The acknowledgments of the next report are described on page 336, the report situation on page 322.

13

ferent in size only and the method used to
change them is exactly the same. However,
the difference in size affects the time required to make the change, as the additional
bulk of the larger bobbin makes it difficult
to handle. This fact is proven by the results obtained in the investigation.

Small Bobbin. The 330 recorded time values for the small bobbin change average .375
minutes per change. This value included not
only the time required to change the bobbin,
but also oiling the bobbin when necessary,
and resewing the portion of the assembly
that was sewed while the bobbin was empty.
Most operators do not oil the bobbin each
time it is changed, but rather every second
or third time the change is performed. All
readings--those during which the bobbin was
not oiled, and those in which the oil function was performed--were averaged together.
It was felt that this resulted in a true
value of the number of times this element
was performed by the average operator.

The fact that the observations were taken
while the operators were working under an
incentive had to be taken into consideration. Since it is desirable to establish
the standard value for a normal operator, it
is necessary to determine how much time must
be allowed to correct the .375 actual average to the normal time required to change
the bobbin. Since all of the 330 accepted
readings were rated as satisfactory, it must
be assumed that even the poorest performance
cannot be given below a zero percent incentive factor allowance. That is, it cannot

14

be rated below normal. On the other hand, the remaining operators work anywhere from zero to fifteen percent over standard. In order to make a blanket allowance for the incentive factor, .025 minutes, or approximately eight percent, was added to the actual average, and the resulting recommended .400 minutes per bobbin change was obtained.

This value represents a reduction of .100 minutes per change, or twenty percent, as compared to the previous figure. An indication of the time saved by using the new value is shown by the following example:

Previous Value

$$\frac{1 \text{ bobbin}}{10 \text{ pcs.}} \times \frac{.500 \text{ minutes}}{\text{bobbin}} =$$

.050 minutes/pc.

Recommended Value

$$\frac{1 \text{ bobbin}}{10 \text{ pcs.}} \times \frac{.400 \text{ minutes}}{\text{bobbin}} =$$

.040 minutes/pc.

The result in this particular case is a savings of .010 minutes per piece.

Large Bobbin. The large bobbin's increased size warrants more time to perform the change. This fact is proven by the .539 minutes per change average obtained from the 15 readings. Using the same analysis as was made for the small bobbin, .041 minutes was added, and the recommended time for this type of bobbin became .580 minutes per bobbin change.

This is an increase of .080 minutes per change allowance over the former value of .500 minutes. However, the number of pieces from each bobbin is very high and the effect on the minutes per piece allowance is very slight.

Previous Value

$$\frac{1 \text{ bobbin}}{50 \text{ pcs.}} \times \frac{.500 \text{ minutes}}{\text{bobbin}} =$$

.010 minutes/pc.

Recommended Value

$$\frac{1 \text{ bobbin}}{50 \text{ pcs.}} \times \frac{.580 \text{ minutes}}{\text{bobbin}} =$$

.0116 minutes/pc.

The loss in this case would be .0016 minutes per piece.

Establishing the Standard Minutes Per
Piece Allowance for Any Length of Sew

The allowance for the bobbin change is shown on the time study as a definite number of minutes per piece. Previously, this figure was calculated by dividing .500 minutes per bobbin change by the number of pieces the operator actually sewed from the bobbin. This method contained a possible source of error.

There are five factors which determine the usage of bobbin thread. They are: size of bobbin, type of thread used, stitches per inch, thickness of penetration (foundation, riser, and material thickness), and the ten-

sion exerted on the thread by the sew. Any
or all of these five factors can cause a va-
riance in the number of pieces obtained from
the bobbin. A discussion of these factors
follows.

Size of Bobbin. As previously discussed,
there are two different size bobbins used
for foundation sewing. Although the small
bobbin is found on most machines, the larger
bobbin is used for some types of sew. Logically, the larger the bobbin the more
thread available for sewing, and the more
pieces obtainable per bobbin. Thus, with a
greater number of pieces per bobbin, fewer
minutes per piece allowance results.

Thread Size. Foundation sewing specifies
the number 24/4 type of bobbin thread. Two
vendors supply this thread and there is a
slight difference in the thickness. One
thread is twisted more tightly than the
other, and, therefore, more thread inches
can be wound on a bobbin. Once again, the
more thread inches available, the greater
the yield per bobbin.

Stitches per Inch. The number of stitches
per inch of sew affects the number of pieces
per bobbin. Fewer stitches per inch in a
line of sew result in less thread inches
being used. By reducing the number of
inches of thread needed to sew a line, more
pieces can be obtained per bobbin.

Thickness of Penetration. If an operation
necessitates sewing only a piece of imitation leather to a foundation, the thread
inches used will be less than if the opera-

tion necessitates sewing through a riser in addition to the leather and foundation. The thicker the penetration, the more thread needed.

Tension. The tension determines how tight the thread will be pulled against the sewed assembly. If the tension is great, then less thread inches will be used.

Determining the Standard Minutes Per Piece Allowance

Since each of the five factors is a prime factor in determining the number of pieces obtained from a bobbin, it follows that if they could be standardized it would be possible to determine this value before a study is taken. Going one step further, with the yield per bobbin known, it is possible to formulate a value in a minutes per inch allowance. Then by multiplying this value by any number of inches in a sew line the minutes per piece allowance can be determined. In formula form this would be expressed as:

$$\frac{1 \text{ bobbin}}{\text{thread inches}} \times \frac{\text{thread inches}}{\text{sew inches}} \times$$

$$\frac{.400 \text{ minutes}}{\text{bobbin}} \times \frac{\text{sew inches}}{\text{piece}} = \frac{\text{minutes}}{\text{piece}}$$

The following paragraphs explain the development and use of this formula:

Bobbin Thread Inches. Bobbin size and type of thread used determine the number of thread inches on a bobbin. The following

18

figures were determined by actually unwinding full bobbins and measuring the number of inches of thread:

1. Small Bobbin - Beta 24/4 thread = 1250 thread inches
2. Small Bobbin - Gamma 24/4 thread = 980 thread inches
3. Large Bobbin - Beta 24/4 thread = 4278 thread inches

The large bobbin machines use only the Beta 24/4 thread.

Thread Factor. The thread factor is defined as the number of thread inches per inch of sew. This factor will vary with the stitches per inch, the thickness of penetration, and the tension of the sew. By measuring a certain number of inches at a specified number of stitches per inch, and carefully removing the thread necessary to sew the measured inches, it was possible to determine thread factors for all types of sew. For example:

Type of Sew: Imitation leather to foundation
Stitches per Inch: 4
Sew Inches Measured: 5
Thread Inches Measured: 7-3/8
Thread Factor: 7-3/8 ÷ 5 =

$$1.480 \frac{\text{thread inches}}{\text{sew inch}}$$

Thread factors of all types of sew can be found on page 79 of the Appendix.

Use of the Formula. Values now can be substituted into the formula to arrive at a minutes per piece allowance. Using a small bobbin machine with Beta 24/4 bobbin thread, and a thread factor of 1.380 inches, the following example of an imitation leather to foundation sew will illustrate the use of the formula:

$$\frac{bobbin}{1250 \text{ thread inches}} \times \frac{1.38 \text{ thread inches}}{1.00 \text{ sew inch}} \times$$

$$\frac{.400 \text{ minutes}}{bobbin} \times \frac{50 \text{ sew inches}}{piece} =$$

$$\frac{.00044 \text{ minutes}}{sew \text{ inch}} \times \frac{50 \text{ sew inches}}{piece} =$$

$$.022 \text{ minutes/piece}$$

By reducing the first three terms of the formula to a minutes per inch value, the minutes per piece value for any number of sew inches can be determined. Minutes per inch values for all types of sew can be found on pages 80 to 84 in the Appendix.

Interpreting the Data

By using the above formula and substituting values correctly, it is possible to accurately determine minutes per piece allowance for any type and length of sew. However, in order to simplify this computation the data are presented in graphical form. It is also felt that with the data presented in this manner, mistakes in calculation of minutes per piece value are reduced to a minimum.

20

Use of the graphs is best illustrated by
taking a typical example of a door assembly
operation, and determining the minutes per
piece bobbin change allowance.

One of the operations of the 10001 door
assembly consists of sewing the bottom
leather and lip of the riser foundation to
the door foundation, and sewing the imitation leather to the door foundation by means
of a bottom seam. (See accompanying drawing
on page 17.) Since the graph values presented are catalogued as to the type of sew,
and the example operation combines two types
of sew, it is evident that two graphs will
have to be consulted to obtain the allowance.

As part of his time study, the observer
records all information relevant to the operation.   Therefore, the following needed
data are recorded:

1.   Bobbin size - small
2.   Stitches per inch - 4
3.   Thread size - Beta 24/4
4.   Inches per sew line
        - 29 (imitation leather, cloth and
          riser to foundation)
        - 29 (imitation leather to founda-
          tion)

To compute the minutes per piece value,
the "imitation leather, cloth, and riser to
foundation" graph on page 25 is first consulted.   The number of sew inches (29) is
located on the ordinate.   Then by following
a horizontal line from this value to where
it intersects the four stitches per inch

curve, and reading the corresponding value
of .016 minutes per piece found on the
abscissa, the allowance for the "imitation
leather, cloth, and riser to foundation" sew
is completed.

Turning to the "imitation leather to foundation" graph on page 22, the same procedure
is followed to find the minutes per piece
value of .0130 for 29 inches of sew at four
stitches per inch.

It should be noted that an additional minutes per inch value is allowed for each inch
of sew out. "Sew out" is defined as that
sewing of a line that does not include any
foundation sewing. Values for sew out were
developed by averaging the minutes per inch
value of each type of sew operation. Sew
out calculations can be found on page 85 of
the Appendix. Referring again to the sketch
on page 17, there are two inches of sew out
on the riser line, and three inches of sew
out on the bottom line. Using the .00056
value found on the riser graph on page 25,
the minutes per piece value for sew out becomes .00112. The .00047 value of the graph
on page 22 becomes a .00141 minutes per
piece. These values must be added to the
two allowances taken from the graphs. The
minutes per piece allowance for this operation is then obtained by adding the four
separate allowances:

1. Imitation
    leather, cloth,
    and riser to
    foundation   .016 minutes per piece

2. Imitation
    leather to
    foundation   .013 minutes per piece
3. Sew out (two
    inches)   .0011   "   "   "
4. Sew out (three
    inches)   .0014   "   "   "
           Total   .0315   "   "   "

Conclusions

Determining bobbin change allowances from
the standard data will result in the following advantages:

1. Increase productive time by reducing
    allowed time for performance of non-
    standard
2. Reduce time required to compute
    allowances
3. Obtain values which are comparable to
    similar operations
4. Obtain accurate and reliable allow-
    ances
5. Allow inexperienced observer to set
    bobbin change allowances.

LAMBDA ELECTRIC STATION ASH
DISPOSAL STUDY

REPORT SITUATION

THIS REPORT is a three-level report. It was prepared by an engineer for the signature of his chief engineer, who then submitted it to top management. (Total pages—16.)

The situation of the next report is described on page 348.

FORMAT

The report was a reproduction of typed copy, single spaced, on one side only. It was stapled in a cardboard cover. The outside of the cover also served as title page.

What is really a list of illustrations appears at the end of the Table of Contents.

Because the main sections are brief, it would have given a choppy effect to start a new page with each new section. Hence the practice shown here.

The format of the next report is described on page 348.

LAMBDA ELECTRIC STATION
ASH DISPOSAL STUDY
EDO 90000

THE SIGMA COMPANY
CHICAGO, ILLINOIS

Mechanical Engineering Department
Mechanical Research Division
December 28, 1953

ME-R-102

PREFATORY MATERIAL

The writer of this report is shown by initials at the end. Also prefatory are the approval signature and the department of origin. Otherwise prefatory material is missing. Such treatment is normal in three circumstances:

1. When a transmitting note or letter is clipped to the cover.
2. When the relationship between the superior and the person transmitting the report is very immediate, and he supplies any needed preface orally.
3. When the situation is well known and the reader anticipates the report.

The prefatory material and report situation of the next report are described on page 348.

TABLE OF CONTENTS

INTRODUCTION

The introduction first states the need and the importance of the problem. Background as to present operation and a definition follow, the latter cut in as a footnote. Next the specific problem is stated and broken into a choice between three alternatives. These serve also as an order of reporting, since the body of the report considers each alternative in the order named. The problem is then limited by excluding the alternative of the sale of fly ash.

No procedure is given, but the standards for judgment are implied in the statement of the problem—the solution must be economical, and must dispose of the ash.

The introduction and report situation of the next report are described on page 348.

LAMBDA STEAM ELECTRIC STATION
ASH DISPOSAL STUDY
EDO 416900

I. INTRODUCTION

Need for Immediate Action

With four units operating at Lambda, an estimated 200,000 tons of ash have to be disposed of annually. The total collection is comprised of 175,000 tons of fly ash* and 25,000 tons of bottom ash. (See Table VI, page 17, for a breakdown of the figures.)

With these amounts, it is estimated that the present ash basin would be filled by about March 1956. Work should be started now to provide another means of ash disposal. If new facilities are available a year or so before the present basin is filled, we can use the present basin for storage of bottom ash and for periods when trouble prevents removal of fly ash to the new area.

Under present operation, the bottom ash is sluiced into a sump from which it is pumped to the ash basin approximately 1800 ft downstream from the plant. The dry fly ash

---

* By fly ash, is meant the fine particles of ash and unburned combustible materials which are carried from the boiler furnace into the gas stream and are collected in the dust collectors which are located between the boiler and the stack. The bottom ash is the coarse, heavy material which drops out of the furnace into the ash pit and is periodically sluiced to the ash sump, and from there pumped to the ash basin.

1

CONCLUSION

The concluding section is in three separate parts. The text of general conclusions is faced with a summary of costs and followed by recommendations. Note the interrelationships here. The introduction set up cost as a criterion. Hence the summary and conclusions are in terms of cost. The three alternatives in the introduction appear in the same order in the summary table, in the conclusions, and in the recommendations. (If Conclusion 1, a re-iteration of the need, is not counted, the symmetry is perfect.) Unquestionably this correspondence was carefully planned after the project was completed. Scheme 3, for example, might well have been investigated first, but has been named last in the introduction to allow for the consistent pattern now shown.

The only significant point where this report could be improved shows here. In the conclusions Scheme 1 is divided into 1a and 1b, but the only way to get any clear idea of the difference is to go to the body of the report. The differentiation could easily have been made in the introduction.

The fact that the body of the report is divided according to the sequence already established adequately keys the conclusions to the body of the report.

The conclusion of the next report is described on page 350, the report situation on page 348.

2

is handled by a pneumatic system, discharged
from exhausters into a sump, and pumped to
fill in the same lines as the bottom ash.

Problem

This project was undertaken to determine
the most economical method of disposing of
the ash at Lambda Steam Electric Station.

The study covered several methods of ash
disposal at the Lambda Plant. These methods
include:

1. Pumping to Tau Island, using existing
ash pumps.

2. Extending the present fly ash handling
system to include storage silos, thus permitting trucking the fly ash to a fill area
in the country.

3. Trucking ash from present basin to a
fill area.

The utilization of fly ash as a means of
reducing the cost of ash disposal is receiving increased attention in this country.
Since we have no immediate market for fly
ash, this report is based on selling no fly
ash. A separate report will be issued
shortly covering the results of a study on
fly ash utilization.

II.   CONCLUSIONS

The following conclusions were reached:

1. Since existing storage space is nearly
exhausted, prompt action should be taken to

TABLE I
ECONOMIC SUMMARY

TABLE I

ECONOMIC SUMMARY

Scheme	Pump - Fly Ash to Tau Island & Bottom Ash to Present Basin		Truck - Fly Ash From Silos to Plot 1, Pump Bottom Ash to Basin	Truck - All Ash from Basin To Plot 1
	North Half	South Half*		
	1a	1b	2	3
Cost of Land & Dikes —	$430,000	210,000	50,000	50,000
Capital Cost —	$0	130,000	365,000	0
		(200,000)		
Operating Expense $/Yr.	81,400	79,000	126,800	177,600
Savings vs Scheme 3	96,200	98,600	50,800	—
Return — $	46,800	44,800	23,800	—
Return — %	67	22	7	—
Storage Life — Years	9-1/2	7	28	25

* Costs apply only if south half of island is used following north half.

12/11/53
M.E.Dept.
ABC:EFG

provide additional storage facilities and
thus allow for bottom ash and emergency fly
ash storage in the present basin.

2. The cheapest way to dispose of the ash
is to pump it to the upper end of Tau
Island. Table I on page 4 shows the economics of this plan, which is called Scheme 1a.

3. The installation of silos and additional handling facilities for trucking to
disposal as shown under Scheme 2, Table I
would lend itself best to the sale of fly
ash sold in segregated carbon contents.

4. If a market could be developed for appreciable amounts of the run-of-pond ash in
the present basin, Scheme 3 would be more
competitive on a cost basis than Schemes
1a and 2.

III. RECOMMENDATIONS

It is recommended that:

1. Facilities be installed to permit
pumping fly ash to the north half of Tau
Island. This work should be completed by
Fall of 1954 to allow ample reserve storage
in the present ash basin.

2. The existing method of pumping bottom
ash to the present ash basin be continued.

3. This study be reviewed when it becomes
necessary to plan the next step, taking into
account possible changes in economic conditions and in the outlook for the sale of
this ash.

DEVELOPING SECTIONS

The sections follow the order set by the introduction, with one section added to exclude other possible solutions. The effect of the added section is to establish that the investigation considered all reasonable alternatives, and that these were hardly worth discussing. Placing them last and not mentioning them in the introduction excludes them from serious consideration. But if they had not been mentioned somewhere and a superior had thought of one of them, a serious doubt might have been raised as to the completeness of the study.

Each section consists largely of interpretation of the tables and diagrams which compose the "appendix" of the report. Note that these tables also are in the sequence established in the introduction. Because they are brief, the sections are not formally opened, and the head is allowed to substitute for a topic sentence.

The developing sections of the next report are described on page 352, the report situation on page 348.

DATA

The introduction implies that the general procedure will be to compare costs. The only mentions of procedure are at the points where Tables II and III are discussed. The assumption is that the procedures used in working out the various schemes will not be questioned. Without doubt the complete account of procedure and original data are in preliminary reports or in the department files.

The cost data here are in tabular form. Three other illustrations also give data. Placement is in the appendix, normal in a report this short.

The data of the next report are described on page 352, the report situation on page 348.

IV.   PUMPING TO TAU ISLAND -
SCHEMES 1a AND 1b

The Sigma Company bought Tau Island for a possible future ash disposal area. The island is about 8800 ft long and 1000 ft wide, and is located in the Theta River opposite the Lambda Plant. Chart I, page 18, shows the relative position of the island to the present ash disposal basin, and the plant.

The island must be protected by dikes to be used as a disposal area. These dikes should be constructed to a height of at least 1 ft above the 1935 flood level. Under this plan, called Scheme 1a, the northern half of the island would be diked to elevation 445 ft, and three 8-inch pipe lines extended from the ash trench alongside the plant, across the river bottom and on to the disposal area on the island. The present ash pumps are capable of pumping this distance without alterations. The piping cost for this Scheme is based on using new pipe. It may be possible, however, to use some of the existing ash piping and save money, providing the pipe is in satisfactory shape and the cost of relocating it is not prohibitive.

As shown on the diagram of proposed flow on Chart II, page 19, fly ash would be pumped through these lines to the island while the bottom ash would continue to be pumped to the present ash basin. We estimate the northern half of the island would provide approximately 9-1/2 years storage of fly ash.

ILLUSTRATIONS

The report contains six tables. One is a summary of costs, five give cost details, and one (Table VI) helps clarify the problem. The report also contained three illustrations not shown here. One was a diagram showing the proposed areas, the other two charts demonstrating how proposed schemes would operate.

Except for the summary chart, all illustrations are in the appendix. Since the text of the report covers only six pages, this arrangement is most practicable—they would have broken up the text badly.

Illustrations for the next report are discussed on page 352, the report situation on page 348.

ACKNOWLEDGMENTS

The only acknowledgment is cut into the body at the point where procedures for getting costs are discussed.

Acknowledgments for the next report are discussed on page 352, the report situation on page 348.

The transmission towers located on the upper end of the island would be protected from the ash water by embedding the tower bases in the dike itself. Also, a considerable quantity of rip-rap would be required around the head of the island to protect the outside of the dike from the effects of high water.

By pumping only fly ash to the island, and bottom ash to the present basin, the following advantages can be realized:

1. A longer storage life available on the island.

2. Minimum wear and less chance of blockage in pipe lines crossing the river.

3. Bottom ash, which is easiest to sell, placed in present basin from which it can be easily removed.

Table II, page 13, shows the cost details of the scheme. The method of arriving at the annual cost was furnished by the System Planning Department after consultation with the Financial Department. Under this method the cost of the dike installation is charged to operation over the useful life of the area.

The reasons why we are recommending Scheme 1a are as follows:

1. Yields highest rate of return of any of the schemes studied.

2. Transportation of ash would be under close control of plant personnel.

8

3. There would be no danger of creating a dust or dirt nuisance from this method.

A test garden has been started in the ash disposal basin to determine the ability of our fly ash to grow a plant or grass cover. If successful we will be able to use this ability to prevent erosion and dusting of ash on the present basin when filled, or on other ash filled areas.

If we wish to continue pumping to the island after the north half is filled, the south half can be diked up and the pipe lines to the island extended to the lower end, as covered by Scheme 1b. Three ash booster pumps would be required on the mainland to operate in series with the existing pumps as shown on Chart II, page 19. The south half of the island would provide an estimated 7 years' additional fly ash storage. In case of blockage in the lines to the island, fly ash could be diverted to the present basin for short periods of time.

Cost details of Scheme 1b are shown on Table III, page 14. Here again, a relatively high dike cost is charged to operation over the estimated storage life of the area. These costs are based on the assumption that the south half of the island would be utilized following the filling of the north half.

V. TRUCKING FROM SILOS TO PLOT 1 – SCHEME 2

This scheme would entail extension of the

present fly ash handling systems to include storage silos. The dry fly ash collected in these silos would be dampened to prevent dusting, loaded into trucks and hauled by a trucking contractor to a fill area in the country.

To collect the fly ash in a dry state in the proposed silos would require extensive additions to the present equipment. The existing Zeta fly ash handling systems for Units 1 and 2 would be retained up to the water jet exhausters. Here the ash from each unit would be discharged into a transfer hopper in a dry state. The present water jet exhausters would provide a vacuum up to this point with the water from the exhausters going into the existing sump and pumped to the ash basin. A single line from each of the two transfer hoppers would carry the fly ash to the silos as shown on Chart III, page 20.

Units 3 and 4 would require less rearrangement and less additional equipment. The existing pneumatic fly ash handling system would be merged into a riser at the silos. At the top of the silos there would be three double swing gates, by means of which the ash from any of the three lines could discharge into either of the two 250 ton silos. In case of future fly ash sale, this would permit us to segregate the various ranges of carbon fly ash. The vacuum to pull the ash to the silos would be produced by three water jet exhausters located near the top of the silos. These exhausters would require a higher water pressure than

10

is now available and therefore, raw water
booster pumps would have to be installed.
The water from these exhausters would discharge by gravity to the ash basin through
two of the present ash lines. The fly ash
would be moistened in dustless unloaders at
the bottom of the silos, discharged into
trucks and hauled to a fill area.

A large ravine, called Plot 1, located a
short hauling distance from the plant, was
chosen as this fill area. This plot is the
best of several studied in the vicinity of
the plant and is well situated for disposal
of ash by truck. The nearest neighbors
would be protected from any dusting by
either a hillside or woodland. Approximately 225 acres of land would have to be
purchased to secure the ravine. Most of the
land is low grade woodland, although a small
farm is included in the area which would
have to be acquired. At the present ash
collection rate, at least 28 years ash storage is available in this plot.

Should a breakdown develop in the silo
system, fly ash could still be pumped to the
present ash basin using existing equipment.
The bottom ash would continue to be disposed
of as it is now.

The details of Scheme 2 are shown on Table
IV, page 15. Although the installation of
silos would be best suited to the sale of
fly ash should a market be developed, the
high operating expense and low return of
this scheme make it less desirable than
pumping to the Island at this time.

VI.   TRUCKING FROM ASH BASIN TO PLOT 1 - SCHEME 3

This scheme would permit continuing the existing method of pumping all ash to the present ash basin.   There would be no additional equipment required nor change in present operation.   A trucking contractor would be given the job of removing the ash from the basin and hauling it to a fill area, such as Plot 1 described above.   An estimated 25 years' storage would be available under this scheme where both fly and bottom ash are trucked.

As shown on Table V, page 16, the $50,000 initial cost of the job is for the purchase of land and construction of a small dike. This is the lowest of any of the schemes on the basis of first cost.   However, the annual operating expense is the highest due to the high hauling charge of $0.70 per ton. If uses could be developed for appreciable amounts of run-of-pond ash in the basin, this scheme would be more competitive to Schemes 1 and 2 on a cost basis.

The ash from the basin contains considerable moisture which could cause excessive spillage while being hauled to Plot 1.   This possible public nuisance factor along with the higher annual cost removes this scheme from further consideration.

VII.   OTHER SCHEMES STUDIED

Several other methods of ash disposal were studied and discarded because they were either uneconomical or impractical.   One of

12

these methods was a scheme to raise the
dikes of the present basin by using a tail-
ings disposal method. This method is used
by several mining companies for building up
large disposal banks from material separated
from various ores. With this scheme, the
present ash basin would be encircled by pipe
lines, and as the area filled, fly ash and
bottom ash which would be deposited near the
dikes would be used to build up higher dikes
or spoil banks. This scheme is not recommended due to its high cost, its question-
able dike strength, and the relatively short
storage life in this area.

Another plan studied was one in which the
ash would be pumped from the plant to the
south area. This area is located downriver
from the present ash basin, as shown on
Chart I, page 18. It embraces a colony of
summer cottages which would have to be removed in order to provide the 4 years' storage estimated for this area. Dikes would be
required on three sides of this area, plus
new booster pumps, and considerable piping.
The cost of this scheme is estimated to be
$15,000 more per year than that for pumping
direct to the island. This fact, plus the
relatively short storage life of this area
and the possible adverse effect on public
relations due to the necessary eviction of
the cottage owners, makes this scheme unat-
tractive.

A.N.J.

N.B. Stubbs

12/28/53
ABC:EFG
M.E. Dept.

TABLE II

COST DETAILS

PUMP TO NORTH HALF OF TAU ISLAND - SCHEME 1a

Initial Cost

Dikes - Including clear- ing, grubbing & rip-rap		$430,000
Equipment		
Piping & Piping Changes	$65,000	
Electrical-Trans. line changes	5,000	
	$70,000	70,000
Total		$500,000

Operating Expense

Dike Charges ($430,000 ÷ 9-1/2 years)	45,400
Maintenance (Present $34,600 + 2% x $70,000)	36,000
Total	$ 81,400

Storage Life - 9-1/2 years

12/11/53
M.E. Dept.
ABC:EFG

TABLE III

COST DETAILS

PUMP TO SOUTH HALF OF TAU ISLAND - SCHEME 1b

Initial Cost

Dikes - Including clearing and grubbing land		$210,000
Equipment		
Piping	$63,000	
Pumps	51,000	
Electrical	16,000	
	$130,000	130,000
Total		$340,000

Operating Expense

Dike Charges ($210,000 ÷ 7 years)		$ 30,000
Operating and Maintenance		
Pump Energy	$ 10,400	
Maintenance (Present, $34,600 + 2% × $200,000)*	38,600	
	$ 49,000	49,000
Total		$ 79,000

Storage Life - 7 years

12/11/53
M.E. Dept.
ABC:EFG

* Includes $70,000 from Scheme 1a.

TABLE IV

COST DETAILS

TRUCKING FROM SILOS TO PLOT 1 - SCHEME 2

Initial Cost

Land and Dikes		$ 50,000
Silo System		365,000
Total		$415,000

Operating Expense

Land and Dike Charges

($50,000 ÷ 28 years)		$ 1,800
Operating and Maintenance		
Labor	$ 8,400	
Energy	4,100	
Hauling (175,000 tons × $.45/ton)	79,000	
Maintenance	33,500	
	$125,000	125,000
Total		$126,800

Storage Life - 28 years

12/11/53
M.E. Dept.
ABC:EFG

TABLE V

COST DETAILS

TRUCKING FROM PRESENT ASH BASIN TO PLOT 1 –
SCHEME 3

Initial Cost

Land and Dikes	$50,000
Total	$50,000

Operating Expense

Land & Dike Charges ($50,000 ÷ 25 years)		$ 2,000
Operation and Maintenance		
Hauling Cost (200,000 × $.705/ton)	$141,000	
Maintenance	34,600	
	$175,600	175,600
Total		$177,600

Storage Life – 25 years

12/11/53
M.E. Dept.
ABC:EFG

TABLE VI

ASH COLLECTION

	Tons/Year of Ash Collected		
	Units No. 1 & 2	Units No. 3 & 4	Total
Fly Ash – Electrostatic Collectors	25,000	60,000	85,000
Mechanical Collectors	80,000	10,000	90,000
Total Fly Ash	105,000	70,000	175,000
Bottom Ash –	17,000	8,000	25,000
Total Ash Collected	122,000	78,000	200,000

12/11/53
M.E. Dept.
ABC:EFG

QUALITY CHECK OF THE CLUTCH GEAR

REPORT SITUATION

THIS REPORT is one part of a continuing test to determine acceptability of a particular part. The writer is responsible for both this and the continuing project. His results are checked and approved before they are reported. Some readers are in the department; others are in the departments responsible for the quality of the gear. (Total pages—3.)

FORMAT

The format is interesting because it shows the value of side heads even in a short report. Note how the reverse indentation of heads makes them stand out clearly.

The original was typed on a typewriter that had no lower case, so the main heads appeared to have less important typographical treatment than the subheads, which were underlined. The reverse indentation saved the situation.

The report had no table of contents because it is short and the arrangement is customary.

PREFATORY MATERIAL

Readers, writer, and other people connected with the project are shown at the end. The occasion—i.e., an assignment—is shown both in the heading and in the "requested by" line at the end.

INTRODUCTION

The introductory material is contained in the identifying part name and number and under the two heads "assignment" and "purpose." The former connects this report to the general project and hence is background material. The latter states the problem—i.e., the purpose of the project, not that of the report. It would have been better to have

ALPHA DIVISION   Progress Report
METALLURGICAL DEPARTMENT   No. 4

Assignment No. 40-36

TITLE: Quality Check of the Clutch Gear.

PART NAME   Alpha Clutch Gear   PART NUMBER   1314646

ASSIGNMENT: A monthly check of the metallurgical quality of the clutch gear.

PURPOSE :   To determine the quality over an extended period of time and
(PROBLEM)   provide information on the part.

CONCLUSIONS:
             1. The gear did not meet the metallurgical specifications for
                 this part.

             2. The case was totally absent on the cone and needle bearing.

             3. Hardness of the cone and needle bearing was one point
                 Rockwell C below the specified hardness of 50 to 56
                 Rockwell C.

             4. The cause and effects of the absence of case and low hard-
                 ness of cone and needle bearing were outlined in Progress
                 Report Number 2 of Assignment No. 40-36.

PROCEDURE: One finished gear, scrapped for a dimensional defect, was
             examined in the Metallurgical Laboratory. The gear was examined
             for material analysis, case and core hardness, microstructure
             of the case and core, and toughness under a hammer test. This
             gear represents January production.

RESULTS AND
DISCUSSION: Laboratory Requisition No. 55153
             Chemical Analysis:

	C	MN	NI	Cr	Mo	Si
SAE 1340H						
Specified	.35-	1.46-	.25	.20	.06	.18-
Check Range	.47	2.04	Max.	Max.	Max.	.37
Observed	.41	1.54	.17	.08	.04	.19

said here that one gear only had been checked in the test being reported. The reader does not know this vital fact until the section headed "procedure."

The entire treatment of procedure is given after the conclusions, as is customary in short reports. In a short report the practice of leaving procedure out of the introduction is perfectly good—the reader doesn't have to look very far to find the procedure if he is curious as to the nature of the check made.

No order of reporting is given. The report is short, the side heads quickly show the order, and this order is always used in this department. But notice that the order of tests listed under "procedure" becomes the order of parts under "results and discussion."

CONCLUSION

No introductory sentence is used here—nor after any other head in the entire report. Consistency is the rule. The conclusions are in the standard position—just after the introduction. The list form is helpful.

The conclusions are in language that is intelligible to the non-specialist. Even a reader who does not know what "Rockwell" is can understand that the part was not hard enough.

The conclusions are not classified as to general and specific, but the first one listed *is* the general conclusion. The last one is not a conclusion at all and normally would be a "note." The writer's justification is obvious—listing it here made sure this vital information would not be overlooked.

The two actual specific conclusions (2 and 3) are not keyed to the body of the report, nor in the same order as the parts of the body. Keying is not essential in a report this short.

Assign. 40-36
Pr. Rep. No. 4

(Results and Discussion continued)

HARDNESS: Alpha Specification No. 13

			Rockwell C
SPECIFIED:			50-56
OBSERVED:	CASE:	Needle Bearing	49-50
		Cone	49-50
		Teeth	54-55
		Racer Bearing	50-50
		Barrel	51-52
		Spline	53-54
		Pilot End	51-52
	CORE:	Pilot End	51-52

MICROEXAMINATION:

The case was martensite with medium low ammonia effect. The core was mainly martensite.

CASE DEPTH:

		Inches
Specified		.005-.010
Observed:	Teeth	.009
	Cone	None
	Needle Bearing	None

HAMMER TEST:

The gear was examined for toughness. It was subjected to a hammer test with a three-pound hammer. The gear exhibited good toughness as five heavy blows were required to break out a tooth.

HEAT TREATMENT:

Carbonitride - Number 5 Surface Combustion Furnace
    Temperature - 1350-1500-1500 °F
    Time - 6 Minute Push, - 1 Hr. 54 minutes total time
    Atmosphere:
        Rx Generator Gas - 900-1000 CFH
        Natural Gas   75 CFH
        Ammonia   15 CFH

DEVELOPING SECTIONS

The two sections—"procedure" and "results and discussion"—have heads, but no other organizational elements. The assumption is that no one except specialists will consult the body of the report. The order of "results and discussion" is the same as that of the tests listed under "procedure."

Note that because the subsection "heat treatment" is not accounted for anywhere, it becomes puzzling. Only those in the department will know why it is there. Probably it is data concerning the treatment this gear received in its manufacture. This defect is immaterial because of the premise that only specialists—that is, people in the department—will read the body.

DATA

Procedures used to obtain data are merely named. The departmental readers know the steps in the procedures and know the writer is competent to perform them. Those outside the department assume that the department knows what it is doing. No unusual features are involved. Some procedure is given at the point of use—under "hammer test." It had to be given because the test is of a nature that cannot be standardized.

The data are tabulated or listed where possible. An illustration identifies the parts tested.

ILLUSTRATIONS

The report makes extensive use of lists and tables.

ACKNOWLEDGMENTS

There are no acknowledgments other than the prefatory "requested by" and "approved by."

40-36 Pr. Rep. 4

(Results and Discussion continued)

Heat Treatment:

Quench	-S-7 oil at 125°F - 150°F
Draw	-Vertical Draw Furnace -Time at heat - 40 minutes -Total time in furnace - 2 Hrs. 25 Min.

Copies to: Messrs.   R. T. Griffen
                                H. B. Richards
                                W. C. Browne
                                R. J Rogers
                                B. D. Clark
                                H. J. Jamieson
                                File

Requested by _B. J. Banks_ Date_____ Reported by _O. T. Ott_

Assigned to _O. T. Ott_ Date _____ Approved by _J. F. King_

                        Date _____

VOLTAGE BREAKDOWN TEST

REPORT SITUATION

THIS IS a semi-routine report situation to answer a specific question. Like most laboratories, this one performs a service function for other departments. Hence some of the readers may not be in this technical field (Total pages—1½.)

FORMAT

The report was typed (single space) and then reproduced. It used marginal heads, lower case underlined, on a line by themselves.

PREFATORY MATERIAL

Here prefatory matter consists only of the signature plus the material which follows "to," "approved," and "observers."

INTRODUCTION

The two opening sentences manage to give the significance of the test, state the specific problem, and give the general procedure (items tested plus kind of test). There is no order of reporting because the report is brief and the sections are in a standard order.

CONCLUSION

The conclusions consist of one specific result and the conclusion that nothing can be inferred.

DEVELOPING SECTIONS

The first developing section reports the procedure used throughout the test. The position is again the standard one for short memos; and curiously, because of the mention of procedure in the introduction, it corresponds to the practice used in three-level reports when the procedure is the same throughout a project, as described on page 85. Both this section and that called "Results" depend on the heading to serve as the opening or topic idea.

IOTA DIVISION
ENGINEERING LABORATORY

Report No. 000-C

To   Q. Hogan   Date   July 31, 1954
      James Island Approved   *F.R. Law*

Observer   J.P. Bartlett

Subject   VOLTAGE BREAKDOWN TEST ON FISH
           PAPER AND MICA SLOT INSULATION IN
           MOTOR ARMATURES, e.g. 1904976

Introduction

Both fish paper and mica have been used as slot insulators in motor armatures for various applications. To make a comparison of the two materials, seventeen 1904976 armatures were furnished, six with fish paper and eleven with mica, for a voltage breakdown test with 750 volts.

Conclusions

One armature from each of the two groups failed, but neither failure was clearly shown to have been through the slot insulation material. No definite preference is clearly indicated by the results of this single test.

Procedure

A commutator bar and the shaft of the armature were connected to the secondary terminals of a transformer. The primary of the transformer was excited by sixty cycle

DATA

Procedure appears in the "Results" section as well as earlier. So this brief report demonstrates the practice of giving procedure in the introduction, in an early section, and at the point of use!

ILLUSTRATIONS

None needed.

ACKNOWLEDGMENTS

None needed.

-2-

A. C. through a controlling resistor. Secondary voltage was increased at approximately 100 volts per second, to 750 volts, rms value, and sustained for one minute. Failure was indicated by the burning out of a fuse in the primary circuit.

Results

Of the six armatures having fish paper insulation, one failed. Likewise one failure occurred in the eleven armatures having mica insulation.

In an attempt to locate the failures, the commutators were isolated from the conductors by making a lathe cut through the conductors just behind the riser bars. The voltage test was applied to each commutator bar and all found to be all right. Each conductor was then tested until faults were located. Failure in the armature with fish paper insulation occurred between a lower conductor and the iron near the commutator end of slot. The slot insulator appeared to be too short or improperly placed longitudinally. The failure in the armature with mica insulation occurred in the same way but it was impossible to locate the exact spot due to unavoidable damage in removing the conductor.

The damaged armatures were inspected by the engineer in charge, Mr. A. B. Sharp, and then salvaged.

Joe P. Bartlett

Joe P. Bartlett

EXAMINATION OF $\frac{1}{8}$ IN. AND $\frac{3}{32}$ IN. ALLEN HEXAGONAL WRENCHES

REPORT SITUATION

BECAUSE a problem situation has developed, one department has requested help from another. A proposed test procedure involving routine methods is being submitted for approval. This report is from the same organization as the one on "Quality Check of the Clutch Gear," page 348. A similar report will come out of this project later. Both will eventually be superseded by a final report. (Total pages—$\frac{1}{2}$.)

FORMAT

This is a variation of memo form, with most prefatory material at the end. The reverse indentation makes the heads stand out sharply.

PREFATORY MATERIAL

The heading at the top of the page, and the routing and other information at the bottom, show the readers, writer, and occasion for writing. Titles or job assignments are not shown because they are known to all concerned.

INTRODUCTION

The introductory function is taken care of by the subject line and the section headed "Problem." No order of reporting is used for three reasons. First, the report is short. Second, a glance at the heads shows what is covered. Third, the order is expected—in this department of this company, these heads customarily appear in this order.

As is very frequent in short reports, no procedure is sketched in the introduction. It is given in full immediately following.

GAMMA COMPANY
METALLURGICAL DEPARTMENT
RESEARCH AND DEVELOPMENT SECTION

PROJECT NO. 703

PROPOSED PROJECT

SUBJECT:

Examination of 1/8 inch and 3/32 inch
Allen Hexagonal Wrenches

PROBLEM:

These tools are twisting under normal application in Factory 11, Department 53
Grinding Room. They were obtained from
the Omega Company and are to be investigated for the cause of their poor performance.

PROCEDURE:

This trouble has been encountered only
with these wrenches currently purchased
from the Omega Company. Three wrenches
were selected as representative of the
group of failures submitted by Mr. D. F.
Backus of the Tool Research Department.

A photograph will be made of these three
wrenches which will then be subjected to
the following tests: hardness, chemical
analysis, and microexamination for structure and quality of heat treatment.

DISCUSSION:

The hardness of this type wrench giving
good service ranges from 49-53 Rockwell C.

1

CONCLUSION

There is no concluding section because not enough has yet been done on the project. Notice, however, that one preliminary result has been given under the heading of "Discussion." It is placed there because it is purely preliminary. (Discussion is a catch-all head under which people put things they don't know what else to do with.)

DEVELOPING SECTIONS

There are no sections to organize—the report has no body other than the "procedure" section.

DATA

Since the project is simply being proposed, there are yet no data.

ILLUSTRATIONS

None needed.

ACKNOWLEDGMENTS

None are needed except the prefatory "originated by."

These twisted wrenches had a hardness
range from 43-46 Rockwell C.

COPIES TO:

B. R. Brick	L. A. Evans	C. H. Darling
A. J. Miles	G. O. Ott	E. T. Cove
K. R. Alfred	H. H. Johnson	George P. Jones
		File

Originated by L. A. Evans   Date: 10-27-50
Reported by George P. James
Assigned to J. P. Jones   Date: 10-27-50
Approved by *S. F. King*

Date: 11-9-50

ANALYSIS OF POTATOES

REPORT SITUATION

THIS IS a routine laboratory test to sample a lot of potatoes. (Total pages—1½.)

FORMAT

Primarily tabular.

PREFATORY MATERIAL

Here are the usual "to" and "from" items, but no full signature. Signature and approval *initials* were on the second page.

The prefatory material of the next report is discussed on page 370.

INTRODUCTION

A single form sentence introduced the table—the problem was to analyze the potatoes.

The introduction of the next report is discussed on page 374.

CONCLUSION

No attempt is made to conclude anything about the lot—the recipient of the report will have this responsibility.

The conclusion of the next report is discussed on page 378.

DEVELOPING SECTIONS

No problem of organization is involved.

Developing sections of the next report are discussed on page 382.

CENTRAL LABORATORIES, PSI CORPORATION

INTERLABORATORY SERVICE MEMORANDUM

TO	John Sadler	IN	PD	DATE June 3, 1954
FROM	Larry Packer	IN	AC	PROJECT NO. PD-4947
SUBJECT	Analysis of Potatoes			NOTEBOOK NO. 10,31,28
				REQUEST DATE

9 ___ samples of ___ Potatoes ___

have been analyzed for the constituents listed below with the following results:

SAMPLES	CONSTITUENTS				
	Wt. Potatoes in sple. gms.	Total Solids	Reducing Sugar as Dextrose	Reducing Sugar d.b.	
	%	%	%	%	%
Potato Sampling Study					
From the same lot of potatoes the following samples were drawn:					
1 Small Potato	106.7	27.1	0.49	1.81	
1 Medium Potato	161.8	26.6	0.62	2.33	
1 Large Potato	250.0	23.3	0.83	3.57	
3 Small Potatoes	294	24.9	0.87	3.49	
3 Medium Potatoes	482	25.2	0.79	3.14	
3 Large	697	22.4	0.61	2.72	
9 Composite	1395	24.7	0.70	2.83	
(3 Small +					
(3 Medium +					
(3 Large					
12 Composite					
(4 Small +	2278	26.0	0.71	2.73	
(4 Medium +					
(4 Large					
Previous Anal		22.1		1.27	

Total Solids - Sand solids with final drying in vacuum oven for 16 hours at 70°C.
Reducing Sugar - Alcohol extraction, clarified with barium hydroxide and zinc
   sulfate. Sugars determined by Somogyi Titration.
Method of Sampling - All except the single potatoes were quartered and then
   ground through a meat grinder. After mixing a subsample of 150 or 200
   gms was blended in the Waring blender with an equal weight of water

NOTE: All results reported on "As Received" basis unless otherwise noted.

cc:

DATA AND ILLUSTRATIONS

The data are in tabular form, with notes to explain the method.

Procedure is briefly given in footnotes to the table. Such a note would be added only to identify one of several standard methods, or if there were variations in the method, or to confirm that it was standard.

Data and illustrations of the next report are discussed on pages 382 and 384.

ACKNOWLEDGMENTS

None used or needed.

CENTRAL LABORATORIES, PSI CORPORATION

INTERLABORATORY SERVICE MEMORANDUM

TO	John Sadler	IN	PD	DATE June 3,.1954	
FROM	Larry Packer	IN	AC	PROJECT NO. PD-4947	
SUBJECT	Analysis of Potatoes			NOTE BOOK NO. 10,31,28	
				REQUEST DATE	

___9___   samples of ____Potatoes____

have been analyzed for the constituents listed below with the following results:

	CONSTITUENTS				
SAMPLES					
	%	%	%	%	%

Methods:

    Method of Sampling (continued) –

        The single potatoes were cubed and blended in Waring Blender with an equal weight of water.

        Single analyses were performed on these 1:1 slurries.

NOTE: All results reported on "As Received" basis unless otherwise noted.

cc:

H. George	/s/ K. Johnson	/s/ L. P.
P. St. John	K. Johnson	Larry Packer

Group Two
Reports Giving Information

THE GEOLOGY OF OHIO

REPORT SITUATION

THIS IS a student report. It is suitable for submitting both to the technical department and to the English teacher. Hence it has the characteristics of a three-level report. In fact, it follows the basic pattern almost exactly. (Total pages—16.)

The report situation of the next report is described on page 390.

FORMAT

The report was typed, single space. Heads are all capitals, main ones centered, and subheads in a side position. It was bound in a cardboard cover. The original report was double-spaced on one side only.

The format and report situation of the next report are discussed on page 390.

[*This page represents the cover*]

REPORT ON THE GEOLOGY OF OHIO
AND ITS ECONOMIC MINERAL
RESOURCES

Submitted by
George Parr

Report on

THE GEOLOGY OF OHIO AND ITS
ECONOMIC MINERAL RESOURCES

Suggested for
ENGLISH 900

Submitted to
Mr. Arnold

By
George Parr
Student

December 8, 1953

PREFATORY MATERIAL

Prefatory material is on the title page and in the letter of transmittal. The former briefly gives the name and status of the author, names the reader, and shows the occasion (for English 900). The latter gives greater detail on:

The Report Situation
> Occasion—an assignment
> Why this subject was selected (second half of paragraph two)

The Reader and Use
> How the report is useful to him, or good for him. (First part of paragraph two, last part of last sentence of paragraph two, and last paragraph.)

The form of this letter is standard semi-block.

Prefatory material and report situation of the next report are on page 390.

2606 Barnes Road
Phi, Ohio
December 8, 1953

Mr. Howard L. Arnold,
Department of English
Beta University
Phi, Ohio

Dear Sir:

In accordance with your request for the
Fall Semester, I have undertaken and com-
pleted my assigned report on the Geology of
Ohio and Its Economic Mineral Resources.

This report was written with the purpose
of giving the reader a minimum amount of
knowledge basic to the understanding of the
historical and physical geology of Ohio and
of the natural resources that have resulted
from its geologic processes. It was noted
that there has been no recent publication
covering all the material presented and that
a knowledge of Ohio's geology has been found
essential to the understanding of the land
forms of the surface and the wealth of natural mineral resources that lie within and
beneath the mantle.

The report should give the reader at least
a basic knowledge of the geology and the
geologically-formed mineral resources of
economic value of the State of Ohio.

Respectfully yours,

George Parr

George Parr

TABLE OF CONTENTS

INTRODUCTION

The introduction opens directly with the purpose—no background was necessary to understand it, and the reader's interest is assumed. Next comes the order of reporting. There need be no heading of "scope," because the scope is clearly implied in the other two parts. For a comment on handling of the order of reporting, see "Developing Sections," below.

The introduction of the next report is discussed on page 398, the report situation on page 390.

I. INTRODUCTION

PURPOSE

This report concerns the geology of Ohio,
both physical and historical. The subject
is considered from the physical standpoint,
as evidenced by the surface land forms found
around us and by the layers of rocks and the
structure of their formations lying beneath
the mantle, and again from the historical
standpoint, from which the problem of the
succession of bedrock formations and glacial
surface remnants will be examined in a
chronological order. The report also deals
with the main economically valuable mineral
resources of the state that have resulted
from geologic processes.

ORDER OF PRESENTATION

First, the pertinent facts of the physical
geography of the state are presented, including the location, physiographic prov-
inces, and the topography of the state.

Second, then, is a background for a sketch
of the historical geology of Ohio. This
includes an introduction to geologic time,
followed by a history of the Paleozoic and
Cenozoic Eras, which alone are represented
by rock formations and surface phenomena
throughout the state.

Third, the physical geology is presented.
The bedrock geology is discussed first. An
explanation of sub-surface geology and a
table of Ohio's geological formations follow. The age, stratigraphic pattern, struc-

1

2

ture and distribution of strata, and the types of rocks found and their distribution are discussed.

The surface geology is explained next. This covers the pre-glacial landscape and the Teays River system. the glaciation of the state, and the effects that weathering has had on topography.

Fourth, the mineral resources, resulting from geologic processes and having economic value are discussed, and defined. The surface deposits are discussed first, followed by the sub-surface ones, on an individual basis, and their distribution and the economic value of deposits and features.

These areas are summarized in the next chapter.

CONCLUSION

Section II is a summary. If placed before the introduction, it would have been called an abstract. Note that it consists of five short paragraphs, each corresponding to one of the main developing sections of the report. Note also that it is not merely a collection of topic sentences, but gives concrete facts.

Taken together with the introduction, the summary gives a good quick picture of the subject of the report. On finishing it, the reader has the main facts. If he wishes more detail, he can continue reading.

The abstract and conclusion of the next report are discussed on pages 394 and 398, the report situation on page 390.

II. SUMMARY

Ohio is a state of low-rolling hills
formed mostly by the Continental-type glaciers that once covered the majority of the
area during the Pleistocene Epoch, or Ice
Age. The eastern half of the state forms a
part of that physiographic province known as
the Allegheny Plateau, and the western sector belongs to what is known as the Central,
or Interior Lowlands. Ohio is bounded on
the north by the glacier-created Lake Erie,
and by Michigan; on the west by Indiana; on
the south by Kentucky and West Virginia, and
on the east by Pennsylvania and West Virginia. The state is drained on the south
and east by the Ohio River and its many
tributaries, and on the north by numerous
streams flowing towards or into Lake Erie.

The geology of the state is represented by
the bedrock formations of the Paleozoic era
and by the glacial drift, lakes, and rivers
of the Pleistocene Epoch of the Cenozoic
Era. The bedrock is all sedimentary, and
was deposited when Ohio was at the bottom of
a shallow sea. Seven times the state was
submerged and later re-emerged as the area,
then within a gigantic trough of unstable
rocks, responded to the effects of gigantic
shifting forces acting within the earth.

The area has been only slightly tilted
from its original horizontal position and
the formations have a slight easterly dip.
This tilting has caused erosion to level the
bedrock and produce a banded, north-south
pattern in the rocks of the state. Along

4

the western border of the state there is a
long, low structural arch of rocks known
locally as the Cincinnati Arch. It was the
upward thrust of this arch during the
Ordovician Period that raised and tilted the
rest of the state's formations toward the
east.

Much of the mantle is the result of continental glaciers such as those presently covering Greenland. The glaciers came down
from the north, swept away pre-existing
mantle, smoothed the landscape, and deposited a great amount of glacial drift. They
blocked and changed the old northward flowing drainage pattern of the Teays River
system of the state, formed the Ohio River,
and in their retreat left the Great Lakes as
one evidence of their existence.

The mineral resources of economic value
resulting from sub-surface geology are coal,
petroleum and natural gas, limestone and
dolomite, sandstone and conglomerate, gyp-
sum, brine and rocksalt, shale and marl.
Those with a surface origin are sand and
gravel, peat, coal formation clays, water,
and molding sands.

DEVELOPING SECTIONS

The order of the main sections is a logical one, from the general to the particular—each is necessary for the understanding of the one which follows.

Section V has been selected as an example of a developing section of this report. Note that it opens by implying the purpose of the section (to tell of physical geology) and specifically naming the two main divisions of the section (bedrock and surface geology). These are named in the same order in which they are discussed.

Note that in the order of reporting in the main introduction, each chapter is analyzed. Because the summary follows, it would have been best simply to name the section topics in the introduction. The material now there, placed at the openings of the appropriate sections, would have served to give a more explicit idea of the contents of each section than do the present openings.

Within Section V, the order of subsections can be considered spatial—from the "bottom" up, or chronological—in order of time of deposit. The same is true of the first subsection. The second subsection (Surface Geology) is more or less chronological.

The section does not end—it just stops. The appropriate section of the Summary, repeated here and suitably introduced, would have made a more effective close.

Developing sections of the next report are discussed on page 404, the report situation on page 390.

DATA

The data are factual. Their authority rests on the bibliography.

Data of the next report are discussed on page 404, the report situation on page 390.

V. PHYSICAL GEOLOGY OF OHIO

Physical geology is represented by the bedrock, or sub-surface geology, and by the surface geology, represented by the glacier-transported mantle and by the evidences of the remains of glaciers that once covered the majority of the state, and also by the topography and the changes wrought in it by the work of erosion.

BEDROCK, OR SUB-SURFACE GEOLOGY

Beneath the mantle of the State of Ohio are found rocks deposited as a result of sedimentation of mud and limy ooze in a shallow sea, and of sand along the seashore. These sediment-lain rocks, formed during the Paleozoic Era, make up the strata of the bedrock geology.

Age, Stratigraphic Pattern, and Structure of Rock Strata: The rocks lying beneath the mantle are all Paleozoic, and range from Ordovician to Permian. Cambrian and Pre-Cambrian rocks are present, but lie far beneath the Ordovician strata that outcrop on the surface. The strike, or direction along the longitudinal axis of the strata, is north-south. The strata have what is known as a banded pattern. This is caused by the almost flat-lying rocks dipping very gently toward the east. The dip is the direction the formation takes, perpendicular to the strike, as it angles into the ground.

Along the Indiana line, or western border of the state, runs a long structural domal feature known locally as the Cincinnati

ILLUSTRATIONS

As the last page of the Table of Contents shows, four illustrations are used. One is cut into the text, as shown; the other three are in the appendix position. The one in the text immediately follows the mention of it. Note that though the text has described the formations, the illustration gives a much more concrete idea than did words.

The illustration shows the value of a sketch in relating parts to a whole and in identification. It is placed in the text at the exact point of use.

The other illustrations are not used or referred to in the text. This is a defect.

Illustrations in the next report are discussed on page 404, the report situation on page 390.

ACKNOWLEDGMENTS

A simple alphabetical bibliography makes acknowledgments. It deviates from the standard recommended in this book in not showing the publisher of books or the place published. The practice here is not unusual, however.

Acknowledgments of the next report are discussed on page 406, the report situation on page 390.

Arch. It is part of a long anticlinal
ridge running from Northern Alabama into
Canada. This arch was pushed up originally
sometime during the Ordovician Period, tilting the strata slightly and causing a
greater amount of material to be deposited
in the eastern part of the state. A later
up-thrusting tilted all the rock formations
of the state and caused the eastward dip.

Illustration No. 1 represents a cross-
section of the stratigraphy of the state
along the 40th Parallel and shows the dip of
the rocks towards the east.

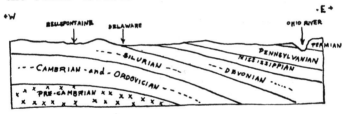

Geologic Profile of Ohio Drawn along 40th
Parallel, Illustrating Stratigraphy

Distribution of Strata Throughout State:
As one travels from west to east anywhere in
Ohio he finds the rock strata becoming pro-
gressively younger and younger. In the
Cincinnati area the rocks are Ordovician in
age and cover an area which includes Brown,
Clermont, Hamilton, Adams, Butler, Warren,
Clinton, Highland, Greene, Montgomery,
Preble, and Miami Counties.

Silurian rocks cover most of the western
one-third of the state, except for the
Ordovician strata in the southwest corner

10

and the two stripes of strata, one Devonian
and the other Mississippian, occurring in a
five-county area in the northwest corner of
the state.

Devonian strata occur on a north-south
line in the central sector of the state, and
also as outcrops east of Sandusky all along
the shore of Lake Erie. Then again, there
is the circular band of Devonian strata in
the northwest corner of the state, and an
erosion remnant of Devonian rocks in the
Silurian strata at Bellefontaine, the highest point in the state.

The western limits of the Mississippian
strata are the Adams-Scioto county line in
the south up to the western half of Huron
County in the north, and the eastern limits
are from the eastern edge of Scioto County
in the south to the east-central edge of
Cuyahoga County in the north. Trumbull
County, along the Pennsylvania state line,
also contains mostly Mississippian strata.

The rest of the state, with the exception
of a five-county area along the West Virginia line, contains Pennsylvanian strata.
The five counties mentioned are Permian in
age.

Types of Rocks and Their Distribution:
General: The exposed bedrock of Ohio is
all sedimentary, made from deposits such as
clay, sand, calcareous ooze and mud, laid
down in shallow seas and later cemented to
form shale, sandstone, limestone, and
dolomite.

11

Specific: Limestone, $Ca(CO_3)$, and Dolomite, $CaMg(CO_3)_2$, are found in thick formations, particularly in the central and
western parts of the state. Shale, or so-
lidified mud, is most important in the
section just east of the middle of the
state, in the Mississippian Series, and
again in the area along the West Virginian
line that contains rocks of Permian age.
Sandstone and coal are found mainly east of
the Mississippian rocks within the Pennsylvanian strata. Important sandstones and
minor coal outcrops are also found in
Permian rocks.

SURFACE GEOLOGY

The Pre-Glacial Landscape: Before the in-
vasion of the three glaciers that covered
Ohio during the Pleistocene, the area was,
as now, in the process of erosion. Throughout the Mesozoic and Cenozoic Eras the land
was eroded as fast as it was uplifted, losing much of the bedrock of the Paleozoic and
forming a dissected type of topography such
as is found in humid climates.

The Teays River System: The greater part
of the state, prior to the glaciers, lay in
the basin of a great river known now as the
Teays. The Teays rose in the Piedmont belt
of Virginia and flowed north across West
Virginia. For a distance it followed much
the same course as the present Ohio River,
but just east of Portsmouth it swung northward, eventually leaving the state near the
present city of Fort Wayne, Indiana. Por-

12

tions of the valley of this great river can
still be seen in certain sections of the
state, but the river itself was destroyed by
the first advance of the glacial ice.

Glaciation: The glaciation caused by the
three ice sheets mentioned earlier covers an
era extending from Hocking to Hamilton
County on the South, northward to Holmes
County, then eastward across the Allegheny
Plateau to the Pennsylvanian line just north
of Jefferson County. The glaciation lasted
approximately 975,000 years. The ice
smoothed the landscape and radically changed
the drainage system of Ohio to the present
westward-flowing Ohio River with its many
southward flowing tributaries, and in its
northward retreat it left much morainal
material and also scooped out the basin of
the present-day Great Lakes.

Effects of Weathering on Topography: The
weathering of the State of Ohio, in the gla-
ciated areas, has not had time to dissect
the topography in most places beyond the
youthful stage of broad flat uplands which
are relatively undissected and small, narrow
river valleys.

In the non-glaciated area of the Allegheny
Plateau, which is higher in elevation than
the western portions of the state, the work
of erosion has been left undisturbed for a
longer period of time and the land is dissected into an area of narrow divides and
deep valleys.

BIBLIOGRAPHY

Emmons, William Harvey, The Principles of
    Economic Geology, pp. 1-7.
Gambs, Gerard C., "Salt Resources," Ohio's
    Mineral Resources, Vol. XV, No. 3, Septem-
    ber, 1946.
Haas, William H., "Influences of Glaciation
    in Ohio," Geographical Society of Phila-
    delphia, Vol. 15, pp. 22-24, 1917.
Hyde, J. E., "Geology of Camp Sherman Quad-
    rangle," Geological Survey of Ohio, Fourth
    series, bulletin No. 23, 1921.
Lamborn, Raymond E., "Geology of Jefferson
    County," Geological Survey of Ohio. Fourth
    series, bulletin 25, pp. 9-19, 1930.
Newberry, J. S., "Geological Relations &
    Structure of Ohio," Geological Survey of
    Ohio, Vol. I, pp. 50-131, 1873.
Peattie, Roderick, "Surface Features and
    Soils," Geological Survey of Ohio, Fourth
    series, bulletin 27, pp. 3-11, 1923.
Stout, Wilber, "Mineral Resources of Ohio,"
    Geological Survey of Ohio, Fourth series,
    information Circular No. 1, 1946.
Wenger, George, "The Story of Ohio's Mineral
    Resources," Ohio Division of Geological
    Survey, pp. 1-14, Information Circular
    No. 9.
Wright, Alfred J., Economic Geography of
    Ohio, pp. 2-6, 1953.

ECONOMICS OF AUTOMOTIVE GEAR STEELS

REPORT SITUATION

THIS REPORT was originally written to be presented at a meeting of a professional society. It is by experts to others in the field not so well acquainted with the specific application under discussion. Reports meant to be read aloud are also common in any business or professional organization. (Total pages—34.)

The next report situation is described on page 414.

FORMAT

The report was bound in a fibre cover. It was mimeographed. Main heads were centered, subheads in the side position.

Because the report was meant to be read aloud, no table of contents or list of illustrations was provided.

Format of the next report is discussed on page 414.

PREFATORY MATERIAL

In the written report prefatory material is found in two places. The title page gives the authors and their affiliation, the readers, and the place of presentation. Section IV (the last of the read report) contains half a page of acknowledgments to people who helped provide information. The position at the end is suitable—thanks certainly had to be given—but imagine a speech starting with such a listing!

The acknowledgments, not shown here, listed name and company of each person who helped.

Although this is all the prefatory material now in the report, the speaker was of course introduced. What was said about him then was also prefatory.

Prefatory material and the report situation in the next report are discussed on page 414.

[*This page represents the cover*]

ECONOMICS OF AUTOMOTIVE GEAR STEELS
AND THEIR HEAT TREATMENT

ECONOMICS OF AUTOMOTIVE GEAR STEELS
AND THEIR HEAT TREATMENT

BY

V. H. Munroe
H. B. Bond
R. E. Tunney

Alpha Division
Beta Corporation

SUMMER MEETING

UPSILON SOCIETY

Nutown, Nebraska, June 7, 1950

ABSTRACT

The quick view is given by an abstract, here called a digest. It abstracts the introduction in two paragraphs, and then devotes a paragraph to each of the developing sections of the report.

The abstract is an example of the "mixed" type. Most of it is informative—it summarizes the main facts. The last two paragraphs are indicative—they simply tell the general nature of the facts.

If you will read the introduction immediately after the abstract, you will find that it seems to cover the same ground, especially at the end. Such repetition often bothers students of report techniques.

It won't seem wrong, however, if you consider the principle of use. This digest was designed so that it could be read and understood quite apart from the report. It is a short report on the same subject. Hence overlapping is necessary.

The next use of an abstract is on page 436.

ECONOMICS OF AUTOMOTIVE GEAR STEELS

AND THEIR HEAT TREATMENT

By

V. H. Munroe, H. B. Bond, R. E. Tunney

Alpha Division, Beta Corporation

DIGEST

In satisfying the requirements of economy, the automotive engineer must specify steels and heat treatments with careful considera- tion of design, quality, material, and proc- essing. These factors are closely related and must be examined simultaneously when determining manufacturing methods for new applications or altering present operations.

The selection of steel specifications and heat treatments should be made on the basis of insuring satisfactory results with proper economy.

The factors influencing the selection of a
steel specification for an automotive gear
application are availability, cost, machinability, heat treating qualities, performance properties, and uniformity.

The heat treatment for a gear must supply
the required quality and uniformity demanded
by the application. Items affecting economy
are equipment, labor, operating, and maintenance costs. Additional factors to be considered are scrap, rework, expense of idling
equipment during down time, and control
cost.

Alpha Division practice in the application
of gear steels and heat treatments is described.

The results of a survey of automotive
manufacturers are shown in tabular form;

these tables show a comparison of steels and heat treatments used by the various companies on rear axle, transmission (conventional, semiautomatic, and automatic), and flywheel ring gears.

INTRODUCTION

The first paragraph is devoted to the importance of the subject. Next come eight paragraphs of general principles. In the last paragraph, the second sentence limits the purpose of the report, which is implied rather than explicitly stated. The remainder of the paragraph gives the order of discussion.

The introduction and report situation of the next report are discussed on page 414.

CONCLUSION

The conclusion used here is the simplest type of ending—the last sentence of the final section (excluding acknowledgments) is so framed as to mention the total subject: "This comparison must be assumed as representing economy in the selection of steels and heat treatment."

The final section is not shown. The conclusion and report situation of the next report are discussed on page 414.

INTRODUCTION

The objective of the engineer is to design and specify a gear for an application that will produce the required quality at the lowest possible cost. The proper selection of steel and the correct processing of this material to produce the desired properties and accuracy, taking into consideration the ease of fabrication, are absolute necessities for true economy.

The economics of automotive gears is influenced by design, quality, material selection, and processing cost.

The design of a gear and the demands of operation are important factors influencing economy in the selection of steel and the heat treatment. The demand for quietness of operation of the modern automobile has made it necessary to go to great lengths in se-

-2-

curing steels of adequate machinability to
meet gear tooth finish requirements, and at
the same time heat treating operations have
been improved to secure the required dimensional uniformity.

It is well to remember that design is important in its influence on the processing
costs and should be such that the gear can
be produced economically within necessary
inspection limits at the required production
rate.

Gear quality or limits of manufacture influence the economy. Such tolerances are
not always indicated on the blueprint.
Using the blueprint as a guide it is sometimes necessary for manufacturing departments to hold closer tolerances than indicated by the design. In applications where
the operating conditions are critical, it is

the tendency to hold to more exacting limits; as a result, the cost is generally increased. It is assumed that with any design or operating condition, the required quality is maintained by the proper amount of inspection.

The cost of the steel for a gear is an important item in the total cost of the part. From one composition to another, the amount and type of alloy generally determines the difference in cost. Inherent qualities of each steel such as uniformity of hardenability, distortion characteristics, and machinability must be considered at the same time that the cost is considered. Availability of a material and the ability of a mill to divert off-heats are important considerations in selecting a steel.

-4-

There are many steels covering a wide
range of hardenability available to choose
from for automotive gear applications.

A correctly applied steel must be capable
of satisfying all requirements of the application taking into consideration the variation in hardenability that must be expected.
This refers not only to properties that are
developed in the finished part but also to
properties that must be developed for processing needs.   The choice of a steel for a
specific gear application is made primarily
to furnish the required properties in the
finished part.   However, it is necessary to
specify a material that can be processed to
production requirements.

In the selection of a steel for a gear
application, it is necessary to consider the
processing characteristics.   The steel must
fit into available facilities, or savings

should justify the purchase of new equipment. The steel should satisfy the conditions of manufacture over the entire range
of properties that must be accepted under
the specification.

   This paper is divided into four parts.
The discussion is limited to the practice
used for rear axle, transmission (conventional, semiautomatic, and automatic), and
flywheel ring gears. In the first part,
economy in selection of a steel for automotive gear applications is discussed. In
the second part, factors influencing the
economics in the selection of heat treatments are presented. In the third part,
Alpha practice is outlined. The fourth part
of the paper includes the results of a survey of automotive gear steel and heat treatment practice. This survey includes data
from a major portion of producers of auto-

DEVELOPING SECTIONS

The order of the main sections is logical, from the general to specific applications. Part I discusses manufacturing factors, Part II heat treatment, Part III a specific practice of one organization, and Part IV practice at other organizations.

The section reproduced here—Part I of the report—shows how the technique for organizing the whole report is also used in the developing sections.

The first paragraph gives a general principle and its importance. Next the subject of this section is stated, implying the purpose will be to consider how manufacturing operations help determine whether a steel is economical. The phase under discussion is then broken into its parts, which are discussed in the order named.

The conclusion of the section is a simple ending, the last few words reminding us that we were discussing factors influencing economy.

The developing sections of the next report are discussed on page 416, the report situation on page 414.

DATA

Except for Part IV, data are based on the experience and authority of the writers. (Part IV tells briefly of a survey to get information on the practice of others.)

Data of the next report are discussed on page 416, the report situation on page 414.

ILLUSTRATIONS

The report contained twelve photographs. Eight were cut into the text at the point of discussion. The others were placed, four to a page, right after the page discussing them. Reference to them followed this pattern: "The accompanying photographs show extremes of finish . . . obtained with Beta steel. Figure 1 shows a very good finish."

-6-

PART I

FACTORS INFLUENCING ECONOMY IN THE SELECTION OF AUTOMOTIVE GEAR STEELS

A steel should be selected because it ful-fills all requirements of an application at the lowest cost. The proper choice can be made only when the engineer understands all conditions of manufacture. The requirements are dictated by the design, application, and quality level. The normal variation in the steel must be taken into consideration.

Cost of a gear is made up of the steel cost plus the cost of manufacturing. It is not possible in a discussion of economy to view steel cost without considering effects upon subsequent manufacturing operations.

Characteristics of a steel that influence economy are availability, cost, machinabil-

When such a report is read, of course, the photographs are projected on a screen. Often, to supplement his words, the speaker points to what he means.

Eight tables were also used. They are grouped at the end of the report in the appendix position. The method of reference is shown in Part I. In reading a report aloud such tables may be projected on a screen or passed around on separate sheets of paper.

Illustrations of the next report are discussed on page 416, the report situation on page 414.

ACKNOWLEDGMENTS

These were prefatory in nature. (See above.)

Acknowledgments of the next report are discussed on page 416, the report situation on page 414.

ity, heat treating qualities, performance
properties, and uniformity.

Availability

A steel must be available in sufficient
quantities to fulfill production requirements, and the limits of manufacture must
satisfy the demands of the application.
Critical requirements caused by design or
quality demands may make it necessary to
restrict the specification and thus increase
the cost. If a particular specification has
little use, it may be difficult to secure
required quantities with suitable delivery.

There are many steels covering a wide
range of properties available to choose from
for automotive gear applications. The survey shows considerable variation among manufacturers in the selection of steel for each

-8-

application. (See Table 1, page 27, Table
IV, page 30, Table VII, page 33, and Table
VIII, page 34.)

Cost

The base cost of the steel, in comparison
with that of equivalent grades, is an important consideration in the selection. Any
increased cost of one grade over another
must be warranted by a necessary quality
improvement or greater economy in processing. Justification of a steel on the basis
of decreased processing costs is often quite
difficult because of intangibles involved.
Items of cost in processing such as tools,
repairs, and scrap can be evaluated only if
adequate records are available for long
production runs.

Machinability

The steel selected must be capable of
being machined to quality requirements at
the specified production rate with a reasonable tool cost. Differences in inherent
machinability between one specification and
another should be considered before a choice
is made. If available annealing cycles are
inadequate for producing a structure with
the required machinability, sufficient decrease in steel cost must be present to allow for the purchasing of necessary
equipment.

Machinability is generally measured in
terms of surface finish and tool life. On
applications such as hypoid gears where excellent tooth surfaces are necessary, finish
is a controlling factor. Where surface
smoothness is readily obtained, as in the

shaving operations on transmission gears,
tool life is the important consideration.
In each case however, the tool cost is a
factor influencing economy.

Improvements in machinability that allow
reductions in labor through greater speeds
and feeds are most easily recognized. At
equivalent production rates and quality,
cost is affected only by tool life

Sometimes improved machinability justifies
the added cost of a sulfur addition. A sulfur addition may improve economy not only in
its desirable effect upon finish, but also
may allow the production of greater tooth
accuracy and less stress from machining.
Sulfur additions which have proved benefi-
cial to many other applications are not
extensively used in steels for highly
stressed gears.

Heat Treating Qualities

The heat treating characteristics of a
steel must allow the securing of the specified properties throughout the range of
chemistry and hardenability that must be accepted. If the demands of operation or
processing are such that the full variation
of a specification will not produce satisfactory heat treating conditions, it is
necessary to restrict the acceptable limits
at an increased cost or be able to divert
extreme heats to other applications. With
some designs, difficulty may be experienced
in securing satisfactory results at the
minimum and maximum extremes of a specifica·
tion. Difficulty with distortion causing
erratic tooth changes and increased
straightening costs are common at the high
side of specifications, while unsatisfactory

response in securing the necessary properties may occur with low hardenability heats.
On jobs with critical requirements, it is
often necessary to exert extra care and control in processing. Production pilot lots
are used in addition to laboratory accept-
ance tests in determining if high and low
hardenability heats of steel will produce
satisfactory results.

Any narrowing of hardenability bands is a
step toward more desirable production conditions and decreased manufacturing cost.

Performance Properties

Usually there is little choice between
steels of equivalent hardenability in their
effect upon final operation of the gear, but
where the design or application is such that
the selection is made because of service

-13-

characteristics, economy is affected. Such items as slight differences in wear resistance, toughness, or uniformity might become important considerations where the design and application are critical.

Steels that prove unsatisfactory generally fail in processing rather than in service requirements.

Uniformity

In the production of gears with great demands for interchangeability and a high production rate, uniformity is very important. Any improvement in uniformity of properties of one material over another cannot be overlooked as a factor influencing economy.

CONFERENCE ON . . . TECHNIQUES

REPORT SITUATION

THIS REPORT was from two members of a Psychology Department who had attended a convention. They were summarizing highlights for others in the department. Readers were people in the general area, but not specialists in this phase. (Total pages—1.)

FORMAT

The numbered list corresponds with the heads of the report. It is a miniature table of contents.

PREFATORY MATERIAL

Besides the material after "To" and the signature, the occasion is shown in the two words "you requested."

INTRODUCTION

The opening sentence gives the purpose—to report upon this conference, plus some identifying facts. Next are named the phases of the subject considered. The last sentence shows these to be identical with the phases to be discussed. The one list thus takes care of scope and of order of reporting. The intervening material is concluding matter.

CONCLUSION

The second paragraph is a general impression or conclusion from the conference, and serves to sum up the report. It could have been set off separately, but integrates well with the introduction.

TAU SCHOOL

Interorganization Letters Only

DATE December 8, 195X

SUBJECT Conference on Minor
Projective Techniques

TO Mr. Simpson
   cc Members of Department

Here is the brief report you requested upon the conference we attended at Omega University on December third. The discussion of minor projective techniques was arranged as follows:

1. Zondi test
2. Sentence completion and proverbs test
3. Case study

The general impression gained was that the field of clinical psychology is showing progress in its present experimental stage. Yet our best testing techniques are still open to question. The clinical psychologist must still depend heavily upon his own experience and ability to gain insight into a patient's personality.

Brief comments on each session follow:

1. Zondi Test (9:00-12:00 A.M.)

The Zondi test was developed in Hungary by Zondi, a Hungarian psychiatrist. The test consists of 48 pictures of mental patients. These pictures are arranged on cards of six to a card. The subject is asked to select the picture on each card that he likes the best and the one that he likes the least.

Dr. Zondi believes that this test will

1

DEVELOPING SECTIONS

The main division is chronological. Two of the sections use a topic sentence to introduce them. Since they are short, that is all they need in the way of formal organizing elements.

DATA

The data are based on the authority of the leader of each session.

ILLUSTRATIONS

None.

ACKNOWLEDGMENTS

None.

help in personality testing. There has been very little work done with it. The theory behind the test has never been tested and there are no norms. Dr. Blanchard presented the test as a good one for clinicians to experiment with.

    2. <u>Sentence Completion and Proverbs</u>
       (1:30 - 4:30 P.M.)

The sentence completion and the proverbs tests are also open to question. They do give results consistent with written tests and projective tests such as the Rorschach and the TAT. However, many of the sentences completed and proverbs selected give information contrary to that obtained from other tests.

Dr. Mason closed the session with this question: "Should we use the information gained from these tests that agrees with other projective tests, or the information that disagrees with other projective tests?" More research is necessary before an answer can be given.

    3. Case Study (6:30 - 8:30 P.M.)

Dr. Barnes presented a case study of a psychotic girl. He gave the data obtained from the case history, a Zondi test, a Rorschach, a sentence completion test, and a proverbs test. The test material showed considerable agreement with the case history. He closed with the caution that we must be careful to consider all the test data obtained, not only the data consistent with the case history.

Paul N. Travers   *John D. Rader*

Paul N. Travers   John D. Rader

MEMORANDUM ON 1953 OPERATIONS

REPORT SITUATION

REPORTS like this one are also sometimes read aloud. It is a report at top level, predicting future operations. Such a report could be part of an annual or quarterly report to the board of directors, or a special interim report. Similar summaries are sometimes made for the benefit of the men just under the presidential level, to brief them on the over-all operations. (Total pages—2.)

FORMAT

Typed, single spaced, with main headings.

PREFATORY MATERIAL

There is none except the signature.

INTRODUCTION

The sole introduction is the title. The importance would be apparent, as would the purpose, in any situation in which such a report was made.

CONCLUSION

The entire report is a summary of information provided to the president by his operating heads. It has no conclusion of its own.

OMEGA MANUFACTURING COMPANY
MEMORANDUM ON 1953 OPERATIONS

FINANCIAL

For the year 1953 we predict a much better financial showing than we have made in the past. We are currently predicting an operating profit for the year of $6,330,000 with profit after tax at $3,150,000.

The expansion expenditures which have been made in the last year are completed and we see no reason for any major capital expenditures in the next year. We do, however, find the necessity for buying some equipment. There are places where we have individual single purpose machines where breakdowns stop our production. It would be unwise to remain vulnerable in this respect. We expect to develop and produce six more automatic assembly machines during the coming year. Our estimated capital expenditures for the year 1953 are slightly in excess of $1,500,000.

SALES

Our most recent forecasts, which we believe to be realistic, show an annual volume for the year 1953 of $49,000,000. The principal unpredictable factor in arriving at this sales forecast is what time in the coming year Alpha and Beta Companies will make changes which will incorporate our parts. Our present predictions are based upon these changes being made in October or November but should these switch-overs be made in mid-summer, a higher rate of sales for the year will be realized. The schedules for Upsilon's chassis parts seem also to be unpredictable.

DEVELOPING SECTIONS

The main headings concern main functions of the organization. The order is arbitrary, but has a relation to the main interests of the organization. Any firm is likely to be in business to make money through sales of manufactured products, well engineered, the whole job being done by competent personnel.

DATA

Nothing is said as to how the facts were arrived at. Here they are simply resting on the authority of the president.

ILLUSTRATIONS

None needed.

ACKNOWLEDGMENTS

None needed or suitable.

-2-

MANUFACTURING

The expansion of the Gammaville facilities including the Mutown installation are now complete with the exception of the delivery of one 60-inch mill which is scheduled for delivery in January and the final piping and hooking up of a new line of presses which are already delivered. By mid-February of 1953, the Gammaville facility will be working all of its new equipment at, we believe, the efficiencies which the expansion has been aimed at.

The Nuburg plant is completed and part of the move to that plant also completed. It is now operating with four assembly crews on the first shift and three on the second. Because these are new crews who have yet to gain real experience, the efficiency is currently only about 60 per cent of standard. We see this improving week by week. We have now recognized Upsilon as the sole bargaining union for the Nuberg plant and are currently negotiating a contract with this union. Part of these negotiations have to do with settling of an incentive system based on the same principles as the one now used in Zetaville, which we are sure will immediately boost the efficiency. The completion of the move of all long run production to Nuburg has been delayed by increases in our customers' requirements and the getting of the present operation at Nuburg up to decent efficiency and it is now anticipated that this move should be completed by the first of March. We are pleased with the type of people we have been able to hire in Nuburg and look forward to this becoming a really good operation in the year 1953.

-3-

ENGINEERING

The designing of parts that we make into the automotive applications has and is proceeding satisfactorily but we have not made the always hoped for strides of expanding our position in other than the automotive markets. We therefore plan in the year 1953 to add to the engineering staff a group of men whose efforts will be completely direcrected at markets which we do not now serve or at least where our present volume of business is small. How soon this can be done depends completely on our ability to find the type of manpower needed, but we are sure that by the end of the coming year, we will be able to report really good progress toward the development of markets in new fields.

PERSONNEL

The original plan at the time of the purchase of the Iota Company of providing it with management and supervisory personnel to insure its future is practically completed. There will always be small changes and additions, but I sincerely believe that there is here now a team of able, loyal and industrious people which will insure constantly better operations of the company.

While the operations for 1953 will not bring Iota Manufacturing to the eventual goals of efficiency and volume, we are committed to the improvements as indicated here which should certainly put this company on the way toward its eventual goals.

George P. Walker, President

BUSINESS CONDITIONS

REPORT SITUATION

THIS REPORT closely resembles the preceding one, except in format. It is a report, sent at regular intervals, from a District Sales Manager to the General Sales Manager. By reading it with the reports from other districts, the latter gets a picture of conditions throughout the country. (Total pages—1.)

FORMAT

The form is that of a letter. A regular letterhead was used. The subject line is added, the salutation omitted.

PREFATORY MATERIAL

This is limited to the letterhead and signature. No more is needed—the report regularly comes from the writer to the reader.

INTRODUCTION

There is no introduction, except the title. The purpose is known, and the topics are all regularly covered each time this report comes in. The order in which they are discussed is evident from the side heads.

CONCLUSION

The entire report is a summary of facts reported to the district manager by other company representatives and by dealers. It has no conclusion of its own.

DEVELOPING SECTIONS

The order of main sections is arbitrary, except that general conditions logically come first. Each section is too short to need formal organizational elements.

THE ZETA COMPANY

121 North Broad Avenue
Gammatown, California

General Sales Department

Nuville, N. J.   March 29, 195X

GENERAL SALES DEPARTMENT SUBJECT:
GAMMATOWN, CALIFORNIA   BUSINESS CONDITIONS

GENERAL BUSINESS CONDITIONS * A seasonal increase in the sale of farm equipment has been apparent during the past two weeks; however, it is not in keeping with previous years demands. Unemployment has increased in this section and apparently reductions in overtime pay have had their effect on business in general. The dealer outlook is good and most dealers expect to at least equal last year's sales.

CROP CONDITIONS * The winter wheat crop is still in good condition and apparently has survived the winter weather and will produce a good yield; however, the acreage is down 25 to 29%. It is still too early to determine the acreage of other major crops; however, in most cases they should equal last year.

SALES AND COLLECTIONS * Dealers report that collections of open accounts have been good; however, they require constant follow-up to keep from getting out of line. The sales demand for heavy equipment is becoming apparent and since we have introduced the tractor, reports from the territory indicate that we will have difficulty supplying the demand during the early portion of the season.

DATA

No attempt is made to establish the validity of the facts. The assumption is that the district manager has gathered them as accurately as he can.

ILLUSTRATIONS

None needed.

ACKNOWLEDGMENTS

None needed or suitable.

GENERAL SALES ACTIVITY * There are now
twelve dealers in the Nuville district territory operating under the DOUBLE OR MORE
program, and the results to date have varied
to a great degree. Some dealers have had as
high as 100 survey forms returned, while
other dealers have had only 20 or 30. All
dealers in the district territory will hold
Open House during the week of April 5th to
10th and this should increase dealers store
traffic.

Several dealers have held Smokers and introduced the new tractor to their farm trade.
Farmers attendance at these meetings has run
as high as 100 per night.

USED EQUIPMENT * Used equipment is still one
of the most serious situations facing most
dealers. It requires constant dealer attention and continuous sales effort to prevent
tying up a great amount of the dealer's
capital. Reports from most zones indicate
that the used equipment inventory is undoubtedly at its highest point. It is expected that this inventory will be reduced
with the beginning of spring sales. Some
dealers still plan to hold public sales of
used equipment.

Yours very truly,

X. X. Jonathan

X. X. Jonathan, District Mgr.

STATUS OF RESEARCH PROJECTS

REPORT SITUATION
THIS IS a very routine periodic report, prepared to show the department head the status of one phase of his operations. He expects it, gets it all the time, and knows what to do with it. (Total pages—1.)

FORMAT
The report is in tabular form.

PREFATORY MATERIAL
None—except name of department concerned.

INTRODUCTION
Just the title.

CONCLUSIONS
The entire report is a summary.

DEVELOPING SECTIONS
None.

DATA
The individual reports of the people concerned were the raw data. They are in the files.

ILLUSTRATIONS
The entire report is a table, which needs no explanation to the reader who uses it.

ACKNOWLEDGMENTS
None needed.

BETA DIVISION
RESEARCH AND DEVELOPMENT SECTION

Status of Research Projects

Number of Projects			778
Number of Active Projects		222	
Code A	110		
Code B	59		
Code C	53		
Number of Inactive Projects		38	
Number of Cancelled Projects		18	
Number of Files		100	
Number of Completed Projects		400	

		Reported		
	Active	Proposed	Progress	Final
Cummings	10	6	34	9
Simons	33	13	29	8
Lang	65	29	10	11
Leggett	67	21	15	46
Utley	39	18	21	5
Schultz	2	0	0	0
Meredith	0	0	56	318

April 30, 195X

DAILY EXPENSES

REPORT SITUATION

Here is routine summary of one day's expenses in one department. The report is purely informational—used to show how the department stands in respect to its budget. The same people regularly make it out and the same readers regularly get it. (Total pages—as shown.)

The next report situation is described on page 434.

FORMAT

This is a form report. For routine reports, forms are desirable. They save time and keep the order of information constant from report to report. They also help to insure that all necessary information is given.

The format of the next report is discussed on page 434.

PREFATORY MATERIAL

It has none. The report is not even initialed. No one *would* make it out except those who are regularly supposed to do so. (Probably, however, the *series* of reports of which this is one part actually did have prefatory material. That is, when the form was originally initiated, a directive concerning its use was undoubtedly sent around.)

Prefatory material of the next report is discussed on page 440, the report situation on page 434.

INTRODUCTION

The title is enough. Everyone who uses the report knows that its purpose is to summarize daily expenses. An order of reporting is not given because the report is both routine and short.

The introduction of the next report is discussed on page 446, the report situation on page 434.

B69-15000-9-50

DAILY EXPENSES

Department Number _____ Date _____

	TODAY			MONTH TO DATE		
Operating Supplies						
Tools Requisitioned						
Tools, Work Orders						
Losses, Errors and Defects						
Efficiency						
Productive Labor						

CONCLUSION

The entire report is a *summary.*

The conclusion of the next report is discussed on page 450, the report situation on page 434.

DEVELOPING SECTIONS

There are no developing sections to organize.

The developing sections of the next report are discussed on page 455, the report situation on page 434.

DATA

The data on which the summary is based do not appear. They are to be found in the individual requisitions, work orders, etc.

Data of the next report are discussed on page 456, the report situation on page 434.

ILLUSTRATIONS

The tabular form, often used in the summary of longer reports, is here used for the entire report—which is simply a summary.

Illustrations for the next report are discussed on page 456, the report situation on page 434.

ACKNOWLEDGMENTS

None were needed.

Acknowledgments for the next report are discussed on page 458, the report situation on page 434.

17

Reports for Supplementary Study

Chapter 16 showed only progressive simplification of the report pattern as the situation became simpler. This chapter shows other ways in which the basic patterns and techniques can be modified.

Study of these samples will demonstrate three things. First, there is no *one* acceptable way in which to write a report. That is why there is no sense in trying to sort reports into a variety of types in order to learn a formula for each. Second, compromises have to be made if the report situation will not let ideal practice be followed. Third, and very important, the basic principle of making the report convenient for the reader is never violated and accounts for most of the variations from pattern.

So that the reports can also be used in connection with the study of each functional part, each analysis follows the arrangement used in Chapter 16. But to emphasize what variations are illustrated, a section has been added at the first of the analysis.

CUSTOMER ORDER CONTROL

THIS REPORT is another excellent example of a three-level report. It also demonstrates these points:

1. The abstract that will be used apart from the report, to give a shorter quick picture than is provided by the introduction-conclusions arrangement.
2. A way of handling a report where the data are not concrete and quantitative.

REPORT SITUATION

This is a three-level report in the full pattern. While the investigation was originally assigned by local management, the report is intended to be useful to other divisions also. The writer's assignment had been to evaluate a procedure and offer alternatives. The problem is of particular interest because it deals with many intangibles. Hence it illustrates how purely quantitative data and measurements cannot always be used. A controlled reasoning process must then be substituted. (Total pages of report—70.)

The situation of the next report is discussed on page 470.

FORMAT

The report used a cover, title page, table of contents and list of illustrations in standard order, as shown. It was lithographed, on one side, sewed, and bound. Heads and subheads were in the positions shown, underlined. The original was double spaced.

The format of the next report is discussed on page 470.

[This sheet represents a "hard" cover, lettered on both front and backbone of book, sewed, and bound]

CUSTOMER ORDER CONTROL

HENRY E. LEE

OMICRON DIVISION

ABSTRACT

In the report as shown here, the abstract is placed inside the cover. Actually it was not bound with the report. It appeared in an index of reports, and was designed to give readers an idea of whether they might be interested in the whole report.

The abstract is an indicative or review abstract, but does give a brief idea of the final outcome.

Saving print or space is important in any index. Hence the incomplete sentences.

The next abstract is discussed on page 490, under "Introduction," the report situation on page 488.

Abstract

An investigation to determine the best system for customer order control to maintain readily available information on orders, schedules and shipments. Report establishes requirements of order control, and studies present methods in relation to these requirements. On same basis evaluates manual posting, transfer posting, and the Alpha, Beta, and Gamma systems. Details conclusions as to how each system meets the requirements. Recommends Beta system if maximum time is desired for follow-up function, but Gamma system if smaller increase in time it provides is considered sufficient.

Report on

Customer Order Control

Omicron Division

by
Henry E. Lee
July 15, 195X

PREFATORY MATERIAL

A preface rather than a letter is used because of the wide readership expected. The occasion is stated as a need plus an assignment. Note that while there is an overlap with the introduction, the statement here is much briefer—just enough to give some idea of the situation. But if a reader begins here, he needs the statement to understand the significance of the project. A glance at the abstract shows a similar overlap. Again it is necessary, for the abstract was planned for separate reading.

Readers are indicated as local and other management, and the report's potential usefulness to them pointed out. The author's authority is implied in mention of the nine months devoted to the study and in the detailed acknowledgments of assistance.

The prefatory material of the next report is discussed on page 472, the report situation on page 470.

Preface

Customer order control at the Omicron Division is the recording and controlling of customers' orders, schedules and shipments.

The present Omicron system of customer order control has functioned successfully for twenty-five years. Frequently, nevertheless, the load on the system has been such that sufficient time has not been available for analyzing and expediting the delivery and shipment required by the customer's schedule.

Previous investigation of this situation has been conducted within the Division but no conclusive facts have been established.

Consequently, the management of Omicron Division felt it would be desirable to make a complete examination of the present methods of order control in comparison with alternate methods. It was believed that the outcome of such an examination might effect an improvement in the conditions for the follow-up function.

Work on this project, which occupied the past nine months, has now been completed, with resulting recommendations for trial of an alternate system. In the belief that the findings might be useful to other divisions, it has been reproduced in this form.

I am indebted to the following for their help in this project:

Mr. John T. Rutlidge, Production Manager, for his support of the project; Mr. Oscar L. Sample, Manager of Material Control,

for his technical guidance; Mr. Frank N.
Cory, Supervisor of the Order Department,
for his departmental assistance; and Mr.
Edward B. Nisbett, Material Tabulating
Department, for machine techniques.

I am also indebted to Mr. Robert R. Hall,
Alpha Company representative; Mr. James O.
Harley, Beta Company representative; and Mr.
Ralph S. Barnes, Gamma Company representa-
tive, for the technical guidance given me on
behalf of their firms.

Henry E. Lee

Table of Contents

List of Illustrations

INTRODUCTION

The first two paragraphs give background: they both define the area of investigation and suggest its importance. Note they are intelligible even to us laymen (and hence to a top-level reader). But they do not attempt to give any detailed description. The third paragraph, in a sense history, is aimed at getting into appropriate proportion the statement of the problem that follows.

The general procedure comes next—and of course shows the limits of the investigation, as does the next to last paragraph. The last paragraph economically gives the order of presentation.

The introduction of the next report is discussed on page 172, the report situation on page 470.

I. Introduction

Customer order control at Omicron Division is a combination of two major functions or responsibilities. Primarily, customer order control functions to maintain on appropriate records complete information concerning customers' orders, schedules, and shipments, and to supply this information to management and all other individuals responsible for the planning, buying, building, and shipping of finished products.

The secondary responsibility is efficient follow-up, a term used throughout this report as the analysis of customers' orders, schedules and shipments, and the contacts and communications required to assure that production and shipment of the finished product are proceeding according to the customers' schedules. Without accurate records any follow-up activity would be useless.

For twenty-five years the present order control system has been operated successfully by the Order Department, a department of the Production Control Organization.

Although this system has operated efficiently, management desired to determine if the present methods were most satisfactory in meeting customer order control requirements.

The problem of the project was then to completely analyze the present system and other possible methods of customer order control. This was done to determine the possible existence of any alternate method which displayed conclusive evidence of being more efficient and more economical.

1

2

The steps of the investigation developed into:

1. Establishing the requirements of order control for the Division.

2. Investigating and evaluating the existing method of order control on the basis of the established requirements.

3. Investigating and evaluating alternate methods of order control on the basis of established requirements. Methods were:

   A. Revision of existing system's forms.

   B. Manual posting to visible card records.

   C. Transfer posting.

   D. Machine posting.

   E. Machine calculating and printing of all information to records.

The five alternate methods were selected because they represented the various general procedures that were functionally applicable to the Omicron customer order control requirements.

The procedure of investigation for alternate system A (Revision of existing system's forms) consisted of physically redesigning the existing system's forms.

The procedure of investigation for each of the remaining alternate methods was basically the same and consisted of:

3

1. Contacting agents of each company offering such systems.

2. Meeting with these men, discussing requirements and responsibilities of Omicron customer order control.

3. Converting these requirements to forms and procedures offered by each company.

4. Applying these forms and procedures to a sample portion of each existing system.

The presence of three Beta system departments within the division, and the partial use of Beta methods, reports, and equipment within the current order control procedures, influenced the investigations and conclusions as well.

Conclusions and recommendations follow this introduction. The organization of the report proper follows the steps of investigation described earlier in this section.

CONCLUSION

In the original report, the introduction and conclusions together gave a total picture of the project in seven typed pages. In the conclusions the systems are arranged in the same order as in the introduction, and also as in the following chapter heads.

The Table of Conclusions (resembling a summary of results) is placed last. The table is not necessary to understand the written conclusions, and if placed first it might give a wrong impression that the evaluation had been a very exact one. As it is, the recommendations preceding it clearly show that the report has simply arrived at a hypothesis which needs to be tested.

Recommendations were to be the final outcome of the project. Since they also are intelligible by themselves, they precede the conclusions.

There is some inconsistency in the lists of conclusions. This is of course a defect.

Note that the table of conclusions compares each system in terms of the criteria set up in the body of the report.

The conclusion of the next report is discussed on page 474, the report situation on page 470.

II. Conclusions

As a result of the study, the following
two methods are recommended under the conditions indicated:

1. Beta, if maximum time is desired for
    the follow-up function. This will
    require an additional two people in
    the Material Tabulating Section, but
    should release forty posting hours
    each day within the order control
    area.

2. Alpha, if increased follow-up time is
    primarily desired, with no additional
    load on outside departments.

It is further recommended that a trial
period of from three to six months be set
during which a selected customer and all
related order activity be carried on the
Beta and Alpha records and procedures.

During this same period, the customer
should also continue to be handled under the
existing system, so that complete opera-
tional comparison can be made of all three
systems.

Specific conclusions as to how well each
system meets the requirements of efficient
order control are tabulated in the "Table of
Conclusions" (Page No. 7).

The remainder of this section follows as a
discussion of the conclusions concerning
each system.

Present Method

1. The present method is satisfactory.

4

5

2. The present system, by virtue of its existence, is the most inexpensive to operate.

3. The present system does not offer sufficient time for follow-up.

4. The hand posting required by this system has a definite influence upon the memory, and does aid in the follow-up.

Revised Loose Leaf Forms of Present System

1. Offers very negligible material savings and no increased time for follow-up.

2. Recommended if rest of present system is kept.

Transfer Posting

1. Requires considerable set-up time and preparation, with little flexibility and inconsistent use of equipment.

2. Not adaptable to an inconsistent posting operation.

3. Not recommended, although possible to use.

Gamma Company System

1. Best combination of manual and mechanical operations.

2. Flexibility and checks of accuracy limited by mechanical operation.

3. Equipment foreign to this division.

4. Equipment would pay for itself in a year.

6

Alpha Company System

1. Best manual method available, offers increased time for follow-up.

2. Offers ease of operation.

3. Previous satisfactory service in Production Control fields of this division.

Beta Company System

1. Most expensive method in regard to outside department labor, but least expensive in overall analysis.

2. Offers maximum time for follow-up.

3. Has performed satisfactorily in other fields within the division.

4. Procedures are incorporated in present method of order control.

5. Will release forty posting hours each day for follow-up within the order control area.

DEVELOPING SECTIONS

The major divisions of the report deal with the systems examined in the order given in the introduction, except that Section III is inserted. It is in a sense introductory. It details the importance of the total operation and sets up and to some extent justifies criteria for judgment.

Section IV uses the basic organization of most of the other developing sections. The section is introduced by stating the phase of the problem with which it deals, reminding the reader of the procedure, and giving an order of reporting. Next the system and its detailed procedures are described, and an evaluation is made in terms of the criteria set up in Section III. A summary of conclusions ends the chapter.

Sections III and IV illustrate how even in the same report there need not necessarily be a consistent pattern in all chapters. Thus the introduction of Section III is simply a topic sentence plus the statement of importance, and the section finishes with an ending (simply states the outcome) rather than with conclusions.

Section V, not shown, discussed a modification of the current system only. Hence it evaluated only in terms of the criteria that applied to the proposed modifications.

Note the contents of the appendix, as shown in the Table of Contents. The detailed description of the current system was relegated to that position because current practice was known by many readers of the report and because it was not needed for the evaluation. But if any reader were not familiar with the system (and out-of-plant readers *were* anticipated) he could readily find the details.

The Appendix also contained two detailed calculations of probable time for one of the proposed systems.

Section IV is organized almost exactly as suggested in Chapter 8, page 87.

The developing sections of the next report are discussed on page 474, the report situation on page 470.

Table of Conclusions

	Present Method	Revised Loose Leaf	Transfer Posting	Gamma System	Alpha System	Calculating and Printing Daily all Order and Shipment Activity through Beta Equipment
Complete and current information	2	2	2	2	2	2
Ease of operation	2	2	1	1	2	1
Accuracy checks provided	1	1	2	2	1	2
Time involved in operation cycle	3	3	1	1	2	1
Flexibility	1	1	4	2	1	3
Mobility	1	1	2	2	1	1
Special equipment involved	1	1	3	3	3	1
Personnel needed	All	All	One each Posting and Operating Clerk	One Posting Clerk	All	Two Operating Clerks
Economy	2	2	4	2	2	2
Time Available for Follow-up	4	4	3	2	2	1
Score	17	17	22	17	16	14

Legend: Excellent ---- 1   ·Maximum Efficiency ---- 9
        Good --------- 2   Minimum Efficiency ---- 36
        Fair --------- 3
        Poor --------- 4

7

DATA

How to handle data in this report presented a major problem because there were no clear quantitative data. These could be gathered only if the experimental procedure recommended in Section II were adopted. Actually, then, the opinions of the author and his consultants had to be presented so that his concluding hypothesis seemed worth testing.

Note that in Section III the author called his assigned values arbitrary and carefully pointed out that they were really not of equivalent value. He is making clear that these are loose quantitative values, but he does not press the point unduly.

In Section IV and the remaining sections he tries to show the logic of his evaluation by carefully describing the particular system and then, under the evaluation, recapitulating or giving critical points. Some checking back to the description is of course required. The illustrations add detail and verisimilitude.

Data of the next report are discussed on page 476, the report situation on page 470.

ILLUSTRATIONS

The report makes use of a tabular summary, numerous lists, and illustrations of the forms discussed. The latter are not shown here. In the original, however, they were on the page on which they were discussed (cut into the text) or on the following page. Size determined the practice followed. Since the report was lithographed, "cutting in" was physically easy to accomplish.

Note that even though the forms were illustrated, the significant things about them are also presented in the text.

Illustrations for the next report are discussed on page 480, the report situation on page 470.

III.   Requirements of Customer Order Control

Any system of order control at the Omicron Division must meet definite requirements in maintaining accurate records of customers' orders, schedules, and shipments; transmitting this information to management -- and following up the production and shipment of finished goods.

The importance of these requirements is illustrated by a recapitulation of the last three years' communications between the customers and the division.

	1949	1950	1951
Production purchase orders received (does not include releases on blanket orders)	7472	10947	13634
Purchase order alterations	2617	1312	2798
Outgoing letters	3139	2410	2793
Incoming phone calls	4192	4434	6846
Outgoing phone calls	714	992	1183
Total phone calls	4906	5426	8029
Incoming telegrams	3787	3748	3256
Outgoing telegrams	3565	4227	3756
Total telegrams	7352	7975	7012
Visitors	18	46	196

This listing shows the frequency in which the records must be referred to, as well as the great amount of direct contact made with the customer. Any improper attitude towards the records or customer will be reflected in both the financial and good will standing of the division.

8

ACKNOWLEDGMENTS

All acknowledgments are for direct personal aid, and are made in the Preface.

Acknowledgments in the next report are discussed on page 480, the report situation on page 470.

To give the personnel of the Order Department an ideal system, a rating of excellent would be expected for each of the following requirements:

1. <u>Complete and current records.</u> -- Information must be complete to show records of all orders, schedules and shipments. Records should give at a glance current daily status of customer requirements.

2. <u>Ease of operation.</u> -- The system and mechanics of operation must be as nearly self-explanatory as possible so as to provide for speed and understanding by the personnel using the system.

3. <u>Accuracy checks.</u> -- Simple checks of accuracy are essential to efficient planning, buying, and follow-up. Those checks of a complex nature tend to complicate and confuse anyone dealing with the system.

4. <u>Time involved in operation cycle.</u> -- This is the time it takes to perform the paper work for orders, schedules, and shipments from the period the forms are received in the department until they are ready for the file. This time will have a relation to the ease of operation and flexibility of the system.

5. <u>Flexibility.</u> -- The system must be flexible enough to absorb daily changes or corrections of orders, schedules, and shipments. Any system

10

impeded by various revisions and minor
changes would lead to an eventual
slow-up of the total function of order
control.

6. Mobility. -- The records themselves or
    their containers must be maintained as
    mobile units. Conversation pertinent
    to a particular customer might require
    the records to be moved to another
    desk or area during the conversation.
    Immobility would prohibit this and
    hinder operations of order control.

7. Special equipment required. -- The
    amount and use of any special equip-
    ment required, which would require
    special operators, installations, or
    additional space, such as posting,
    calculating, or printing machines, or
    special files, cabinets, ledgers, or
    forms, will influence the time, speed,
    ease, and flexibility of the opera-
    tion.

8. Personnel. -- This refers to the num-
    ber of people required for the system
    and may include those people required
    in other departments which supplement
    or contribute to the Order Department
    operations - such as special equipment
    labor.

9. Economy. -- The most efficient system
    may not always be the most economical.
    Total cost must be considered and will
    be reflected in all of the above
    items.

11

10. Time available for follow-up. -- A
     prime requisite of any system is to
     permit time to perform a completely
     adequate follow-up operation. The
     result of which will increase customer
     satisfaction and goodwill for the
     division, as well as minimize expen-
     sive telephone calls and wires.

In order that the existing system and the
alternate methods might be evaluated, four
values have been arbitrarily established.
These, and arbitrary numerical equivalents,
are arranged in descending order of consequence.

                Excellent ---- 1
                Good --------- 2
                Fair --------- 3
                Poor --------- 4

These values are assigned each method by a
comparative ranking with the ideal system.
Although a poor rating does not indicate any
failure to function, such a rating is to be
regarded as highly significant in both the
No. 1 and No. 10 criteria. Although all
elements are rated as equal, No. 1 and No.
10 are the main criteria for any system.
Any system with a "poor" rating in both of
these criteria would not be considered
acceptable.

These values have been applied to each
method as an indication as to how well the
particular method met the criteria for the
customer order control.

IV. <u>Evaluation of the Existing</u>
     <u>Method of Order Control</u>

[*Note: This space contained a photostat of the customer
Orders and Shipping Record. Five other illustrations of existing
forms are in the original report. One of these is cut in like this
one. The others are on the first page after the discussion of them
begins.*]

The first phase of the project was to
evaluate the existing method of order control. This evaluation was made on the basis
of how well this system met the ten previously described requirements for customer
order control at the division.

The remainder of this section gives:

1. Description of the system.
2. Forms and procedures.
3. Evaluation.
4. Conclusions.

<u>Description of the system.</u>

The Order Department employs nine clerks
and five stenographers under the direction
of the Order Department Supervisor. Each
clerk is responsible for a prescribed number
of customers and item set-ups.

Information of customers' orders, schedules, and shipments, is posted and entered
to loose leaf records maintained in ring
binders (Figure No. 1). The number of
binders for each customer depends upon the
number of items ordered by that customer.
These binders contain the records for each
particular part ordered by the customer, and
are arranged by item classification as
follows:

12

```
Generators
Cranking motors
Distributors
Item parts
Horns
```

Each item within the binder is represented by a historical and current record. All entries to these records are hand posted. Because this hand posting has a definite influence upon the memory, it does aid in the follow-up function.

Forms.

The historical record (Figure No. 3) lists:

Customer	- Order number
Location	- Date of order
Shipping destination -	completion
Delco-Remy part	- Quantity of order
number	- Total ordered
Customer part number	- Monthly shipment
Part name	- Total shipped
Date	- Balance due orders.

Basically, it presents the status of customer orders through the relation of total shipments to total quantities ordered.

The current record (Figure No. 4) which is maintained for each month, lists:

Omicron part number	- Total shipments for
Part name	- each month
Customer part	- Balance due the
number	- month
Month	- Balance due customer
Customer	- order for the
Date	- month

14

```
Daily schedule        - Carrier
Order scheduled       - Total planned sched-
                        ule for the month
```

The current sheet presents the daily status of customers' requirements and shipments.

From both the historical and current records, authorization is made to build and ship the finished item. Management, and the other departments concerned, must be notified of the customer's schedule in order that production may be planned, and the correct quantities of material purchased. These schedules are taken from the binders' records and listed on a building schedule ticket (Figure No. 5).

This record lists the following:

```
Customer         - Code
Part name        - Date
Part number      - Monthly scheduled quantity
Class name       - Unscheduled quantity
```

This information is transferred to punched cards and listings are printed and distributed to management and the Planning and Material Departments.

Any transaction of cancellation or addition to schedules occurring within the current month may necessitate a revision of the month's scheduled quantities. This is transferred to a revision form which lists the following:

```
Quantity of addition or cancellation
Customer
Quantity involved
Part number
Part name
```

Total schedule
Date of change

The new monthly figure is required in the
respective monthly column of the building
schedule ticket. Thus, both the Planning
and Shipping Departments are informed of the
schedule change.

The records requesting and recording shipments are Beta company punched cards. Originally, there is a punched master order card
for each order. Quantities are released for
shipment on this card. From this master
card, a shipping card is produced listing:

Date	- Clerk Number
Quantity	- Quantities shipped
Shipped via	- Item weight
Date shipped	- Clerk checking
Terms	- Postage
Number of items	- Back order
Item number	- Case number
Invoice number	- Packed by
Waybill or B/L number	- Tax
Number of skids	- Month
Number of cases	- Day
Shipping weight	- remarks

All of these forms supply the information
required to plan, build, and ship the finished product to meet customers' requirements.

Procedures.*

Customers' orders are received and checked
in the Sales Department and sent to the
Accounting Department for pricing. Two

---

* Complete details of procedure are in the
Appendix, page 56.

16

copies of the order (Figure No. 2) and the master order card are received by the Order Department.

The date of promised shipment is listed on the copies, and serves as information for order acknowledgment to the customer. The order is now entered on the history card, and the quantity is scheduled for shipment on the current record.

If the monthly total is revised by a schedule or new order, it is corrected on the Shipping Record and the new figure transferred to the Building Schedule Ticket which is taken from a file maintained in the desk of each clerk. After every such entry, the form is sent to the Material Department and reflects the new building requirements to the Material and Plant Production Control Departments.

The previously mentioned master order card is kept in a temporary file until the date the customer has listed as the release date of his shipment on the current record. The date and quantity of release are written on the card which is then sent to the Shipping Department. The card now serves as authorization for shipment, and from it is produced a shipping card (Figure No. 6).

When the material is ready for billing and shipment, all necessary information is written on the shipping card. From the completed card is printed an eight copy shipping order (Figure No. 7).

One copy of this notice is returned to the Order Department, and the shipping information is posted daily to the current record.

This quantity is accumulated each month and transferred to the history record.

Frequently, changes or revisions in the current month's shipping schedule are requested by the customer. Any such change is listed on the current record, the Building Schedule Ticket, and the Revision Form (Figure No. 8).

Complete and current records. -- Good; information is complete and more than adequate, to the point of offering information that is maintained by other departments of the division.

Ease of operation. -- Good; fundamentals are simple and easily performed. Records are self-explanatory. There are three different locations of record forms, however, and an order entry requires posting to from four to nine forms.

Accuracy checks. -- Excellent; several methods of checking entries to controlling figures. Errors can be traced and determined easily.

Time involved in operation cycle. -- Fair; customer order books are maintained vertically in metal cabinets.

To analyze or post to any record requires:

1. Determine and obtain correct book.

2. Leaf through book until correct part number is found.

3. Leaf through building schedule tickets until correct one is found. All records and forms are arranged by item

18

classification and part number, but
are blind filed.

4. Post or analyze.

5. Close book, lift, and return to cor-
    rect space in cabinet. Place building
    schedule ticket in basket.

Flexibility. -- Excellent; changes or revisions can be made easily within this
system, but are subject to the previously
mentioned items of evaluation.

Mobility. -- Excellent; the system has mobility with its books. Each book weighs
approximately six pounds and can be taken
from the cabinet and carried easily to any
location. These books contain approximately sixty part number set-ups each.

Special equipment involved. -- Excellent;
equipment is now in use. Twenty-seven metal
cabinets purchased from an outside source
along with the 126 customer order books
which they contain.

Personnel involved. -- All personnel of
the Order Control function are required by
this system, as each performs his share of
posting, and of entering orders, schedules,
and shipments.

Economy. -- Good; although savings would
be possible if expensive telephone calls and
wires were minimized. This could happen
only if more time were available for
follow-up.

Time allowed for follow-up work. -- Poor;
follow-up is usually done after the cus-

19

tomer has called or complained. This is
evidenced by the presence of twenty to
thirty "hot" or "ship immediately" items,
and the fact that the order clerk spends
from six to eight hours each day maintaining
the customer order book. This leaves little
time, or no time, for follow-up.

Conclusions

The following conclusions are based on the
previous evaluations:

1. The present method is satisfactory.

2. The present method of customer order
   control at the Omicron Division offers
   complete and accurate records with a
   great degree of flexibility, as well
   as many checks of accuracy.

3. The present method offers no provisions for visible filing and hence
   does increase the time required to
   post to or analyze any records.

4. The present method has a separation of
   related records which also increases
   the time required to post or to analyze records.

5. The present method does not provide
   for sufficient time for follow-up for
   the order clerks, and does not point
   out exceptions of schedules and shipments before they occur.

ALPHA STEAM ELECTRIC STATION

HERE IS the interesting way in which one company organizes its three-level reports to make them easy to use. The company's formula achieves the necessary goals by modifying practices customary in short reports. Hence this report retains some things which appear to be vestiges of such reports. Actually, however, the company has simply generalized report practice so that all reports can follow almost the same pattern, whether short or long, or whether telling of an investigation or giving information.

Unusual features, in order of their significance, are:

1. The placement of the Table of Contents.
2. The minimizing of procedure.
3. The break-up of the introduction.
4. The use of the heading "Discussion" even in a long report.

These are treated in detail below under "Format," "Introduction," "Developing Sections," and "Data."

REPORT SITUATION

The report was prepared by an engineer for the approval signature of his chief engineer, who transmitted it to top management. (Total pages—ten.)

The next report situation is discussed on page 488.

FORMAT

The report was stapled into a cover. The outside cover served as the title page shown here. Main heads were at the margin, all capitals, underlined. Subheads were side heads, indented halfway to the paragraph indentation, lower case, and underlined.

The most striking feature of the format is the placement of the Table of Contents. It comes *after* the material that top management is expected to read.

ALPHA STEAM ELECTRIC STATION

SUPPLYING COAL TO BUNKERS

FOR NO. 10 AND 11 BOILERS

EDO 416815

THETA COMPANY

NU, IOWA

Mechanical Engineering Department
Mechanical Research Division
December 28, 195X

ME-R-101

The arrangement has several advantages. It gives a detailed order of reporting. It does not force the reader to leaf over it before getting the quick picture. In case he questions part of the conclusions, he finds on the next page the necessary means of getting to the appropriate part of the report. Thus the function of keying the conclusions to the body is fulfilled.

The only drawback of the practice is the shock effect it gives when encountered for the first time—people are not used to finding a table of contents at this position. But once the practice is established in any organization, this consideration has no force.

Format of the next report is discussed on page 488.

PREFATORY MATERIAL

This is almost limited to the title page material and the signatures, exactly as in short reports. The first paragraph also is really prefatory—it relates this report to other reports.

Prefatory material in the next report is discussed on page 490, the report situation on page 488.

INTRODUCTION

Normally an introduction includes the items here called "Object" and "Scope." In a short report, these can be the total introduction. Here they are left as main heads, but preceded by a section called "Introduction."

Examination of the content shows that except for this detail we have a regular introduction. Paragraphs 2, 3, and 4 are what are usually called "Background," and include a brief account of the history and the particular situation or need (high costs) which gave rise to the problem. The material head "Object" (of the project, not of the report) is what we have called the "Problem." "Scope" is a breakdown of the general problem into the specific areas of in-

ALPHA STEAM ELECTRIC STATION
SUPPLYING COAL TO BUNKERS
FOR NO. 10 AND 11 BOILERS
EDO 416815

INTRODUCTION

This report is part of the Alpha continuing station study, and covers methods of supplying raw coal to the west side bunkers for use in No. 10 & 11 high pressure boilers. Because of expected future station loading, changes in the method of unloading coal for the low pressure boilers were not considered. A study of the inside coal handling facilities is in progress and a report will be issued in the near future.

Alpha's high pressure boilers have been in operation since 1943. They are modern in design and should provide efficient steam capacity for many years. The plant is strategically located on the system, being close to heavy load centers and large coal fields.

However, the present method of manually unloading coal from railroad cars into the raw coal bunkers is time and labor consuming. This method has been in practice since 1913 when only "Z" coal or larger was burned and labor was cheap. The smaller sizes burned now will not flow from the cars without hand labor.

A comparison of 1952 coal handling costs in cents per net ton for Alpha, Beta and Gamma, shows the cost at Alpha to be double that of Beta and approximately six times that of Gamma. Beta uses a car shakeout and Gamma a car dumper to unload coal from cars. Also, Beta and Gamma can fill their bunkers in eight hours, while Alpha requires two shifts per day.

OBJECT

To reduce operating expense and improve working conditions by the installation of modern coal handling equipment.

SCOPE

This report includes evaluations of:

1. Installing a belt conveyor system extending from a pit in the coal yard to the gallery over the west side bunkers.
2. Installing a heavy duty car shakeout, over the west side coal bunkers.
3. Utilizing the west coal bunker that now serves boilers 1 to 4 for the storage of "X" coal.

CONCLUSIONS

1. The installation of a belt conveyor system would provide an economical and efficient method of coal handling. Coal unloading could be done on one shift and the coal handling crew reduced by an estimated 24, resulting in a total labor savings of $107,000 a year, equivalent to a return of 19.5%. (Tables I & II, Pages 7 & 8.)

1

vestigation. These areas approximate an order of reporting. They are not intended to perform this function, however, as can be seen by the fact that they do not account for all the sections of the report.

Note that the statement of the object (problem) follows short report practice in that it is an incomplete sentence.

Obviously this opening section competently does most of what an introduction is called upon to do. All that is lacking is an account of the general procedure and of the actual order of reporting. But as we shall see later, the Table of Contents serves for the latter, and this report was not expected to explain the source of its data.

The general heads of "Object" and "Scope" can be used in both the informative and investigative situations. (The heads are not so specific, of course, as those we have used.) To get a fairly usual short report practice we simply need to leave out the heading called "Introduction" and the material so labeled.

The introduction of the next report is discussed on page 490, the report situation on page 488.

CONCLUSION

Here the concluding section is split into conclusions and recommendations. The short report practice of not using a topic sentence is followed.

Clearly these two sections could be combined—each recommendation combined with its related conclusion. Since these headings are standard practice in the company, however, the split is justified—people are expecting both headings.

In a sense the conclusions are keyed to the body, as discussed under "Format."

The conclusion of the next report is discussed on page 492, the report situation on page 488.

2. In order to realize maximum labor savings with the above belt system, it would be necessary to operate the coal preparation plant during peak load periods.

3. The side girders of the "X" raw coal bunkers are badly corroded and stressed to the maximum allowable limit.

4. The installation of a car shakeout over the west coal bunkers would cause excessive noise and vibration which may be harmful to the building structure and equipment.

5. Utilizing the west coal bunker which now serves boilers 1 to 4 for storage of "X" coal is not necessary.

RECOMMENDATIONS

1. A belt conveyor system be installed, including a car shakeout, car unloaders and accommodations for additional "X" coal storage. This scheme is estimated to cost $238,000. Chart I, Page 9, shows the proposed arrangement of this equipment.

2. With the belt conveyor system the preparation plant be operated during peak load periods to reduce coal unloading to one shift. (Chart II, Page 10).

3. The "X" raw coal bunkers be reinforced and united. This work is extra maintenance, not chargeable to the job, and is estimated to cost $33,000.

TABLE OF CONTENTS

DEVELOPING SECTIONS

The head of "Discussion" used in short reports has been retained. Hence the brief repetition of the introduction is needed. The slight awkwardness that results must be weighed against the advantages of standardization of practice.

Ignoring the head of "Discussion," the arrangement of sections is "Present Method," "Proposed Method," "Rejected Alternatives." Grouping the latter preserves better proportion than handling them separately.

Note that the present system is not described—everyone knows what it is like. Instead it is briefly analyzed.

Developing sections for the next report are discussed on page 498, the introduction on page 488.

DATA

A striking difference between this and the report which follows is in the handling of procedure. Here almost none is given. Four reasons lie back of this omission. First is the fact that if one scheme is better than others in terms of criteria such as cost, it doesn't much matter how it was arrived at. Second is the fact that a design problem is a creative activity that involves a good deal of trial and error, both mentally and on paper. To trace these steps in detail and justify each decision in terms of principles of basic design would be an elaborate process. Third, the actual plans were reviewed by the man whom the organization considers most competent in the field. On the purely technical aspects of the problem, he ought to be right. And finally, sketches of the proposal are included, in case anyone wants to offer modifications.

Standards of judgment used are not made as explicit as in the report which precedes this one, but they can easily be picked out. They are:

<u>DISCUSSION</u>

This report deals with methods of unloading coal into the west side bunkers supplying high pressure boilers No. 10 and 11 for the purpose of reducing coal handling costs. A study of inside coal handling facilities is in progress and will be covered in a separate report.

<u>Present Method of Handling Coal</u>

The original method of unloading coal into the bunkers is still in use. Coal is delivered to the plant by rail or by truck. Coal coming in by rail can be taken to either the bunker room or storage bank for unloading. Trucked coal is dumped from a ramp into railroad cars and then shifted to the bunker room for unloading.

Due to inadequate bunker capacity, coal unloading must be done on two shifts, 8:00 AM to 4:00 PM and 12:00 PM to 8:00 AM seven days a week. The work is done by 25 bunker attendants, divided into three groups, each working 40 hours per week. In addition, two train crews are required for day shift operation and one for night shift operation. Each train crew is composed of a locomotive operator, trainman and switchman. Table II page 8 shows job titles and pay rolls of the coal handling crew.

Unloading the coal into the bunkers is a time consuming and laborious job. "Z" coal runs out of cars easily, while "Y" coal usually runs out with the aid of some hand labor. "X" coal will not flow freely from the cars and requires excessive hand labor. The men must poke the coal and pound the sides of the car and hopper and then get inside with shovels to clean out the coal which did not flow from the car.

Although all safety rules are followed closely, working in a hopper bottom car is hazardous. Modern unloading equipment would eliminate these poor conditions.

<u>Proposed Method of Coal Handling</u>

The installation of a belt conveyor system would provide an economical and efficient method of coal handling. Loading coal into the west bunkers could be reduced to a one shift operation.

This proposed system includes the installation of a car shakeout, track hoppers, railroad car unloaders and belt conveyors. About 300 tons of additional storage would be provided by increasing the height of the west side raw coal bunkers. Chart I page 9 shows the proposed arrangement of the above equipment.

In this scheme cars would be shifted from the yard to a shallow unloading pit located under the curved track leading to the bunkers. A car shakeout would be provided to vibrate the cars and facilities complete unloading without hand labor. The pit would be about six ft deep and contain three hoppers with sufficient length to accommodate both 50 and 70 ton cars.

Ability to do the job

Now
In Future

Cost

Of installation
Of operation (especially labor)

Safety

Of personnel
Of structures

Data for the next report are discussed on page 498, the situation on page 488.

ILLUSTRATIONS

The report contained four illustrations, as listed at the end of the Table of Contents. All are referred to in the concluding section. Table I and both charts are also referred to in the body. Though three of the references in the concluding section are minimum, it is clear from the preceding statements what each illustration will show. More elaborate references are used in the body.

Illustrations for the next report are discussed on page 500, the situation on page 488.

ACKNOWLEDGMENTS

One textual acknowledgment is made on page 491 for information provided.

Acknowledgments for the next report are discussed on page 500, the situation on page 488.

Each hopper would have a control gate to regulate the feed of coal to each of three car unloaders located in the pit beneath the shallow hoppers. When unloading 50 ton cars, two unloaders would operate each at 150 tons per hour. When unloading 70 ton cars, all three unloaders would operate at a total rate of 300 tons per hour. The unloaders would feed the No. 1 conveyor which is a 42" belt. This conveyor would be provided with a discharge chute to transfer the coal to the 36" belt conveyor No. 2 which carries the coal to the bunker gallery. The 36" belt would be installed as high as practical in the gallery over the bunkers in order to provide maximum storage space in the bunker below. This belt would be equipped with 14 V-type discharge plows spaced at 15 foot intervals to distribute the coal evenly over the bunker sections. By using the side walls of the bunker gallery for a height of 3 feet above floor level, an additional 300 tons storage can be obtained. This will provide approximately 750 tons of active storage of "X" coal in the two bunker sections now handling this fuel. The belt conveyor system is designed to transport up to 400 tons of coal per hour directly into the bunker room.

The "X" coal storage bunkers have been in use since 1913. We have no records of repairs or alterations since that time with the exception that they were gunited in 1940. An inspection of these bunkers was made to determine the present condition of the bunker steel and the supporting members. The side girders of the north bunker had not been gunited and have corroded to the extent that with present loading the metal is stressed to the allowable limit. The side girders of the middle bunker are gunited and could not be given a complete examination at the time of the inspection. The bottom section of the bunkers are gunited and appeared to be in good condition.

The reconditioning of these bunkers should be done as a maintenance item. The side girders should be reinforced and gunited while the belt system is being installed. This work is estimated to cost $14,000. The bottom section of the bunkers should be given a complete examination and if necessary, regunited at an estimated cost of $19,000.

Information received from the System Operating Department on expected future operation at Alpha, after the first two units are installed at Phi Creek, estimates "X" coal requirements at approximately 1,000 tons per day. Present day "X" coal consumption is approximately equal to that estimated for the future. The belt conveyor system would require about 6 hours to take the daily coal requirements into the plant. This will allow for any external delays which could slow down the operation.

To unload 1,000 tons of coal on one shift, the operating schedule of the preparation plant will have to be changed. At present the preparation plant is shut down from 8:00 AM to 12:00 M to gain additional station output and to allow time for maintenance of this equipment during the day shift. With the present operating practice 750 tons would not be adequate storage capacity. However, by referring to Chart II, page 10, it can be seen that by shutting down the preparation plant during the off-peak period and operating at full capacity when the coal

unloading crew is on shift, 750 tons is sufficient capacity for expected coal load requirements. Also, during normal operation the pulverized coal bins would not drop below 480 tons. This 480 tons plus 270 tons of dry coal storage would provide sufficient fuel for about 15 hours operation at full load. By operating the preparation plant 8:00 AM to 12:00 M, during peak load hours, station output is reduced by about 3 megawatts. This loss in output is estimated to cost $10,000 per year.

Future operation of boilers 5 to 9 is estimated to require 27,000 tons of "Y" coal per year. Most of the "Y" fuel will be required during outages of a high pressure boiler in order to provide sufficient 25 cycle generation for the Xi Co. and the Pi Company. The dryer stokers will burn an additional 8,000 tons. Two bunker attendants are to be retained for unloading "Y" coal into the east bunkers.

The entire coal handling crew on the night shift would be eliminated. Coal unloading would be done on one shift, 8:00 AM to 4:00 PM. Three handymen would operate the belt system. Two of these men would open and close the car hopper gates and operate the car shakeout. The third man would operate the discharge plows distributing coal in the bunkers and be responsible for operation of the conveyor system including general care and lubrication. This is in contrast to the 16 men required each day, 8 men on each of two shifts, to fill the bunkers under present conditions.

By installing the belt system, it is expected that the coal handling cost at Alpha would become comparable to those of Beta. The car shake-out can unload cars faster with less men. Manpower requirements would be reduced by 24, and a labor savings of $107,000 realized. Bunker attendants would be cut from 25 men to 4, two of whom would be reclassified as handymen, and a train crew of 3 men eliminated. Table II, page 8, shows a comparison of present and proposed labor requirements with the belt system.

The cost of this scheme is estimated at $238,000 with the return estimated at $46,000 or 19.5%. Table I, page 7, shows a breakdown of the estimated investment costs and savings.

Other Plans Considered

Installation of Belt System Using a Deep Pit

An alternate belt conveyor system considered was one in which a pit approximately 35 ft deep would be used. This pit would be large enough to accommodate a 60 ton hopper. This deep pit plan would provide the same labor savings and coal handling operation as the recommended belt system, but is estimated to cost an additional $120,000. $40,000 is due to the extra cost of the deep pit and the balance of $80,000 due to changes of the railroad track system.

Since the increased cost of this plan provided no additional labor savings or operating advantages, it was eliminated.

Installation of Car Shakeout Over Bunkers

In an attempt to keep investment costs as low as possible, the installation of a car shakeout in the bunker room was investigated. Although savings provided by this coal unloading scheme were only slightly less than that of the belt system, the job could be done for one-half the cost.

A test was conducted at Alpha using the car shakeout from Gamma to determine the effect of vibrations on the building structure. Readings were taken with a Sound Level Meter and a Vibrometer on the track girders, and floor and roof beams. The maximum vibration reading was .008 inches recorded on the top flange of the track girder. The highest sound reading was 130 decibels, which is equivalent to the noise of a pneumatic rock drill.

This scheme was eliminated because:

a. Although the vibrations caused by the shakeout had no immediate effect on the building structure, it is highly possible the vibratory impulses of 1000 per minute would set up fatigue failure of the riveted structure. Also the effect of vibration on the piping, ducts and other equipment could be quite harmful.

b. Since the major portion of the estimated cost to make this installation is in building changes, that part of the cost could be a total loss if the vibrations proved harmful to the building and the scheme had to be abandoned.

Utilizing South Section of West Bunker

The south section of the west side bunkers feeds "Z" coal to boilers No. 1 to 4. Since these boilers are expected to be taken out of service in the near future, we considered utilizing this bunker for "X" coal.

To gain this additional storage of approximately 250 tons for the belt system would require an expenditure of $50,000. This cost of coal storage space at $200 per ton is very expensive. At Phi for instance, the cost estimate for steel bunkers amounted to $100 per ton.

The $50,000 required to utilize this bunker capacity would provide for the installation of a 15 inch vertical Redler Conveyor connecting the existing 15 inch and 17 inch horizontal conveyors. New rack and pinion gates and chutes would be required to allow free flow of "X" coal out of the bunker.

As previously explained, by changing the operation of the preparation plant, no additional storage of "X" coal is required. Therefore, this work is not recommended.

Coal Delivery by Truck

In this report no additional provisions were included to receive trucked coal. About 100,000 tons were trucked to Alpha during the past year. It is expected between 10,000 to 60,000 tons maximum will be trucked during the coming year. Present facilities are adequate to receive much more trucked coal than is expected in the future.

A considerable expenditure is required to improve present facilities. Therefore, we do not feel that provision should be made for any additional truck unloading facilities at this time. If, in the future, we are forced to receive a considerable quantity of trucked coal, additional provisions can be made without altering the proposed belt system.

P. D. Scornia
P. D. Scornia

A.N.T.
A.N.T.
12/28/52
M.E. Dept

IMPACT DAMPING

In this report the concept of the "quick picture" is carried an extra step, as discussed below under "Introduction." At first glance the conclusions also seem to depart from basic principles in that the language is technical. Reasons are explained below under "Conclusion."

Otherwise, except for omission of a table of contents, the report exactly follows the principles stressed in this text. But it is particularly interesting in view of its heavy emphasis on procedure, in contrast to the sample report just ahead of this. (Total pages—13.)

REPORT SITUATION

This report had distribution to interested people in several organizations. Most readers were on the higher technical levels. It was used to help determine how their products would be built.

The next report situation is discussed on page 532.

FORMAT

The report is in a cover, with a window opening to display the center of the title page. Main heads are centered and capped. Subheads are centered and underlined. Each new main head begins a new page, but no Roman numerals are assigned to them.

A departure from most long reports is in the absence of a Table of Contents.

Format of the next report is discussed on page 532.

GAMMA TESTING DEPARTMENT
Nu, Iowa

L. D. Morgan - Director

October 1, 195X   Copy No. 59

Report No. 3587

IMPACT DAMPING OF AUTOMOBILE
OUTER DOOR PANELS: A FUNCTION
OF DEADENER SURFACE DENSITY

Report Prepared By
Alfred N. Gertz
William P. Shaw
Noise and Vibration Laboratory

PREFATORY MATERIAL

Little is used. There is some on the title page, and some in the last sentence and the note of the Foreword. The last two pages of the report list the readers. (Total distribution—58.)

Prefatory material for the next report is discussed on page 534, the report situation on page 532.

INTRODUCTION

In effect, this report has *two* introductions. The one named "Foreword" exactly resembles a brief indicative abstract, but its function here is introductory—it tells the reader all he needs to know to understand what the conclusions are about.

Note that, brief as it is, several introductory functions are touched upon. The reader knows the problem—to establish a certain relationship. The procedure is sketched: the method of test (knuckling, etc.) is named, as are the nature of the data and the fact they were plotted and reduced to equations.

The second introduction, which follows the conclusions, is the standard pattern, except for the absence of any order of reporting. It begins on page 495.

The introduction of the next report is discussed on page 546, the report situation on page 532.

FOREWORD

This report presents results of a study
leading to a relationship between the surface density of deadener materials applied
to automobile outer door panels and the effective damping when they are "knuckled" or
impacted by other means. Subjective data of
this relationship are plotted, and mathematical equations are given to fit these
curves.*

This study was conducted during the period
of June, 195X, to March, 195X.

---

* Curve fitting was done by Mr. N. J.
Winters, Testing Section.

CONCLUSION

The "Conclusions" seem to violate what was said about avoiding technical terms in the concluding section of a three-level report. But no defect actually exists. The relatively few non-technical readers can quite easily get the significance of the last paragraph—and that is the gist of the findings. Except for the abbreviation of decibel and possibly "decay rate" the first conclusion also will give no trouble.

Thus the formula is the only really technical language used. It certainly must come here in view of the much larger number of technical readers and the objective of the project.

The conclusion of the next report is discussed on pages 540 and 544, the report situation on page 532.

CONCLUSIONS

1. For impact excitation:

   a. The surface density of the deadener materials applied to outer door panels is the important factor in determining their damping effectiveness.

   b. The db/second decay rate of deadener materials applied to outer door panels is not a significant factor in determining their damping effectiveness.

2. From data thus far obtained, the relation between impact of a door panel and surface density of applied deadener is best expressed by the equation

$$Y = 116 \ (X)^{.57}$$

   Y = percent damping (100% damping is assigned to a well damped door).

   X = surface density of deadener material (lbs./ft.^{2}).

   Thus, to obtain an agreeable, quality-sounding effect when car doors and roofs are given the knuckle test, the deadener must be selected on the basis of surface density (lbs./ft.^{2}) and not on the basis of damping rate. The same consideration applies to the case of rain and hail impact on car tops, doors and panels,

INTRODUCTION

The thick plate method has become the accepted method in the American automobile
industry of rating the vibration damping
properties of various applied materials.
Briefly, this consists of determining the
rate of decay of free vibration in db/second
of a 1/4 by 20 by 20 inch steel test plate
with the material attached. This method is
appropriate for the evaluation of damping
properties of materials used to control free
and forced vibrations as found in the
automobile.

However, it has been observed that the
thick plate rating does not correlate with
what is heard subjectively in the case where
a panel with deadener material applied is
set into vibration by impact. Examples of
impact excitation of practical importance in
relation to automobile bodies and panels are
rain and hail impact, and "knuckling." As a
specific example of lack of correlation between thick plate ratings and the effectiveness as applied, two materials evaluated by
the thick plate method were observed to have
the following damping and surface density:

Material	Surface Density (lbs./sq.ft.)	db/second at 150 cps
Chi	.4	2.2
3/4 inch Beta	.03	16.0

These materials were applied to the under-
side of two car roofs, and it was observed

that the car with the Chi applied gave a lower degree of disturbance inside the car in a simulated rain.

A laboratory check of this result was made by applying these materials to automobile outer door panels. Subsequent knuckle tests indicated that the one with the Chi applied was by far the quieter panel, confirming the car top observation.

DEVELOPING SECTIONS

The order of developing sections is almost inescapable: the preliminary investigations, the resulting major investigations, and the application of the results.

The organization of each section is classic. Thus "The Investigation of Some Theories" opens by stating the phase of the over-all project reported here and divides it into two heads, which are then discussed in the order named. The last paragraph gives the final outcome.

The section on "Effect of Surface Density . . ." is a different variation of the pattern. The first paragraph explains the situation which led to this phase of the investigation—here a hypothesis. Next materials tested and the nature of the test are given. No order of reporting is needed—obviously the tests will be reported in the order performed.

Developing sections of the next report are discussed on page 550, the report situation on page 532.

DATA

In sharp contrast with the sample report that immediately precedes it, the body of this report gives great emphasis to procedure. Under "Higher Mode Damping," for example, the reason for the testing procedure, its limitations, and the materials used are carefully described. In the section on "Effect of Surface Density" we also get reasons, materials, and specific steps. In addition, we are told how the data were processed.

The differences between this situation and that of the preceding report are obvious. Here the result reverses certain previous theories and must be evaluated by many critical people. If the chief engineer in the earlier situation had doubted his engineer's results, he could raise his questions directly. In this instance some readers had to evaluate the results many miles from the files and personnel of the department in which the tests were performed.

INVESTIGATION OF SOME THEORIES

Preliminary investigations were made in an effort to find the reason for this apparently anomalous behavior. These include the investigation of damping at higher vibration modes of the thick plate and the effect of initial amplitude on observed thick plate damping rate.

Higher Mode Damping

The reasoning behind giving consideration to this aspect of the problem is as follows: When a panel such as a car door is impact-excited, as by "knuckling," all the many possible modes of vibration are excited, and included, of course, are many high frequency modes. It was considered possible that different materials might exhibit radically different damping characteristics at these higher modes and frequencies, and that the rating at the 150 cps mode of the thick plate would thus not be an indication of the higher frequency performance. The effect considered here is in addition to the expected proportional increase in damping as the vibration frequency is increased. This latter consideration results from the fact that the energy extracted by a viscous damper, per cycle, is a fixed percentage of the total present; raising the frequency means more cycles per second and, hence, a higher db per second decay rate.

The raw data have been tabulated and are first presented in that form, then reduced to curves and a formula. The sections carefully interpret and evaluate these data.

Data of the next report are discussed on page 550, the report situation on page 532.

ILLUSTRATIONS

The original report contained five tables inserted in the text at the point of use. In reproducing the report, some of these have been changed to the "facing" position. The paragraph under Table I clearly demonstrates the value of explaining a table rather than leaving the entire job to the reader.

At the end of the report are two graphs and a photograph. Both curves are referred to in the text. The photograph is placed at the very last for the good reason that most of the readers are familiar with the door panel pictured and hence don't need the picture. Reference is made to it early in the second developing section, as part of the discussion of procedure.

Illustrations for the next report are discussed on page 550, the report situation on page 532.

ACKNOWLEDGMENTS

No acknowledgments are made or needed.

Acknowledgments of the next report are discussed on page 550, the report situation on page 532.

Report No. 3587

To investigate the higher mode effect, it was decided to excite the standard thick plate at its higher modes. This method does not provide for the separation of the effects of frequency and of higher vibration mode upon damping. But until the extent of these effects was roughly evaluated, it was not considered justifiable to design and build entirely new testing facilities which would allow separate evaluation of these two effects.

Using the same materials as in the door panel test, the thick plate was excited at the next three higher modes; the frequency which corresponds to these modes, as well as the damping obtained for the two samples in these modes, is listed in the following table:

		Damping, db/second				
Frequency		5122X			Fiberglas	
Chi	Beta	Obs.	α Freq.	Obs.	α	Freq.
151	155	2.44	2.44	16.6		16.6
392	402	14.5	6.3	26.3		44.
754	775	46.	12.2	48.6		84.
1710	1755	415.	27.7	140.		190.

These data indicate that the Beta maintains its standing as the better damper for the first two modes. In the third mode, about 760 cps, Chi is equally as good as Beta, and in the only mode higher than this which was investigated, the Chi has surpassed the Beta, thus continuing the trend shown in the lower modes.

These data were interpreted as not consti-
tuting an answer to the problem on the basis
that the important door panel frequencies
elicited upon impact of a moderately or well
damped door are below 750 cps.

In passing, it should be stated that with
the standard magnetic drive for the thick
plate, the resulting amplitudes at these
higher modes were quite small. The exact
configuration of the vibration patterns are
known only for the two lower modes, which
had one and two closed nodal curves, respectively. Little is known of the two higher
modes except that the small, closed nodal
circles were formed in each of the corners.

Also shown in the Table above is the
damping in db/second which might be expected
at the higher frequencies on the basis that
db/second damping is proportional to frequency. It is interesting to note that in
the case of the Beta, the observed damping
was less than what might be expected, while
for Chi, the observed damping was more than
this figure.

The bare plate damping values corresponding to each of the higher modes were not
determined.

The Effect of Initial Amplitude on Damping Rate

In conducting thick plate damping tests, a
choice must be made of the starting, or
initial, amplitude of the free vibrations,

Report No. 3587

the decay of which is a measure of the damping rate. Some variation of the damping
rate with initial vibration amplitude has
been observed, and the damping rate may
either decrease or increase as the amplitude
is diminished depending upon the material.

One material tested, Theta, was observed
to have a negative coefficient. By measuring the rate of decay at various times along
the decay record, it was found that an initial damping rate of 18 db/second fell to
15/second when the amplitude was reduced
20db. Another material, Epsilon, was found
to have an essentially flat characteristic.
The coefficients of still other materials
were determined by making separate observations of decay rate for each initial amplitude. In this way a material designated
Delta, 1/4 inch thick, was found to have a
negative coefficient of 1 db/second per 7 db
of amplitude. 1/2 inch thick Xi was found
to have a positive coefficient of 1 db/sec-
ond per 4 db. Lastly, the bare test plate
upon which these materials are tested was
found to change from 58 db/second to .51
db/second when reducing the initial amplitude by 20 db/ in both cases the decay rate
was averaged over a 10-db decay range.

These data have been accumulated over a
period of years and are presented here as
bearing on the problem even though the two
specific samples used on the car top test
were not included. In any case, it is clear
that these amplitude effects are small, of
the order of .2 db/second per db of amplitude, and so are not capable of accounting
for the anomalies observed.

EFFECT OF SURFACE DENSITY ON
IMPACT DAMPING

The effect of surface density on impact
damping was the major concern of this project. It was reasoned that under conditions
of impact excitation the initial displace-
ment of the panel represents conditions of
large acceleration and, hence, the panel is
probably mass-controlled. That is to say,
that initial amplitudes are essentially controlled by the mass of the damper rather
than by its resistance (damping) element or
stiffness.

It was decided to determine the relationship, if any, between surface density and
impact damping effectiveness by the application of various deadeners to the automobile
outer door panel shown in Figure 3. Several
materials having various combinations of
surface density and thick plate ratings were
selected. They are tabulated on the next
page.

Particular attention is called to Panels
1 and 6, which have the same damping but a
2:1 ratio of surface densities. Similarly,
samples No. 3 and No. 9 have the same damping and a 17:1 ratio of surface densities.
On the other hand, samples No. 4 and No. 5
have approximately the same density and a
12:1 ratio in damping, and Panels No. 7 and
No. 8 have identical densities and a 2:1
ratio in damping. These deadener materials
were applied to 10 automobile door panels

Report No. 3587

TABLE I

Panel No.	Material	Surface Density (lbs./ft.^{2})	Thick Plate Damping (db/sec. at 150 cps)
1	Omega	.77	26.8
2	Zeta	.77	30.1
3	Omega	.55	15.4
4	1 inch Xi	.31	111.2
5	1 inch Omicron	.25	8.9
6	1/2 inch Pi	.167	26.8
7	1/2 inch Xi	.104	8.9
8	1/2 inch Upsilon	.104	3.9
9	3/4 inch Beta	.031	15.4
10	Bare	--	--

and were suspended by means of ropes. A number of observers were asked to knuckle these panels and to rank order them according to the tinniness. All observers rated these 10 panels in the same order as they are tabulated above; that is, in order of their surface densities.

Subjective Tests - Increment Basis

These results are somewhat startling, yet constituted the answer we were seeking. In order to be able to "put a number" on the effectiveness of these materials which, as indicated by the knuckling test above, was primarily governed by their surface densities, additional tests were conducted. The best damped door, the one with the heavy, "quality" sound when knuckled, Panel No. 1 in Table I, was arbitrarily assigned a 100 percent rating. At the other end of the scale, a bare panel was given a zero rating.

TABLE II

Subjective Evaluation of Damping by Increments

TABLE II

Subjective Evaluation of Damping by Increments

Panel No.	lbs/ft.²	Observers' Rating							Average Rating
		DH	HL	ML	JH	RR	GV	DA	
1	.77			Assigned Rating					100.0
2	.77	95	99	100	95	100	95	95	97.0
3	.55	87	98	90	85	100	90	90	91.4
4	.31	70	93	75	70	90	80	82	80.0
5	.25	65	85	60	60	85	75	78	72.5
6	.167	60	80	60	50	77	70	74	67.3
7	.104	55	70	55	45	70	65	70	61.4
8	.104	50	65	50	40	70	60	65	57.1
9	.031	30	50	40	30	60	45	55	44.2
10	Bare			Assigned Rating					0

Seven observers were asked to rate the 8
other doors on an individual and independent
basis, given the two reference doors and
their ratings as "markers." They were asked
to do this on an increment basis; that is,
in rating a door their thinking would be in
terms of, say, 5 or 10 points between two
given panels, as estimated by comparison
with the total increment of 100 points between the markers. The values given by the
observers are tabulated in Table II.

There is a relatively large variation between observers' ratings for a given door
panel. The greatest difficulty seems to lie
in determining the increment to be assigned
between a bare panel and the one with the
minimum damping. In spite of this difficulty, however, it is interesting that there
is complete agreement regarding the rank
order of the panels.

The average of these seven observers' ratings for each panel is tabulated in the last
column and this average is plotted against
the corresponding surface density of the
material in Figure 1. A mathematical expression to fit this curve was determined.
This equation is

$$Y = 33 \sqrt[4]{100X}$$

where Y is the average of the observers'
ratings (on an incremental basis), and X is
the surface density of the materials applied
to the panels in lbs/ft^2. The steep slope
of this curve from zero to 50 (corresponding
to low surface density materials) reflects

TABLE III

Subjective Evaluation of Door Panels by Ratios

TABLE III

Subjective Evaluation of Door Panels by Ratios

Observers' Assigned Ratios

Panel No.	D	H	M	R	V	A	N	Average Ratios
1:3	1.3	2.0	1.1	1.0	1.2	1.1	1.5	1.31
1:4	2.0	—	1.25	1.3	1.3	1.4	2.0	1.54
3:5	1.7	2.0	1.2	1.1	1.4	1.2	1.5	1.44
4:7	2.7	—	2.0	2.0	1.8	1.4	1.5	1.90
5:7	2.0	2.2	1.5	1.2	2.0	2.0	1.5	1.63
7:8	-1.2	—	1.0	-1.1	-1.1	1.1	1.0	.96
7:9	2.0	1.6	2.0	1.2	2.5	2.0	2.0	1.90
8:9	2.5	—	2.0	2.0	2.0	2.5	2.0	2.16

the difficulty which was encountered in establishing a value for the increment between a bare door and one with a small amount of damping.

Subjective Tests - Ratio Basis

The Weber-Fechner Law indicates that an evaluation on a ratio basis is much more in order. This law states that physiological responses such as hearing, seeing, feeling, etc., follow a percentage increase in the corresponding physical stimulus rather than an incremental increase.

Accordingly, seven of the 10 outer door panels which were used in the two earlier tests were used and the best panel was assigned a reference point of 100 percent. Seven observers were asked to individually and independently knuckle and rate each consecutive pair of panels, giving a decimal number representing their conception of the damping ratio. Each observer thus rated eight pairs. The findings are given in Table III.

Here Panels 7 and 8 were reversed in order, but the average ratio is nearly unity; these two samples have identical surface densities. The average ratios were then converted to percent damping values by starting with the 100% panel and working downward. These converted values are shown in Table IV.

TABLE IV

Subjective Percent Damping on Basis of Ratios

Panel No.	Surface Density lb/ft²	Percent Damping				116 (X)$^{.57}$	114 (X)$^{.5}$
1	.77		100	100		100	100
3	.55		76.3	--		82.5	84.5
4	.31		--	64.9		59.6	63.5
5	.25		53.0	--		52.7	57.0
7	.104	32.5	32.5	34.2	34.2	31.9	33.6
8	.104	33.9	--	35.7	--	31.9	33.6
9	.031	15.7	17.1	16.5	18.0	16.0	20.1

In Table III it will be noted that Panel 7 is related to Panel 1, the reference, via two means: (1) 1:3, 3:5 and 5:7; and (2) 1:4 and 4:7. These "routes" lead to values of 32.5 and 34.2 for Panel 7. The agreement here must be considered as extremely good in view of the small number of observers. Similarly, Panel 9 is rated with respect to Panel 7 in two ways, and this in combination with the two figures for Panel 7 leads to a total of four values for Panel 9. Again, these four values check closely, all lying within the range of 15.7 and 18.0.

These subjective damping figures are plotted in Figure 2 and an average curve drawn through them. The mathematical equation which fits this curve is

$$Y = 116 \ (X)^{.57}$$

Y and X being the damping and surface density, respectively. This equation is fairly close to a square root function

$$Y = 114 \ (X)^{.5}$$

Both of these expressions are shown in Figure 2. The square root function, while more desirable because of its simplicity, obviously does not have the precision of fit that the other function possesses.

APPLICATION

Thus, there is good evidence that the aural impression obtained by an observer when an automobile panel is impact excited is largely controlled by the surface density of the damping material applied. The surface density characteristic outweighs the importance of the damping characteristic. Referring to Table I, it seems especially significant that Panel 3 outranks Panel 4 because it has the higher surface density, and this is so even though Panel 4 has a damping 7.5 times as large as Panel 3. Apparently, even when the surface densities are identical, the damping is not an important enough factor to determine the better plate. There are two examples where this occurs; Samples 1 and 2 (Table II), and Samples 7 and 8 (Table III). In both instances, the lower damping was preferred, although by a slight margin.

The principles disclosed in this report apply to body and roof panels where the damping material is applied to the full area. Whether or not impact damping is controlled by surface density to this same extent in cases where the material is applied to a limited area of the panel will have to be determined by further investigation.

Further, the effect of completing the door assembly should probably be assessed. For

example, a curve similar to those of Figure 2 may result, but completing and trimming the door may tend to compress the horizontal (density) scale, either rather uniformly or on one end or the other. As desirable as additional investigation may be, the study reported here should help designers in their problem of what material to specify by properly relating the physical characteristics which control various effects.

This is essentially the state of affairs previously existing, when materials were chosen on the basis of their damping rate alone; that is, completed door performance could not be predicted from that figure. The difference now is that the additional information should lead to a more discerning choice.

In this connection, it appears that the ideal damper for automobile doors and tops would have high surface density for best impact performance, as well as high damping rates for absorption of steady-state and free vibrations. Further, it appears that the requirement for a high surface density could profitably be relaxed for materials to be applied to floors and other panels where impact damping performance is not of primary concern.

Report No.   3587

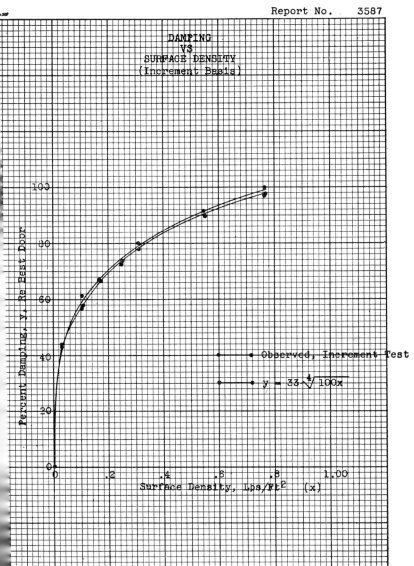

DAMPING
VS
SURFACE DENSITY
(Increment Basis)

Percent Damping, y, Re Best Door

Surface Density, Lbs/Ft² (x)

← Observed, Increment Test

$y = 33\sqrt[4]{100x}$

Figure 1

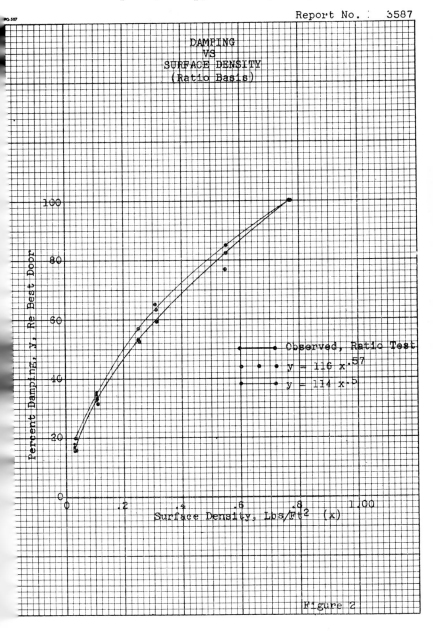

DAMPING
VS
SURFACE DENSITY
(Ratio Basis)

Percent Damping, Y, Re Best Door

Observed, Ratio Test
$y = 116\ x^{.57}$
$y = 114\ x^{.5}$

Surface Density, Lbs/Ft² (x)

Figure 2

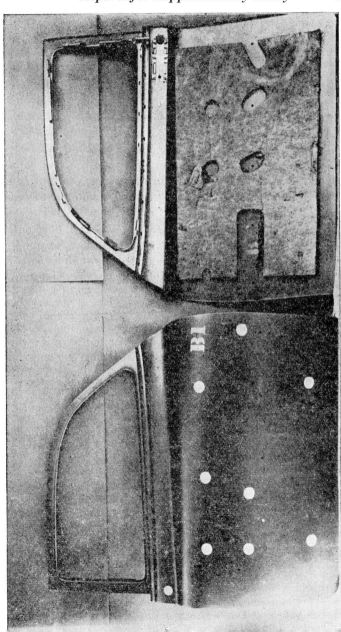

2962.42A. Example of Outer Door Panel and Position of Deadener Material.

SOYBEAN LOSSES

This REPORT is included as another example of a variation in giving the quick picture. It resembles the preceding report in placing the Conclusions before the main introduction, and preceding them both by another element. Here instead of a brief foreword, the element is a complete summary.

The report also gives another instance of the influence of short report practice on longer reports. It is a successful adaptation, but might have been more successful without being partially strait-jacketed in a form suitable to less extensive material.

It shows how a good and careful job can overcome obstacles. But it also shows what obstacles can be put in our way if we *don't* learn to design a report in virtue of the particular situation, including materials. The only defects of this report come from having learned too well the rigid pattern of certain short reports.

REPORT SITUATION

This is a *student* report which won first place in a national contest of a professional association. (Total pages—31.)

The situation of the next report is described on page 564.

FORMAT

The report was bound in a fibre cover which contained the usual identifying material. Only main heads were used.

Look next at the format of the reports on pages 564 and 576.

[*This page represents the cover*]

SOYBEAN LOSSES
AT THE CUTTER BAR OF THE COMBINE

by

Edwin J. Halter   February 26, 195X

PREFATORY MATERIAL

The main prefatory material is in a letter of transmittal in standard form. Here the letter is placed *before* the title page, a frequently used position. The first sentence both transmits the letter and gives the occasion for doing so. The original occasion and readers are designated next. The last sentence qualifies the recency of the data.

Other prefatory material is on the title page—the author's status and the advisors.

A graceful acknowledgment is the last item of the report. The information it gives was not pertinent to the purpose of this particular letter, but the author rightly wanted to show his obligation and appreciation. The separate section was the best solution (see page 563).

There is also a prefatory footnote on page 1.

The next prefatory material is described on page 578, the report situation on page 576.

2396 Simonds Avenue
Phiville, Illinois
February 26, 1954

Mr. F. Charles Leeds, Chairman
Section on Student Paper Awards
Sigma Equipment Association,
3300 S. Brand Street
Alphaville 12, Kentucky

Dear Mr. Leeds:

The following report entitled "Soybean
Losses at the Cutter Bar of the Combine" is
submitted to your committee for consideration in the Student Paper Award contest.
This report was originally prepared and
written to fulfill the requirements of Agricultural Engineering 613 and 702 at Delta
University. It recently was adapted for the
Gamma Student Paper Competition. The data
presented in this report were collected during the summer and fall of 1953.

Respectfully yours,

Edwin J. Halter

Edwin J. Halter

vjs

SOYBEAN LOSSES AT THE CUTTER BAR

OF THE COMBINE

by

Edwin J. Halter

February 26, 1954

Student at

Delta University

Alphaville 12, Kentucky

Class of 1954

Advisors

Byron K. Schultz, Assistant Professor

Donald R. Hunt, Assistant Professor

Department of Agricultural Engineering

TABLE OF CONTENTS

ABSTRACT

The summary provided here could also be called an abstract, for it demonstrates exactly the rules of abstracting. That is, it follows the order of the main report and keeps the space devoted to a topic in the abstract and in the whole report as proportional as possible. (It is like a photographic reduction of a big picture.)

Overlap between it and the conclusions is inevitable. And the overlap is very apparent when the conclusions are brought forward from the end position to a position near the front. Hence the arrangement shown here is desirable only when the abstract or summary is likely to be reproduced separately from the report. That was the situation here.

As an abstract, this exhibit is nearly ideal.

This is the last sample report containing an abstract.

SOYBEAN LOSSES AT THE CUTTER BAR

OF THE COMBINE[1]

I. Summary

Since the soybean losses at the cutter bar
of the combine represent the major proportion of the harvesting losses, it was felt
that a study of the factors that influence
these losses would be of considerable value
to both the farmer and the manufacturer.

The objective of this study was to investigate the cause and the significance of the
losses that result from the action of the
cutter bar knife and reel.

One of the biggest problems in the investigation of these losses was that of separating the losses that were caused by the

1. The study of these losses was conducted
   as a partial fulfillment of the requirements of the 613 and 702 Agricultural
   Engineering classes, and as a phase of
   work under the Research and Marketing
   Project No. 38 of the Delta Agricultural
   Experiment Station.

2

knife from those that were caused by the
reel. The magnitude of these losses should
be known by the designer and the operator so
that they can place their emphasis at the
proper place. One method of doing this was
that of mounting a reel on a tractor in
order to determine the loss caused by the
operation of the reel without the use of the
cutter bar. Another method was that of
operating the combine without the reel.
These two methods indicated that the loss
caused by the reel under normal conditions
was relatively low.

A self-propelled combine was used in this
study to permit the selection of any desired
forward speed. Since the reel on this combine had only two speeds, an electric speed
changer and a portable generator were
mounted on the combine to provide a means of
varying the speed of the reel. It was found
that an increase of either the forward speed

3

of the combine or the speed of the reel caused an increase in the cutter bar losses.

The Delta Experimental Reel, which was used in two tests, did not indicate any major difference in the losses over those that resulted from the use of the conventional reel.

The most time consuming task encountered in the conducting of the field tests was that of collecting the shatter and cutter bar losses. The time lost in taking these samples made it necessary to reduce the area from which these losses were collected in order to provide enough time to conduct the required field tests.

Because of the limited amount of time that was available for the conducting of field tests, this report does not give all of the answers to the questions that have arisen during this investigation, but this study

CONCLUSION

Conclusions are clearly stated and appropriately listed. They are shown to be under the influence of short reports in two ways. First, they are not introduced by a topic sentence. Every other section is. Second, they are not keyed to the supporting evidence in any way. We cannot use the Table of Contents, as it shows only the generalized head of "Discussion of Results." Finally, the order of the conclusions does not correspond to the order of the main sections of the report. If a reader doubts one conclusion he is not given help in finding the supporting evidence, but must leaf through the report.

4

has confirmed the need to continue this investigation.

II. Conclusions

1. Reel losses increase as the speed index of the reel increases, but it is relatively low for normal reel speeds.

2. Cutter bar losses increase as the forward speed of travel increases.

3. There was no noticeable difference in the losses caused by the Delta Experimental Reel and those caused by the conventional reel.

4. Shatter losses increase as the time of harvest is delayed beyond the date of maturity.

5. There is a need for a faster method of collecting shatter and cutter bar losses.

6. The losses at the cutter bar of the combine are high enough to warrant further investigations.

INTRODUCTION

The introduction here comes after the short view has been given. Only those interested in the detail will read it and the rest of the report.

It contains most of the major elements of the full pattern. Its use of history as background is effective, because it leads directly to the development of the problem in paragraph two. Next the problem is broken into its parts, and two of them excluded.

Normally, the reader would expect the report to continue with two more sections—one on each phase studied. Since it does not, an order of reporting ought to have been given.

Procedure is likewise missing, but this is not a defect, for two reasons. First, a brief view of procedure has already been given in the summary. Second, an account of general procedure follows at once, without intervening material.

5

III.   Introduction

During and after World War II, the farmer
had a great deal of difficulty in securing
extra help. In order to alleviate the labor
situation and to become more independent,
the farm placed considerable emphasis on
obtaining harvesting machinery which saved
labor. Since the combine met the demands of
those farmers who grew small grains, it became accepted in many localities as the best
method for harvesting these crops. Now that
the combine has been accepted and is widely
used, the farmer is becoming more concerned
with the efficiency of this machine.

Since the losses at the cutter bar* of the
combine represent as high as 80% of the
total harvesting losses in soybeans,[1] it was
felt that a study should be made to reveal
the nature and the magnitude of these
losses; therefore, the purpose of this study
was to investigate the sources and the

* See Definition of Terms, page 25.
1. Hurst, W. M. and Humphries, W. R. Performance Characteristics of Five and Six
   Foot Combines, U.S.D.A. Circular No.
   470, May 1938.

6

causes of the various losses that occur at
the cutter bar and to make recommendations
pertaining to both the design and the operation of the combine which will materially
reduce these losses.

There are four principal places where
losses occur at the front of the combine.
These places are (1) the cutter bar knife,
(2) the bats of the reel, (3) the grain dividers, and (4) the platform of the combine.
Since it is believed that the losses caused
by the action of the reciprocating knife and
the bats of the reel compose the greatest
percentage of the cutter bar losses, this
study was primarily concerned with investigating the knife and reel losses.

IV. General Procedure

One of the first problems encountered in
conducting field tests that will give valid

data on cutter bar losses is that of developing a method of evaluating the preharvest or shatter loss. Basically, the method must be such the grain is collected from a known area so that it can be converted to a loss per acre basis. The use of a fixed frame of a definite area is not practical since its use would cause many beans and bean pods to be knocked to the ground. This is especially true in fields that have been drilled.

In an attempt to get a definite area and still not disturb the soybean plants, a method was devised so that four yardsticks, which were placed individually by sliding them on the ground, were used to form a sample area of one square yard. Before field tests were started, the beans and bean pods that were enclosed in the square yard were picked up at three or four randomly

DEVELOPING SECTIONS

As the Table of Contents shows, the main sections are in the order of those of a short report. Note the relatively large number of pages given to discussion of results (14).

This "discussion" section, not shown here, was itself very well organized. The principle of organization was chronological. The section was arranged in the same order as the tests were conducted. This arrangement now explains the order used in the conclusions.

Note the effective use of topic and transition sentences in the sections on procedure.

DATA

The procedure sections are given here as another example of careful explanation of methodology. Such detail and careful evaluation are required whenever a procedure is new or the results open to serious question.

Data were presented in photographs, tables, graphs, and drawings, which were interpreted in the text.

ILLUSTRATIONS

The photographs shown here give a concrete picture of the apparatus and how it was mounted. Drawings and text gave the details.

Note that the position of the photos allows a simple "See Figure 1" reference.

ACKNOWLEDGMENTS

The acknowledgments are prefatory, except on page 541, where a footnote is used and on page 558, where an acknowledgment is in the text.

8

selected locations. In order to prevent the collection of erroneous data that would result from having one of these areas fall within a test area, these shatter loss sample areas were either located between test plots or they were located so that the affected area could be removed by combining a preliminary swath.

In order to evaluate the cutter bar losses, a wooden frame which had an area of 1/10,000 of an acre was placed at five different locations in each test plot. These locations were chosen in the middle of each swath in an attempt to eliminate the influence that the grain dividers might have on the cutter bar losses. The loose beans, bean pods, and stems with pods attached were collected from each test plot and placed in separate sacks. These samples were taken to the laboratory where they were separated and

9

weighed. Net cutter bar loss was found by subtracting the weight of the shatter loss from the sum of the above mentioned losses.

Test plots of 1/100 of an acre were laid out by placing two range poles perpendicular to the direction of travel at each end of the test plot. In all tests the combine was operated so that it was cutting a full swath; therefore, the length of the plot was a function of the cutter bar width only. The plots were located so that the combine had time to stabilize before it entered the test area.

As a reference point on when the combine entered the test area, a stop watch was started and the grain from the discharge spout was collected in a sack. As the same reference point passed the end of the test area, the stop watch was stopped and the sample grain sack was removed from the grain

10

spout. The stop watch gave very accurate data from which the forward speed of the combine and the speed of the reel could be determined. The weight and moisture content of the grain sample were determined as a first step in the calculation of the yield. The moisture was determined by the use of a Steinlite Moisture Tester.

All discharge from the combine was collected in a large canvas which was either fastened or held against the bottom of the shoe. Since the discharge that was collected contained the threshing and separating losses, the beans that remained on the ground represented the sum of the shatter and cutter bar losses.

A combine efficiency of 90% was used in calculating the yield. This was the approximate efficiency that the 613 Agricultural Engineering class found for the combine on

11

October 20, 1953. The yield was needed so
that the losses could be computed on a
percentage basis.

V.   Special Procedure

The logical approach to the problem of
reducing cutter bar losses would be to find
the magnitude of the component losses and
strive to decrease the ones that are the
most significant. Since it is generally
believed that the major proportion of the
cutter bar losses is caused by the action of
the knife and the bats of the reel, it would
be quite desirable to be able to separate
the losses caused by the knife from those
caused by the reel.

The previously tried method of attaching a
canvas to the rear edge of the cutter bar on
a mowing machine to determine the loss

12

caused by the knife was not very satisfactory. One limitation was that the specifications and characteristics of the cutter bar of a mower are quite different from those for the cutter bar of a combine. Another limitation of this method was that the material bunches up on the cutter bar and pushes the uncut plants forward. This causes abnormal losses since some of the stems fall forward and are then cut again at a point above some of the lower pods.

Since the idea of using a mowing machine was not successful, a search was made to find other methods that would work. The idea of mounting a combine reel on a tractor and operating the reel independent of the combine and the cutter bar seemed like a possible solution even though the results obtained would only give a relative instead of a true value for the losses caused by the

13

Fig. 1.   The Mounted Reel

reel.   See Fig. 1.   To test this method, a
reel was mounted on a tractor and fitted
with several pulleys so that different speed
indexes could be obtained.   The tests consisted of running this reel through the test
area at given conditions of speed and speed
index and then to collect the resulting
losses by the method used to determine
shatter loss.

14

A second method that was tried was that of operating the combine without the reel. This was done by disengaging the conventional reel and removing two or three of the bats to prevent them from touching or interfering with the grain. Since the platform canvas did not extend clear out to the dividers, the straw tended to bunch up on the cutter bar close to the dividers. Yardsticks were used to keep the straw from bunching up on the cutter bar.

The combine used in these tests had a variable-speed pulley drive system which made possible the selection of any speed within the speed range of the combine. Since the reel on this combine only had two speeds which were driven independently of ground speed, it was possible to get only two speed indexes for each forward speed

15

used. The relationship of forward speed to
speed index is shown in Fig. 2.

Because of the desirability of using the
same speed index for several different forward speeds and of selecting different speed
indexes to be used with given forward
speeds, a method was developed to permit the
selection of any desired speed index for any
given forward speed. This was done by
mounting an electric speed changer and a
portable generator on the combine. See
Fig. 3.

The Delta Experimental Reel, which was
designed by Professor Benson and his 613
Agricultural Engineering class in 1952, was
mounted on the combine and tested. See Fig.
4. This reel was designed so that the bats
would enter the grain in a vertical plane
with no motion parallel to the direction of
combine travel at a speed index of 1.5:1.

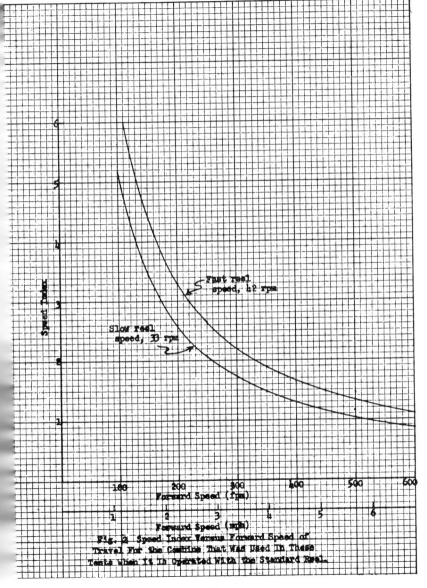

Fig. 2 Speed Index Versus Forward Speed of Travel For the Combine That Was Used In These Tests when It Is Operated With the Standard Reel.

Fig. 3. The Electric Speed Changer and the
Portable Generator as They Were
Mounted on the Combine.

Fig. 4. The Delta University Experimental
Reel

18

The collection of the shatter loss in undisturbed areas was a very time consuming
process, but no substitute or improvement of
the previously stated method was found. In
the case of the cutter bar losses, it was
thought that the use of a vacuum cleaner
would speed up the collection of these
losses. Because of the importance of reducing the time required to pick up these
losses so that more tests could be run on a
given day, the vacuum cleaner method was
tried. The same frames that were used for
the hand method were randomly placed in the
test area and then the open end of the
vacuum hose was moved back and forth over
the area inside of each frame. This system
picked up the losses fairly well, but the
strong vacuum required to pick up the beans
removed most of the top one inch of soil.
This method was discontinued because of the
difficulty experienced in separating the
losses from the soil.

.   .   .   .

APPENDIX C

ACKNOWLEDGMENTS

The writer wishes to express his appreciation to all of the people that have helped to conduct these investigations. The author feels indebted to Professor B. K. Schultz and Donald R. Hunt for their constructive criticism and helpful suggestions. Credit should also be given to the members of the 613 Agricultural Engineering class for their contribution in the investigation. This is especially true for David Cashman and George Corey, for they worked on this study for their class project, and for Robert Weeks, who helped with the drafting work.

EXPLORATORY WORK ON
ELECTROLYTIC RECOVERY

THE FINAL report on a long-term project may be handled in many ways. One way is to integrate the entire story, including all data, in a final report organized as a single unit that supersedes all earlier reports. We have seen such reports on pages 279 and 390.

Here is illustrated another practice. The first report shown, called a "completion report" does not supersede earlier reports. Instead, it is a summary of them. If all were gathered in a single cover, this report would come first, giving the required quick picture of the entire project. The total report of the project, then, would consist of this report, plus the three progress reports (one of which is also shown) plus the laboratory notebooks of data.

In practice, these are either bound together or placed together, unbound, in the file of the originating department.

Twelve pages of tables and graphs were appended to the progress report.

January 27, 1953
J. B. Bailey

Subject:

Exploratory Work on Electrolytic Recovery
of White Metal Composite Scrap

Project:

No. 389 - Completion Report

References:

1. "Exploratory Work on Electrolytic Re-
    covery of White Metal Composite
    Scrap." - Project 389 Progress Report.
    J. B. Bailey 1-10-51

2. "The Electrolytic Recovery of Steel
    Backed Theta Scrap." - Project 410 -
    Completion Report.
    J. B. Bailey 10-14-52

3. "Investigation of Electrode Character-
    istics for White Metal Recovery."
    Project 389 - Progress Report.
    G. D. Boyle 1-26-53

Object:

This project was undertaken in order to
investigate the possibilities of using
electrolytic methods for the recovery of
white metals from steel-backed scrap.

Conclusions:

1. Technologically, it appears possible
    to recover white metals from steel-
    backed scrap by simultaneous anodic
    solution and cathodic deposition. It
    has been indicated, however, that re-
    covery will be less complete than in

the case of electrolytic Theta recovery, because of the formation of insoluble metal rich anode slime or mud.

2. The following two considerations make the electrolytic recovery of white metals appear less attractive economically than was the case for copper-base alloys:

    a. White metals would not be recovered in a premium-value form, as would the copper-base alloys. (Reference 3)

    b. Existing thermal methods for recovery of white metals are at present considerably more profitable, so far as realization of metal value is concerned, than is the direct sale of Theta scrap.

Recommendations:

Should further work on the electrolytic recovery of white metals be undertaken, it is recommended that pilot-plant operations be instituted, using initial conditions established in the work covered by references #1 and #2. Such operations would make possible the development of the essential details of process technology, as well as a more complete economic evaluation of the process.

It is suggested that any such work be undertaken only when and if electrolytic recovery of copper-base alloys has been proved profitable on a production basis.

Discussion:

I - Technology

In the work covered by references #1 and #2, it was shown that selective anodic corrosion of white metals in the presence of steel could be obtained in alkaline solutions by proper potential control. Complete solution of the white metals was not obtained, however. Using the best anion combination studied, a 10% to 15% loss of metal in the form of anode slime or mud was encountered. In practice, this metal would be wasted, or would be recovered only by operation of a second refining process. It is possible, but by no means probable, that mechanical tumbling of the anode charge (which would be obtained in a cell such as the one used in the pilot plant studies on clevite scrap), might decrease this loss. It seems doubtful, however, that metal loss as slime could be ignored even under these conditions.

Loose, coarsely crystalline cathode deposits of both tin and lead have been obtained at high cathode current efficiency. The physical characteristics of these deposits (adherence to cathode, ease of removal, etc.) appeared to be suitable from the standpoint of cathode handling in an operating process. Further study of the cathode processes would be necessary to work out the problems of balancing deposit composition and deposition rates with scrap composition and corrosion rates. Preliminary experiments have indicated the probability of obtaining such balance, and it is felt that further experimentation would best be carried out in connection with pilot plant operations.

II - Economics

In studying the potential economies of electrolytic recovery of copper base scrap (reference 3) it was evident that profitable operation would depend to a considerable extent on the fact that these alloys could be recovered in a premium value form (i.e., as alloy powder). Realization of that premium in value would require the use of the powder in that form, without further refining or melting.

In the case of the white metals, there seems at present to be no reason to consider the re-use of recovered metals without melting and re-alloying. Under these conditions, it seems very doubtful that an electrolytic process could compete with existing thermal methods of recovery, which are themselves capable of returning a substantially higher portion of the metal value of the scrap than is realized from the direct sale of copper-base scrap.

In the light of these comparisons, it appears that further investigations (which should be on pilot plant scale) would best be deferred until such time as the electrolytic recovery of copper-base scrap has been proved out on a production basis.

J. B. Bailey

J. B. Bailey

/jw

January 10, 1951
J. B. Bailey

Subject:

Exploratory Work on Electrolytic Recovery
of White Metal Composite Scrap.

Project:

No. 389 - Progress Report

References:

Laboratory Notebook #210 pp. 1-41.

Object:

To investigate the anodic corrosion of
steel-backed white metals in various solutions, and to select a basic anion system
for the recovery of the white metals from
composite scrap.

Summary & Conclusions:

1. No suitable acid electrolyte for the
    separation of white metals from steel
    has been developed.

2. The general suitability of alkaline
    solutions for this purpose has been
    indicated.

3. A fairly effective alkaline system has
    been obtained and its performance at
    the anode under one set of conditions
    defined quantitatively.

4. The general drawback of alkaline baths
    has been found to be the tendency to-
    ward the formation of insoluble anode
    smut and consequent loss as sludge
    of metal from the electrolytic system.

5. Cathode deposits containing all the
    metals present in our white metal

alloys have been obtained from alkaline solutions.

Recommendations:

The following outline for future small-scale experimental work is recommended:

1. Determination of optimum conditions of current density, solution motion and chemical concentration in the alkaline cyanide-tartratenitrate-carbonate system, from the standpoint of minimum loss of metal as smut.

2. A similar quantitative re-study of the effects of chloride and bromide ions, and the possibility of omission of cyanide and tartrate ions.

3. A study of cathode reactions for the purpose of cathodic recovery of the dissolved metals.

4. A study of the treatment of anode smuts for metal recovery, if smut formation cannot be substantially eliminated in the work of 1 and 2 above.

Experimental Procedure:

The work discussed in this report was done in 2 and 3 liter still baths, using white metal anodes cut from production bimetal stock and equipped with a removable Lucite shield for use when one side only of the anode was to be exposed. Except where noted, 2" x 6" rectangular anode blanks were used. Steel and stainless steel cathodes were used, of size equal to or greater than that of the anode.

Current-voltage curves were obtained by using shielded anodes (steel side exposed for steel current values), and reading current values as rapidly as possible with ascending voltages. This was done in order to minimize the effect of anode passivation with time. For determination of stability of current, constant currents were held until anode passivation necessitated a sudden increase in voltage. Passivation was considered to be rapid in cases where such a voltage increase occurred within 30 minutes from the beginning of electrolysis with an initially clean anode surface.

A setup for the complete stripping of F-11 from steel was made by connecting a large (2" x 6") shielded anode in parallel with a $\frac{1}{4}$" wide strip from which most of the alloy had been removed by filing. By using a separate ammeter for each anode, it was possible to maintain a constant current density on the large anode (100% alloy surface) while permitting the current to the small anode to drop off as the alloy area decreased. Smut accumulations were removed by periodic brushing. This arrangement simulated the conditions which would exist during a stripping operation -- i.e., the presence in the bath of parallel-connected anodes ranging from 100% steel to freshly charged material. The quantity of metal tied up as anode smut was determined by brushing the smut from the anode under water, filtering and washing the material thus collected, igniting, weighing and analyzing for metals.

Experimental Data:

The selective action of a number of elec-
trolytes is shown in Figs. 1-6, together
with the approximate current densities
above which rapid alloy passivation
occurred.

The nature of the corrosion of white
metals in alkaline baths is shown in
Tables I and II. Table III summarizes the
effect of the various additions made in
obtaining the date of Table II.

The current-time relationships existing
during the complete stripping of F-11 in
an alkaline bath are shown in Fig. 7, and
the calculations of deplating rates for
this experiment in Table IV.

Table V shows a summary of the performance
of an alkaline cyanide-tartrate bath with
added nitrate and carbonate.

Compositions of the baths used in this
work are given in Table VI.

Discussion:

To be suitable for the separation of the
non-ferrous portion of composite scrap by
anodic corrosion, the anion system used in
the electrolyte must make possible the
following.

1. Selective action - the concentration
    of anode current and action on the
    non-ferrous portion of the anodes.

2. Continuous action - corrosion of the

non-ferrous metals without the formation of passivating films or smuts, or
with the formation of only such insoluble material as can be easily dis-
lodged from the anode surfaces.

Economic considerations would favor the
use of an electrolyte which produced maximum solution of the metals to be recovered
with as little loss of metal as anode smut
or slimes as possible.

From the standpoint of the ability to form
soluble compounds of the constituents of
our white metals, two general systems were
indicated -- acid, such as chloride, fluoborate or fluosilicate, and alkaline, possibly with the addition of one or more
complexing ions such as cyanide or tartrate.

Past experience in our plating operations
did not indicate the probability of obtaining selective action in acid solutions. Several trials were made with
fluoborate solutions to determine whether
such selectivity might exist at low poten-
tials, or be promoted by the addition of
an oxidizing ion (dichromate) or by prior
saturation of the solution with iron.
Figs. 1, 2 and 3 show that only in the
case of the iron-saturated bath was any
selectivity indicated. It was found in
this case that prolonged electrolysis at
the point of greatest spread between steel
and alloy currents resulted in pronounced
steel corrosion. It was also found, in
connection with tin-splatter removal in
plant 3, that anodic corrosion of steel in

inhibited hydrochloric acid proceeded just
as in uninhibited acid. For these reasons, no further work was attempted with
acid systems and attention was devoted to
investigation of possible alkaline systems.

The data of Table I show that, in simple
alkaline solutions, corrosion of F-1
(tin-base) took place in a fairly clean
fashion at low current densities, although
considerable smut was formed on the lead-
base alloys. Fig. 4 shows that pronounced
selective action was obtainable at current
densities below those causing rapid alloy
passivation (approx. 20 amp/ft^2). The in-
clusion of tartrate and cyanide ions appeared to somewhat diminish the smut forming tendency.

A number of additions were made to a basic
alkaline cyanide-tartrate bath in an effort to further reduce the formation of
anode smut. The results of these trials
are shown in Table II and summarized in
Table III. It appeared that some improvement resulted from the addition of chloride, bromide, and particularly nitrate
ions. Carbonate ions, not found to be
harmful to white metal corrosion, resulted
in still greater improvement in selectivity (Figs. 5 and 6). Prolonged electrolysis in nitrate containing baths resulted
in rapid alloy passivation at current

densities above 20 amp/ft^2. It was also
found, upon prolonged electrolysis, that
F-1 corrosion resulted in appreciable smut
formation -- a fact which had not been
apparent in previous short run tests.

The possibility of completely stripping white metal from composite scrap in an alkaline solution was demonstrated by the results shown in Fig. 7 and Table IV. It was shown that, with regular removal of anode smut, 100% stripping was achieved, and at a substantially constant corrosion rate -- indicating complete concentration of electrolytic action on the white metal.

A quantitative measure of the effectiveness of the alkaline cyanide-tartrate-nitrate-carbonate system for white metal corrosion was obtained from the work summarized in Table V. Under the test conditions, 17% of the F-1 and 19% of the F-11 were lost as insoluble anode smut. The dissolving tendencies of the various alloy constituents are indicated by their separate solution ratios. The determination of such solution ratios for a given bath and set of conditions would appear to be the most valid method of evaluating performance at the anode, and should probably be applied in future work.

The composition of the cathode deposits obtained (Table V) indicated the possibility of cathodic recovery of the metals taken into solution at the anode.

J. B. Bailey

J. B. Bailey

JB:mp

SUGGESTION PLAN REPORT

This report consists of a memo (letter) plus a printed report. The nature of the main report is such that it is not reproduced here. However, it will be analyzed below.

The report is an interesting handling of a report situation, but the main reason for analyzing it is to show that an accompanying letter often has a summarizing and interpreting function in addition to a transmitting one.

REPORT SITUATION

The report which this letter accompanied was printed in black and red on a single sheet, which folded to three parts, each 8½ by 12. When opened, the first third seen was a summary of the year in the same terms as in the list in the letter shown here. Also on that page was a table breaking payments down by certain classes.

The first page, then, was a tabulated quick view of the year. It had no explanatory text—nor did the rest of the report.

The remaining two "pages" of this side of the sheet showed, in terms of a composite figure, standings of divisions and of plants. They were arranged from first to last, with the corporation average placed in its order. Those below that average were shown in red; those above it in black.

The entire opposite side of the sheet was a breakdown by plants of the items summarized on page one.

In short, it was a report entirely in tables, proceeding from a summary in the front to detailed data in the back.

The entire report went from a corporation office to corresponding offices in plants and divisions. The readers got a similar tabulated report and memo every quarter. The tabulated report was extensive and important, but routine.

Hence no text was needed to explain the tables. But something was needed to prevent the report's being handled as routine. Hence the memo. (Total pages of memo—2.)

Jan. 23, 1953

SUBJECT   SUGGESTION PLAN REPORT
            FOR THE YEAR 1952

TO   SUGGESTION CHAIRMEN   ADDRESS

We are sending you this report closing out 1952 with mixed
feelings. There are two things which stand out in examining
the report. First is your remarkable record of accomplishment
for 1952. Second is the serious problem with which we are
faced in view of the extremely high backlog of open suggestions.

First, let's look at the great progress you made in 1952 as reflected in the comparisons shown below--

	Fourth Quarter 1951	Fourth Quarter 1952	Year 1951	Year 1952
Number employes Participating				
Per Cent Employes Participating				
Number Suggestions Submitted				
Per Cent Suggestions to Eligible Employes				
Number Suggestions Reviewed				
Number Suggestions Adopted	(Here were four columns			
Per Cent Suggestions Adopted	of figures)			
Total Amount of Awards				
Average Award				
Number Maximum Awards				
Number Awards $1,000 or Over				
Time and Material Savings Awards				

We are sure that all of you will get a great deal of satisfaction
out of examining this outstanding record because it shows clearly
how well your efforts have paid off. The cooperation of supervision, Suggestion Committee members and everyone in management
who helps to investigate suggestions, has resulted in a continuing
enthusiastic response from employes. They obviously like the new
Plan and the way their ideas have been handled. And the quality
of ideas submitted has been good. Of the total amount paid in
awards, two thirds was paid for suggestions which save labor or
material.

In addition, the thousands of constructive management-employe
contacts on suggestions have, we believe, helped materially to
improve employe attitudes.

PREFATORY MATERIAL

Besides the usual memo fill-ins, obvious prefatory material is the "I am sending you." The rest looks like a re-hash of the report, with a comparison of a previous year and quarter.

But is it? Recall that prefatory matter makes clear the relationship between reader, writer, and material. (Why are YOU giving THIS to ME.)

The answer the writer is giving is this: "It isn't just for routine information. I looked at this material and compared it with last year's material. You did mighty well here in one place, and we can all be proud. But here's another place we can both do better. Let's do so."

Assuming the letter was read first, it was necessary to abstract from the report the things that most needed highlighting. If the reader had had to flip back to the report, some of the force of the letter would have been lost.

Whenever important interpretation and emphasis need to be given, then, the letter should repeat the most significant material. It saves the reader from having to turn back and forth between letter and report.

However, the tone of the treatment ought to be personal—"Here is what this material means to me and you."

REMARKS

Note the first two sentences of the letter give the purpose. The subject is then broken into two phases, each discussed in its order. The ending asks for action on the one phase.

So, if the same high level of activity can be maintained during 1953, we will continue to gain much in the two important areas of improved employe relations and cost reduction. A year ago I recall mentioning that you would have a tough job equaling your 1951 performance in 1952. After looking at your 1952 record, we believe there is no reason to entertain such doubts for 1953. With the momentum you have at present, there is no question that 1953 can be another outstanding year.

You may have noted that one line was omitted from the comparisons on the previous page. Here it is --

	Fourth Quarter 1951	Fourth Quarter 1952	Year 1951	Year 1952
Suggestions Open End of Period	---	---	----	---

The situation with regard to open suggestions is the other thing we mentioned. The fact that investigations had not been completed on this many suggestions at the end of the year means that many employes have been waiting for nearly three months for a final decision on their suggestions. Naturally, we cannot expect employes to keep up their interest in offering ideas if they wait too long for answers on suggestions already submitted. I'm sure you appreciate that this problem calls for prompt action in taking whatever steps are necessary to effect a substantial reduction in the number of open suggestions.

H. P. Jordan

Attach.

COMPOSITE REPORTS

THE REPORTS described here illustrate a technique used in many reports. They are made up of several reports, each by a different individual, exactly as they were first submitted. At the head of them stands a report summarizing them from the position of one who takes an over-all view of the entire situation.

The technique can be suited to many applications. Before me now, for example, I have these:

1. The annual report to the board of the president of an organization. His report, which comes just inside the cover, summarizes operations from an over-all point of view: financial position, record of achievement, and future plans. There follow reports from each of the main divisions of the organization, just as submitted to him.

2. A report which reads exactly like a textbook, or manual, discussing a new maintenance procedure and how to carry it out. The main report is purely informational. Bound with it, however, are individual studies of different machines, made by different people. These provided the basis for the integrated report.

3. A very similar report which tells how a certain test should be run in the future. Individual test reports run according to the procedure are appended.

4. A report made up of three reports, arranged as follows:

 a. A report describing major features of plans for a new installation, for the information of all concerned.

 b. Detailed directions to each group concerned.

 c. The original report recommending the installation and detailed reasoning which led to the recommendation.

Reports for Supplementary Study

5. A similar project taking a variation of the investigation pattern. The department head's report comes first. It makes recommendations, with brief reasons given for them. Next comes a report from the man under him. It makes no recommendations, but interprets the effect on current operations of certain technical findings. The language is not highly technical. Last comes the very detailed original report, done by the specialist. Even in its conclusions it is a mass of mathematical formulas and equations.

APPENDIX

Answers to Problems on Page 261

A. (a) Harlan Hatcher
   (b) Bobbs Merrill
   (c) Indianapolis
   (d) $4.00
   Source—Cumulative Book Index—under "Western Reserve."

B. Edward Ricketts, *Sea of Cortes,* 1941.
   CBI 1938-1942, p. 2312.

C. Yes. From Engineering Societies Library, 29 West 39th Street, New York.
   Article also in Industrial Arts Index under "Titanium Carbide," but without reference to "Fatigue Strength."
   Source—Engineering Index—under "Carbide."

D. "Eggs from a Slot Machine," in *Farm Journal* (Dec. '53) 77:67.
   Source—Readers Guide—under "Eggs."

E. Remington Rand, "Work Analysis Cuts Fatigue," *Mill and Factory,* Volume 54 (January, 1954) p. 127.
   Source—Industrial Arts Index, 1954, under "Fatigue."

F. Vertical File, Volume 21, 1952, p. 38 under heading "Electromagnets."

G. *Bibliographic Index,* 1951 ed., p. 46 and 1952 ed., p. 98.
   (Note: There will probably be later lists by the time you use this book.)

H. A test for the determination of the melting point of bitumen for use in building or road-making.
   Source—Chambers Technical Dictionary—also in handbooks.

I. One who "uses scissors to cut off loose ends of threads from cloth and to trim and thin out thick places in fabric. Uses burling iron to remove burls (threads), rough ends, slubs, and other imperfections."
   Source—*Dictionary of Occupational Titles,* Volume 1, second edition, March, 1949. (On p. 1234 under "Slub

Picker," reader is referred to "Burler," p. 161, where definition is given.

J. Hutchinson Brothers Leather Company, 1928 W. 8th, Cincinnati and MacGregor Sports Products, Inc., 4861 Spring Grove Ave., Cincinnati.

Source—Thomas' *Register of American Manufacturers,* Volume I.

K. Yes, *Titanium,* 1953. (Reprint from *Minerals Yearbook,* 1951). (b) Bureau of Mines. (c) J. Cszervenyak and Alfred Tumin. (d) $.10.

Source—U. S. Government Publications, month Catalog, Item 2017, Index "Titanium."

L. $1,532,000.

Source—*Statistical Abstract,* 1951, p. 417 (Chapter 16, Banking and Finance).

Using a Letter to Apply for a Job

YOU MAY never have to write a letter of application. The odds are, however, that you will. You may have to write one to get your first job. Later, you may use one when you hear of a really good job or when you feel you must find greater opportunities for personal development.

There is no more important piece of practical writing. If the letter is effective, you may get a chance at the job you want. If it is bad, you won't.

The importance of the letter becomes clear if you consider the two major situations in which it is used.

The first situation occurs when a definite job opportunity is known to exist. The company has advertised through a "blind ad" or used other channels to spread information about the opening. There may be anywhere from a dozen to a hundred or more applicants.

For any job there are certain critical essentials of experience or education. The first step the employer takes is to match these job specifications against the qualifications of the applicants. Selected letters are then evaluated in detail and more or less "ranked" according to how well the applicant's qualifications match the job. Chances are that several will prove to be about equal. Employers then take into consideration other factors besides technical competence. They particularly look for clues as to the applicant's personal adjustment, ability to get along with others, and leadership. Though such qualities may not affect the applicant's competence to perform the immediate job in a satisfactory way, they are good indicators of his potential for future growth and advancement. Many employers consider these qualities the most important ones—they point out that few employes are ever rated unsatisfactory because of technical incompetence.

Selecting the top few applicants who have survived this careful comparison, the company next consults the people whose names were given as references. This check may be made by telephone, since a person is more likely to say what he really thinks in conversation than in writing. Tonal inflections, hesitation, or obvious enthusiasm give valuable clues, and points of particular significance can be checked in detail.

The last step is to interview those that appear best qualified. If time is short, several may be called in. Otherwise the candidates are interviewed in the order established by the investigation, or according to how close they are geographically.

The purpose of the letter written in this situation, then, is to get an interview on favorable terms—an interview in which the employer will think well of the candidate even before he meets him. If the applicant does not get the job, the letter is still not a failure if the application is placed in the "live" file, for then it gets the same treatment as if it were written in the second situation under which applications are made.

The second situation exists when the application is made "cold." The applicant doesn't know if an immediate opening exists, but he does know that the company sometimes needs people with his qualifications. Most people just graduating from college are in this situation.

Such a letter has the advantage that it is first read by itself—not along with others. If the letter establishes that the applicant does have qualifications which interest the company, he will be sent an application blank. It and the letter are then placed in a "live" file. When a job opening occurs, the material in the files is reviewed, exactly as if the application were for that specific job. Excluding promotion from within, this is the way in which most jobs above the hourly or clerical level are filled.

The objective of the letter, then, is to get the application into the "live" file, with the eventual objectives of an interview and a job.

From the use of the letter certain things follow:

1. The application should make a good first impression.
2. It must "hold up." That is, it must stand being looked at time and time again.
3. It must make information easily accessible. The employer should be able to pick out the information he wants as quickly as possible.
4. The information should be sufficiently full that the employer can judge whether the applicant is suited for whatever job becomes open.

A letter will not make a good first impression if it is slipshod in appearance, misspells the name of the employer, is full of overstrikes and crossed out words, or uses language associated with semi-literates. The more times an employer looks at such a letter, the less highly he regards the applicant. If the writer does such sloppy work in applying for a job, what can he be expected to do in his routine everyday work?

A letter that uses a "cute" opening or a trick device will not hold up either. It may catch attention on the first reading, but when looked at repeatedly will become more and more stale, until at last it becomes offensive.

A letter that buries information in the middle of a long paragraph forces the employer to re-read large sections of it each time he wants a particular piece of information. Will he prefer the applicant who wrote it or the one who has arranged material in a clearly headed table?

The letter which merely implies that the writer has certain qualifications or that leaves them out altogether stands no chance against the one that clearly states those qualifications.

The application that best meets these tests is one that has been carefully planned to fit the particular situation. It will not merely be a letter. It presents all significant data in a tabulated summary, and it uses the actual letter to highlight the writer's most significant qualifications. If the letter results in an interview, the applicant must then conduct himself to increase the good impression he has already made.

The remainder of this discussion therefore takes up:

1. Analyzing the situation
2. Designing a summary of qualifications
3. Writing the letter itself
4. Handling the interview

ANALYZING THE SITUATION

If you are going to show that your qualifications match a particular job you need a clear picture of both. You can start with either, but since you are likely to know more about yourself, that is a good place to begin.

ASSESSING YOUR QUALIFICATIONS

Any good salesman needs to know his product. You are selling yourself. The more you know about yourself, the better.

Begin by making out a preliminary summary of your qualifications. Don't worry about length or order. Just jot down the information. Points to cover are discussed in full on pages 593 to 600. They include such facts as your name, address, age, marital status, education, experience, and activities. Don't skip any of the items.

Next consider what you are like and how you react to different situations. Professional abilities can be employed under a variety of circumstances. A lawyer who likes variety, likes people, and still likes to "be his own boss" may do his best working by himself in a small community. One who hates to appear in court and finds himself uncomfortable in novel situations may do his best at a desk job in a large corporation, specializing in contracts. Some engineers enjoy solving theoretical problems and hate to work with "merely" practical applications. They will be happiest in a research laboratory. Others detest being pinned to a desk or drawing board. They need a job in the field or out on the floor of a plant.

Making your own personal inventory is easiest if you do it in terms of specific situations. What about that summer job did you like? What bothered you? What is there about *you* that made you like or dislike these things? How do you react when you are told to do something? Are you upset when put entirely on your own?

The more complete and exact you can make your personal inventory, the surer you can be about the kind of job for which you are suited. No matter how good a job looks financially, you won't want to apply for it if it will keep you constantly battling against your weak points. *You want a job where your strong points can show.*

Be honest in your inventory. No man can be happy in a job to which he is not suited.

LOOKING OVER THE JOB

The next step is to get a clear idea of the job for which you are applying. You need this information for three reasons: to determine if you really want to apply for the job, to decide what facts to emphasize in the summary and letter, and to carry you through the interview without blunders.

If the application is submitted in reply to a "blind ad," the best you can do is to imagine the nature of the job from the clues and specifications it gives. In all other circumstances you will have heard of a specific opening or will at least know the name of the company.

Much about the job and its desirability will depend upon the nature of the company itself. Find out as much as you can about it.

Sources of information are in the library. If the firm is of any size, it will be listed in Standard Corporation Descriptions, Moody's, or the other sources of financial information discussed on page 257. Its products may be discussed in Sweet's or other catalogs like those listed on pages 256 to 257. Also talk to instructors or other friends in your field.

If you know the name or title of the job, you can get a rough idea of its duties from the USES Dictionary of Occupational Titles.

DESIGNING A SUMMARY OF QUALIFICATIONS

You are now ready to put the summary of your qualifications in a form that will be most useful to the employer and will display you to best advantage.

Arrange the summary in tabular form, with headings that stand out clearly. If the employer wants to compare your education, say, with that of another applicant, he doesn't want to hunt through several paragraphs to do so. He'll like it better yet if he doesn't have to read even a single paragraph to pick out precisely what he wants. So arrange things so that he can go to a particular column under the heading of "Education."

Under each heading, place first those qualifications that you think will be most significant. How to do this will be explained in more detail below.

You will have more room for explanation if you place the material lengthwise on the paper.

The content of the summary is much the same as that of standard application blanks. In fact, later you may have to duplicate much of the information when requested to fill out such a blank. Make out your own summary anyway. In the first place, it will convince the company that it is worth while to send you the blank. In the second place, your own summary can be set up to emphasize your own strong points.

Now for the specific items to show.

GENERAL INFORMATION

At the top of the first page come some general facts about yourself. These are not the most important ones, but they are pieces of information that give the employer a feeling of acquaintance with you as an individual. They include the following:

NAME

Center your name, in capitals, at the top of the page.

ADDRESS

Put the address right under your name. If you have two addresses—school and home—show the one that will reach you best, or note when each should be used.

TELEPHONE NUMBER

If the employer wants to call you to make an appointment, he needs your telephone number. If you can be reached only at certain hours, give them.

PHOTOGRAPH

In an upper corner, staple a recent portrait-type photograph. It should not be large or glamorous, but neither should it be a snapshot. The size that fits in a pocketbook is good. The picture is to give the employer a mental image on which he can hang the rest of the facts about you. It makes him feel better acquainted with you.

AGE, WEIGHT, AND HEIGHT

These again are mostly for acquaintance. Sometimes an employer does have a certain range of ages in mind, and he will always expect more experience in an older man. For some sales jobs, he may even want a man six feet or over. Such "standards" are of course always flexible.

HEALTH

Describe your health as excellent or good, and mention any physical handicaps that might influence your job placement. Don't hide such handicaps—they would appear later in a physical examination anyway. Sometimes people add a remark such as "No absences caused by illness in the last five years."

SEX

Your picture and name cover this item.

MARITAL STATUS

State if you are single, married, or divorced, and give the number of your children. Again this item is mostly to acquaint the employer with you. Few employers nowadays use this information as a critical item in filling a job.

NATIONALITY

If American, state whether you are native or naturalized. If you are citizen of another land, you should give the status under which you are in the country.

RACE, RELIGION

In some states it is illegal to ask for information on race and religion. Omit it.

EDUCATION

The information given so far has been relatively unimportant. It was placed first to give a general picture. The next two items, education and experience, are critical ones.

Which should come first? It depends on you. If you are a student just finishing school, you don't have much work experience. The main proof you have that you can handle the job is the training you have for it. Education will come first.

On the other hand, if you are thirty-five years old, you will have had substantial experience. You will have proved in action whether you have been able to profit by your education. Experience will be the significant point and will come first.

Here education will be discussed first because so many letters of application are written for beginning jobs.

One caution—make sure that all your time from high school graduation to the present is accounted for under either education or experience. Any missing year will cause suspicion. If you were in jail, you might as well say so. (Count military service and travel under experience.)

Since you want to put your best foot forward, start with your highest education. In other words, put the latest years first. College and graduate work ought to be given in some detail. The high school record should not, and can be omitted.

The following column heads should be used:

DATE　SCHOOL　DEGREE　MAJOR　COURSES　REMARKS

The last two columns will need to be much wider than the others. Under "date" give beginning and ending dates. Under "school" name the school and give its address. The abbreviation for the degree is enough, unless it is an unusual one. Under "major" state the area of specialization, unless it is clear from the degree. If the column adds nothing, omit it. For some jobs (like teaching) a column to show minors should be added.

The next column, "courses," is very important, since the requirements for any given degree or major vary widely from college to college. You must therefore be specific. On the other hand, don't try to reproduce your transcript of credits.

One good arrangement groups things by general subject, showing the total hours. If you use it, be sure that the hours shown total to the number required for graduation. Ones you regard as of less significance can be grouped under "other."

The order in which you list the courses should vary according to the job you are seeking. Show first those which you think will be most useful for that job.

The "remarks" column can also be headed "explanation." It is used to point up significant values in the courses listed or in a combination of them. Don't try to explain *all* courses—just the ones you think are most significant to the job for which you are applying.

EXPERIENCE

The experience section of the summary is arranged on the same principles. Latest experience is placed first, because the last job held is likely to be the most important one and of most interest to the employer.

If you are just graduating from college you may feel that your experience looks pretty skimpy. Don't worry about it. No sane employer is going to expect extensive experience in a young person of twenty-two. He isn't going to refuse to hire you because you lack it. If your other qualifications are satisfactory, he will be willing to invest in giving you the necessary experience.

On the other hand, any experience you may have had is

all to the good. It shows that you can handle the day-to-day responsibilities of an actual job. So if you have little experience, include such things as summer jobs, part-time jobs in college, or cooperative experience.

Military experience should be included here rather than under a special head. Here it is in proportion—just one of those things a citizen expects to do and does. Under a separate head it may give the impression that you are trading on it—that you are a kind of professional veteran. Yet don't omit describing any significant elements in it. The man who has handled a platoon in combat is not likely to explode under the minor crises of day-to-day employment.

The labels of the columns under "experience" will be these:

DATES   EMPLOYER   SUPERVISOR   POSITION   SALARY   DUTIES

Under "dates" show the beginning and ending date of each job. If a summer job, show it as "Summer, 1955."

"Employer" calls for the name of the company or organization for which you worked. Underneath the name give the mail address.

"Supervisor" calls for the name of your immediate superior. It is the person whom the prospective employer would contact if he wanted to find out about your work. Give his name and title, and department if useful.

Under the column "position" list the title of the job you held.

The information under "salary" should be given in the same terms as you were paid—per hour, per week, or per month. If the pay varied, give the range. Don't be afraid the employer will try to buy you as near to your last figure as possible. He won't. If he does, turn down the job. Any respectable employer knows that you are moving to another job in order to advance yourself. To make a move worth while, you need substantially more than you have been getting. Moreover, the employer has a "price range" for the job that is open. This range is established by what other people in the organization are getting for jobs requiring similar education, experience, and responsibility. He won't hire you at the *top* of the price bracket, because he wants some room to advance you in that job. But he won't hire you below what you should get. Although salaries are confidential, he knows perfectly well that information gets exchanged. If you were to learn that you had been bought at a bargain rate, you'd be an unhappy employe. No unhappy employe is a bargain at any price. So don't be afraid to tell what your salary was.

Right here is a good place to take care of a related problem. Should you give the salary expected? Unless requested, do not do so, for the reasons given in the last paragraph. Salary is a matter for negotiation at the end of the interview. It is affected by your qualifications, the policy of the company, the nature of the job, and the opportunities you see in it.

The last column, "duties," will be much wider than the others. For jobs which are standard from organization to organization, the column won't be needed. Thus a "rate clerk" does about the same thing everywhere. So does a foreman, but did his department contain five men or fifty, male or female employes, skilled or unskilled personnel? If such major variations might exist, state them and give the actual things you did to carry out the job. Keep things in honest proportion, but place first and give greatest emphasis to those duties which fit the job for which you are applying.

CLUBS AND ORGANIZATIONS

All companies want people who are more than technicians. They want employes who can get along with others—

who can work on a team, who are socially adjusted, who can both accept and provide leadership. One indicator is the organizations to which people belong. The man who belongs to a professional society is striving to better himself, yet is sharing his knowledge with others. The leader in a community activity such as the Parent-Teachers Association shows that he feels responsibility for the development of his own children and those of the community at large. The man who is a church deacon shows he is willing to give his abilities to a worthy cause. The country club member probably likes people.

Undoubtedly you belong to several organizations. If not, now is a good time to join. Your employer will consider these affiliations important.

In the summary of qualifications, list the organizations by full name or standard abbreviations. The employer may not understand their "first letter" abbreviations. If you have held offices, show the fact after the specific item, like this: (president 1953-54, secretary 1952-53, member of council 1951-52).

Occasionally the title of an organization will not tell what it is. Add a brief parenthetical explanation.

List the clubs in order of their importance from the employer's point of view, not according to your own feeling. A good order would be professional societies, honor societies, community groups, church groups, social clubs, and fraternities.

SPECIAL HEADS

If the heads discussed so far do not display all your activities to their best advantage, add ones that do. The college student—especially the athlete—may wish to list "sports and hobbies." One who has received scholarships, fellowships, and other prizes should have a special heading for "honors and awards." Those who have published professionally will add "publications." Others might have a listing of "patents." Use any category needed to show you at your best.

REFERENCES

The last section is headed "references." List at least three people who can testify to your professional competence. Former employers and teachers are excellent. Also give as references some of the people with whom you have worked in club and community activities.

For each reference give name, title or position, company or other affiliation, and address.

Use judgment in listing references. Select people who know you well, not people with big titles who recall you only vaguely. Then be sure to ask their permission to use their name. If they seem the least bit hesitant, thank them cordially and later quietly cross their name from your list. Many an applicant has had his application undermined by a reference who "hardly remembered him" or who remembered without enthusiasm. Pick people you know and trust. The prospective employer will not check your references unless he is already favorably impressed with your personal record. What they will say will determine whether you get the final interview for the job.

CAUTIONS

The summary is now complete. Before final typing examine it to see that you have included all information that is pertinent to the job. Then type it neatly, planning it so that both main heads and column heads stand out sharply.

Do not print or mimeograph the summary. Some employers will not object, but others will gain the impression that you are sending out applications wholesale. Besides, the duplicated summary cannot be adapted to a particular employer and makes obviously false any statement at the time of the interview that you have a particular interest in the company to which you are applying.

Also avoid unusual art treatment or use of a folder in a kind of "prospectus" arrangement. The summary is employed in a utilitarian way. It gives the best impression by making the facts easy to find. The only possible exceptions are if you are applying for a sales, promotional, advertising, or art position. Then most employers do not object, considering the application as a sample of the type of work the applicant will do. Especially avoid trick devices which may backfire. Don't be like the applicant who gathered his materials in a folder which opened with a front-view photograph and closed with a close-up of the back of his head.

WRITING THE LETTER ITSELF

The next step is to write the actual letter. Since a summary of qualifications is used, the letter can be short—a page or less.

Its functions are to make the application, to give emphasis to your most important qualifications, to get the reader to the accompanying summary in a receptive state of mind, and to make it easy to call you for an interview.

The letter has a sales function, it is true, but an unusual one. Any intimation of pressure tactics will be resented. You cannot brag of your accomplishments without seeming obnoxiously immodest. Even your product, yourself, must be mentioned unobtrusively.

The two basic guides are these:

1. The executive who will be your reader is conservative in most things. He prefers the solidly efficient to the flashy.
2. The executive is more interested in the objectives of his company than in your personal objectives. He

wants to know what you can do for the company, not what the company can do for you.

Both form and content are affected by these guides.

FORM

Good form is unobtrusive. It doesn't attract attention to itself. An executive is used to receiving business letters that are neat, well-spaced, and standard in form. That shown on page 617 is acceptable.

Notice these features:

1. It is typed. The hand-written letter of application is no longer expected or desired.
2. Each paragraph is single spaced, but double spacing is used between paragraphs.
3. The margins are ample, and no part of the letter violates the margins.
4. The whole is balanced on the page.
5. Just within the boundaries of the upper right hand corner is the heading. It shows

> Street address
> City, zone, and state
> Date

The style is block; that is, each line begins directly under the preceding one. The punctuation is open— none at the end of each line. Closed is also acceptable; that is, a comma could follow each of the first two lines and a period the last. Avoid abbreviations, unless a very long line will result.

Do not use letterhead paper of the company for which you now work, or of the club or hotel at which you are staying. The former is in bad taste because you are not writing on company business. The latter may be your permanent residence, but the letterhead may lead to the inference that you simply appropriated it to your use. A regular heading is best.

6. Flush with the left margin comes the inside address. It too is in block style. In punctuating it, use whatever practice you followed in the heading. Again avoid abbreviations.

If you know the name and title of the recipient, place them as in the sample on page 620. If you know only the title—and possibly have to guess at it—you'll have to omit the name.

Suppose you know the name of both the head of the department in which you want to work and of the Personnel Director or Employment Manager. To whom should you address the letter? Either will do. The department head does have final say, and he sees fewer letters than the personnel department, so there is some advantage in writing to him. If he has no vacancy, he will transmit the letter to the personnel office for possible alternate placement. On the other hand, if he requisitions a man, Personnel will supply him with selected names, and your application will get to him in the end.

Be sure of the proper spelling of the name of the person addressed and of the company. Both are misspelled with amazing frequency. (Ask yourself how you like to see your own name misspelled!)

7. After the inside address comes a double space and the salutation, followed by another double space. The salutation is a conservative one. Don't try any tricks. Use

Dear Sir:
Dear Mr. Jones:

Notice that the colon is used even after "Dear Mr. Jones." A comma would be perfectly all right, but it is less formal and some people don't like it. Play safe and use the colon. (NOT a semicolon!)

8. Next comes the body of the letter. Indent the paragraphs or keep them block—just so you are consistent.

9. The complimentary close is again set apart by double spacing. It begins just to the left of the center of the page. Use "Yours truly" or "Yours sincerely." Add a "very" and change the word order if you wish, but that is all.

10. Directly under the complimentary close comes your typed name, with enough space between for your signature. Don't sign with a flourish.

11. Note the generous margins. Never have them less than an inch and a half on the left and an inch elsewhere. If possible, use wider ones yet, especially at top and bottom.

12. KEEP THE LETTER TO ONE UNCROWDED PAGE.

CONTENT

The entire content of the letter should be as conservative as the form. For a job of any importance—and that includes a good beginning job—you don't have to pull any hat tricks. You are not selling soap or a gold brick security. You are writing about you, and you are a good substantial product. Your reader knows that the success of his business depends on how good people he hires. He knows that his competitors have a good product, good buildings, good machinery, and adequate capital. One thing only can keep him ahead or get him ahead—BETTER PEOPLE.

A company gets better people by hiring good potential at the lower levels of responsibility and then giving opportunities for growth. The man who hires a beginner hopes he is also hiring tomorrow's executive. He doesn't hire him on the same basis he buys a toothpaste.

The whole content of the letter, then, should give the impression that you are earnest, sincere, competent in your field, and modestly confident of your qualifications.

It is a large order, for even minor slips may spoil the impression. A good letter needs a good beginning, solid developing paragraphs, a definite close, and good standard English throughout.

Here are some suggestions for each phase.

THE BEGINNING

The first sentence or two should be pleasant and direct. The beginning should get right down to the business at hand—the reader shouldn't have to wait to find that he is dealing with a letter of application.

The particular approach depends on the situation.

The most favorable situation exists when someone known to the company has told you of the job or has suggested that you apply. His name is in effect an introduction. If you use this approach do so without making it seem that you are using pressure, and be sure to ask permission of the person concerned. The opening then becomes something like these:

> Mr. Arnold Brice tells me that you now have an opening for a junior process engineer. This letter is to request that you consider my qualifications.

> At the suggestion of Mr. John P. Jeffers, your distributor in this area, I am writing to inquire about a position with your organization. As this letter and the attached summary of qualifications show, my education, experience, and interest are in the field of cost accounting.

Note that each beginning uses the name to good effect. The employer, "you," is brought in early. Emphasis is on *qualifications,* and "I" is submerged. The first example shown above mentions a specific job, the second a general area in which the young man is competent.

The name beginning can be badly used. Here are common pitfalls.

1. If the man is your uncle or other close relative, and is employed by the company or is one of its customers, don't mention the relationship. If he is sure to be known, give only his name. Otherwise give his name and title or company. The recipient will doubtless unearth the relationship, but if you seem to be trading on it, the impression will be bad. Even the relative may then be offended. One important man, whose name was misused, replied to an inquiry from the company, "Your applicant comes from a very good family." That was all!

2. Even if he isn't a relative, if the man is very important and well-known in the company, be sure *not* to mention his title. Avoid all appearance of pressure.

3. The man whose name you use doesn't have to have a "big" job for the approach to be helpful. All he needs is a good reputation as an honest, dependable worker.

A second good beginning takes off with a reference to some other source of information about the job. The letter will be in response to an advertisement or some similar device to solicit applications.

    The Delta State College Placement Bureau
    informs me that....

or

    This letter is in response to your ad-
    vertisement for....

The hardest beginning to write is the one for which there is no ready-made point of contact. A forthright application is best here, as:

```
Will you please consider my qualifications
for possible placement in your Labor
Standards Department?  These qualifica-
tions are summarized on the sheet that
accompanies this letter.
```

All good beginnings have several things in common:

1. They make contact at once, either through a common point of acquaintance or directly.
2. The letter mentions the reader early, using the "you" approach.
3. "I" is submerged and does not appear at the first of any sentence, yet no circumlocution such as "the writer" is used.
4. There is no question as to the purpose of the letter. It is a straight-forward application.
5. The job or the nature of the job is stated early. Thus you show that you know what you want and that you have an objective. The employer likewise knows what you want. If he doesn't have the job open, but has other positions that you can fill but that you wouldn't know about, he will tell you. If you apply for just anything, he will suspect that you have no enthusiasm for the area in which you were educated. Remember, he *wants* good people. If he thinks you are good and has any job for you, he will want to place you just as much as you want to be placed.

To these points can be added certain things to avoid.

Don't use the shock or the hide-and-seek beginning. These "attention getters" may also get jobs, as some writers say, but the average employer dislikes them intensely. (Except in the sales, advertising, and promotional areas, where employers are resigned to almost anything.)

Here is a "shock":

> If you could get a man who led the field in sales last year, you'd want him, wouldn't you?

or

> You've got something I want. I've got something you need. It looks like we ought to get together.

Another:

> Your decision on this letter can cost you money.

These beginnings are arresting, but they lead the reader to expect more than the remainder of the letter can deliver. Even if they are backed up by facts, they give an impression of arrogant self-confidence. They are not popular with employers.

Now for the hide-and-seek beginning, complete with flattery:

> From an investigation of your company, I know it is the leader in its field. Last year it was first in sales in the world. It is a progressive company. It was first to [here is listed a whole string of alleged "firsts"]. And even now it looks to the future. It has announced the beginning of experiments with atomic power and with solar rays [and so on].
>
> It is with a company such as yours, that looks to the future, that I want my future to lie . . .

The employer who begins to read such stuff is puzzled for a moment as to why these things are being said to him. When he does find out, he is sure to suspect the sincerity of the applicant.

An especially annoying hide-and-seek approach is the one

which offers gratuitous advice about the company's operation, as

> The seller's market is a thing of yesterday. The buyer's market has arrived. Competition is keen. Only the well-designed product that offers a real value can hope to meet the fierce competition ahead.
>
> In the field of household appliances this situation is particularly acute. . . .

Eventually the writer of the letter got around to applying for a job as product designer.

A final caution is that you should apply *for a job*. Do not apply for a training program instead (unless you have been specifically invited to do so). Many firms offer such a program, and they may decide to place you in it, but applying for the program instead of the job sounds as if you were looking for free education. Let the employer have the feeling that you expect to really work for your money.

THE DEVELOPING PARAGRAPHS

The function of the developing paragraphs is to call attention to the accompanying summary—if the beginning has not already done so—and to stress one or two qualifications that you believe will be most attractive to the employer. Do not try to cover all the points, and don't simply repeat what the summary gives. The two sample letters on pages 617 and 620 show the general idea. The first letter is written by a young man who must emphasize his educational qualifications. The second stresses experience that should prove useful in the prospective job.

Neither letter *argues* its point at length or specifically states that these qualities will be especially valuable to the company concerned. The employer is allowed to reach this conclusion for himself.

Keep away from any discussion of your ambitions or goals, your interests, or what the company can do for you.

THE CLOSE

An effective close suggests the action wanted but does not push. It can mention the references, ask for an interview, or do both. An example:

> The references listed in the attached summary will give further information concerning my qualifications. If you believe an interview is desirable, I can be reached at the address or telephone number shown.

Although you certainly want an interview, handle the request for it with caution. The phrasing given above as an example has the virtue of suggesting the interview without seeming to demand it. It is a logical suggestion if the applicant is within a half day's drive of the office of the employer. If he is not, the suggestion becomes a touchy one. No fair employer wants to ask an applicant to absorb the expenses of a longer trip unless almost certain of offering him a job. Then many companies expect to pay his expenses. To them, asking for an interview becomes something like asking for an expense-paid trip.

A distant candidate sometimes suggests that he will be in town on a certain date. This device in effect sets the date for the interview, taking the initiative from the employer. It also may give the impression, false or not, that the applicant will really have to make a special trip. If you do visit in the employer's city occasionally, say so without setting a date. Or omit mention of the interview, and if you are in town a few weeks later, telephone the employer to inquire as to the current status of your application. Most employers will then suggest the interview themselves.

What it amounts to is this—there is no harm in suggesting an interview, but if your qualifications are those that the employer wants, he certainly will think of the interview all by himself.

THE LANGUAGE

The language of the letter must be carefully chosen, accurate, and conventional. "I" must sometimes be used, or the letter may sound stilted and unreal, but the use should be sparing. The letter that begins each paragraph and sentence with "I" gives the impression that the writer is centered entirely in himself. To avoid this effect, examine the first draft to see how many times you have used "I." Then recast some of the sentences to get rid of all except three or four of them. Make sure that none of those remaining stands at the first of a sentence.

Next check, sentence by sentence, for the possible errors in standard usage discussed on pages 187 to 219 of this book. Especially check spelling, for poor spelling is noticed by people who overlook most other errors in English.

Finally, type the letter as many times as necessary to get a copy that has no overstrikes, crossouts, or noticeable erasures.

Your letter is now ready to represent you at your best. Send it off and hope for an early favorable reply. If instead you get an answer saying that the application has been filed, don't be disappointed. Most letters of application have a delayed action. Yours will be ready to do its job when an opening actually occurs.

HANDLING THE INTERVIEW

Suppose that an opening has occurred, your application has been checked and rechecked, your references have done their job, and you are called in for an interview. What can you expect and what should you do?

Prepare for the interview as well as you can. Review the

facts that you know about the company. Plan some of the questions you will want to ask about the job or about living conditions in the town. Anticipate the employer's probable questions. Some college placement bureaus will even help you by giving you a preliminary interview as a sample. If yours does not, a friend may consent to "role play" the employer for you.

When the day arrives, dress neatly and conservatively, and arrive on time or a very few minutes ahead.

Don't worry if you are a little nervous. Almost everyone is who is really interested in the outcome of such an interview. Of course, there is a point beyond which nervousness is bad. But a little nervousness may even key you to do your best.

The actual interview is a two-way street. The employer is trying to confirm his favorable impressions of you and to see how you handle yourself and react as a person. You will want to know more about the company, the job, and the city itself. Since the employer's decision must be made before you can make yours, be flexible to any situation that may arise. Save most of your questions to the end of the interview.

The interview is not an exact measuring device, and most employers know it. The discussion will be general, not in the nature of an oral examination. Introduce yourself and then let the employer take the lead.

There is no set pattern for an interview—different individuals have their own ways. Expect almost anything and be ready to modify your conduct to fit the situation. Certain things, however, are almost sure to be covered.

If you are from out of town, an interview may start with questions about your trip. If you used a "name" beginning for your letter, you may exchange comments about your mutual friend. (Be sure you say only pleasant things about him!) Very often the interviewer asks questions as to where you live or went to school—almost anything you have already told him in your application. He is trying to warm you up and put you at ease by letting you talk about something with which you are familiar.

As the interview continues, you may be asked questions about your field. From factual matters, the interviewer may switch over to asking your opinion on something. If so, give it honestly but not belligerently. Don't get drawn into extended arguments and don't give any long speeches.

Other questions asked may include:

> What are your personal objectives?
> Why do you want to work for us?
> Why did you leave your last job? (Or why do you want to leave your present one).

Answer the first question in terms of the kind of work you like to do and feel you can do well. You can also speak of the jobs to which you hope to be able to progress. Stop short of president of the company, but don't be afraid to show that you have professional goals and ambitions beyond the immediate job. Unless asked specifically do not reply in terms of money—don't mention that till the end of the interview. Don't get led astray into a discussion of family and personal plans.

If asked why you want to work for the company, answer as honestly as you can. Your prior investigation of the company can help here. Don't try to tell the man the details of his business or to flatter him. Answer in terms of what you know of the job opening, of what you like about the size of the company, of what you know of how they do business, and so on. Be brief. If you do well here, the interviewer is likely to take over and tell you more about the job, the company, and the opportunities for advancement. If so, listen with interest and ask any natural questions that occur. *Don't* ask about salary or training programs.

If asked why you left your last job, sensible reasons are to accept or seek work more nearly in your field, more challenging work, or advancement. If you were fired or laid off, you might as well say so, but interpret the former employer's action charitably. Any indication that you had trouble with your former boss and fellow employes will be a red flag of danger to the interviewer. At the same time, you don't want to accept a job under false pretenses, and your former employer is almost certain to give his interpretation of the situation. The best thing to do is to be frank about the situation, report it unemotionally and objectively, and not dwell unduly on any aspect of it.

Toward the end of the interview you will be asked if you have any questions. Ask those still unanswered about requirements of the job, company, or town. It is also perfectly in order to ask where the job may lead—what the lines of promotion are.

By this time, something will probably have been volunteered about salary. If not, you can ask how the salary for the job is determined. This should elicit the information desired.

After you believe the interview is about over, don't be surprised to find that you are also expected to talk to other people. You are almost certain to be interviewed by the man for whom you are to work directly, and other executives may also be introduced.

Endure necessary repetition patiently, and repeat your answers to new people as often as questions still come. You will be making progress.

Throughout all interviews be sure not to fall into any of six common errors. The first is talking salary too soon and too often, so that your primary interest seems centered there rather than in the job. The second is telling your troubles, especially those about your family, your former job, your former associates, or your former instructors. The third is giving an indication that you are not amenable to supervision. One applicant, for example, ruined a good impression he had made because he didn't eat dessert when he was taken to lunch. As the others ate, he held the floor, and finally swung into an elaborate story of how he had disagreed with his boss's policies and had successfuly organized other employes to thwart them. His story was entertaining, but his prospective employers had no wish to have their policies skillfully undermined. A fourth error is going on the defensive, as when an unusually fat boy spent most of his time explaining why his excess weight was not a handicap. The fifth error is explaining what seem to be the deficiencies in the company's present practices and suggesting what should be done to improve them. The sixth is going into an elaborate monologue on a point which can be handled in a few sensible statements.

The interview will end in a definite offer or in a remark that the employer will let you know the outcome. If the former, you can accept at once or ask for a day or two for reaching your decision. The latter will not be held against you, but you must then make your decision as quickly as you can and let the employer know what it is. If you are told that you will be informed later concerning the decision, do not show disappointment. Some companies make no decision until several candidates have been interviewed.

When the interview seems over, take your leave promptly but not abruptly. Whatever the outcome, thank people in a genuinely friendly way for the time they have taken and the information they have given you.

After the interview, a thank-you letter is in order. It can be simply a note of appreciation, or it can be used to reiterate tactfully your interest in the company and their job. This demonstration of thoughtfulness may swing the job your way.

If not, try again, profiting by what you have learned. If

you have the qualifications for the openings for which you apply, if you present them well, and if you think of the job instead of yourself during the interview, it will not be long before you get a job you want.

The following letters are samples of letters of application. They should not be used as models, of course, but they give an idea of the kind of applications employers understand and approve.

One is from a young man just graduating from college. The other is from a man established in his field.

365 Western Avenue
Epsilon 1, New Hampshire
June 21, 1954

Personnel Director
Delta Manufacturing Company
Gammatown 4, Colorado

Dear Sir:

This letter is to make application for a job with your
organization in sales engineering or sales. A summary
of my qualifications is attached.

These qualifications include recent graduation from
Beta University with a B.S. in Sales Engineering. The
course provides training in basic engineering subjects
during the first two years, and an additional engineering course each semester of the final two years.
The primary emphasis of the second two years is on
economics, business administration, and sales. The
objective is to produce men who know something of both
engineering practice and business theory and techniques. My average in the course placed me in the upper half of the graduating class.

Summer work experience has given me some acquaintance
with both sales work and the inside of a factory.

The references listed can furnish information concerning my job performance and personal characteristics.
It is my earnest wish that you will judge these qualifications to be ones that can make me an asset to your
sales organization.

Yours very truly,

Donald R. Roberts

Donald R. Roberts

DONALD R. ROBERTS
365 Western Avenue
Epsilon 1, New Hampshire
Telephone MAin 7245

(Photograph
Here)

Age - 24   Single   Height - 5 ft 11 in.   Weight - 170
Health - Excellent   Native American

EDUCATION

DATES	SCHOOL	DEGREE	MAJOR	COURSES	REMARKS
1950-54	Beta Univ. Gamma Oregon	B.S.	Sales Engineering	Economics - 33 hrs. Engineering and Related - 34 hrs Psychology and Social Science - 18 hrs English and Speech - 18 hrs Languages and Arts - 22 hrs Other - 18 hrs Total - 143 hrs	Combination of engineering and economics courses designed to give sound engineering background for sales and management work. Some special courses were Ind. Org. and Mgt., Sales, Acct'g, Business Law, Corporation Finance, Labor, Transportation, Drawing, Mathematics through Advanced Calculus, Chemistry, Physics, Metallurgy, Heat Treat and Welding.
1943-47	Nuberg H.S. Nuberg N.H.	Diploma	College Prep.	---	---

EXPERIENCE

DATES	EMPLOYER	SUPERVISOR	POSITION	SALARY	DUTIES
Summer 1953	Alpha Rubber Co. Epsilon, N.H.	A. C. Close Press Room Supt.	Press Operator	$1.95/hr	---
Summer 1952	Omicron Sales Epsilon, N.H.	L. G. Walton Sales and Service Manager	Asst. Sales and Service Rep.	$275/mo	The company, a small concern, leases and sells shuffle boards and mechanical game devices. Went with representative to assist in repairs and adjustments. When not busy there, called on sales prospects, the last two months by myself.

618

Page 2 (Donald R. Roberts)

EXPERIENCE (Cont'd)

DATES	EMPLOYER	SUPERVISOR	POSITION	SALARY	DUTIES
Summer 1951	Psi Camp Zeta, Vermont	P. N. Larga Director	Counsellor	$180/mo	Supervising recreation, and usual camp counselling of boys 8 to 14
Part time 1951-54	Beta Univ. Gamma, Ore	B. D. Horton Supervisor, Student Jobs	Clerk	$1.25- 1.40/hr	Performed various clerical jobs in different college offices.
1947-50	U.S. Army		Sgt. First Class at time of honorable discharge		Longest assignment as administrative assistant, headquarters (18 mos)

CLUBS AND ACTIVITIES

American Mgt. Assn. (president, student branch, 1953-54; sec'y 1952-53). Society of Automotive Engineers.
Member Presbyterian Church. Boy Scouts - leader. De Molay. Zeta Zeta Zeta (Social fraternity, house mgr. '52).

REFERENCES

FOR JOB PERFORMANCE -- ANY OF EMPLOYERS LISTED ABOVE

FOR EDUCATION
Prof. G. D. Downes
Dept. of Economics
Beta University
Gamma, Oregon

Prof. A. G. Williams
Dept. of Mechanical Engineering
Beta University
Gamma, Oregon

PERSONAL
O. O. Maas, M.D.
100 Main Street
Epsilon, New Hampshire;

Rev. John P. Briggs
First Presbyterian Church
Epsilon, New Hampshire

Mr. D. D. Potter
62 Main Street
Epsilon, New Hampshire
(Real estate broker)

1268 East Merket Street,
Nuville 2, Missouri,
May 3, 1954

Mr. George P. Gregory,
Director of Public Relations,
Omega Corporation,
Chi 2, Illinois.

Dear Mr. Gregory:

Mr. Davis of Smith-Davis Associates tells me that
he understands that you are planning to add an experienced man to your public relations group, and that my
qualifications might interest you.

In the five years I was with Tau Brothers, they
gave me a splendid grounding in many phases of public
relations. As you no doubt know, they are a forward-
looking manufacturing organization which, like yours,
employs some 10,000 people and has customers throughout the country.

Since leaving them four years ago to strike out
on my own, I have done just about everything conceiv-
able in the field of public relations. To give a
really concrete picture, there are enclosed with this
letter the following:

1. A summary of the main facts about me.

2. A list of clients over the past two years.

3. A tabular summary of the types of public
   relations activity engaged in this past
   year.

4. A brief synopsis of the program just planned
   for one of my small business clients.

If from this material it looks as if I might be
the man you want, just let me know when I should come
to your office to talk it over.

Yours very truly

Joseph P. St. John

Joseph P. St. John

PRACTICE SUGGESTIONS

1. Select some job for which you might now apply. Write an appropriate summary sheet and letter.
2. Assume it is ten years from now. Apply for an appropriate job.

Index

623

Key to Chapter 12—"Writing and Checking"